Education
in the Development
of Tanzania
1919–90

EASTERN AFRICAN STUDIES

Swahili Origins
Swahili Culture & the Shungwaya Phenomenon
JAMES DE VERE ALLEN

A History of Modern Ethiopia 1855–1974
BAHRU ZEWDE

Control & Crisis in Colonial Kenya
The Dialectic of Domination
BRUCE BERMAN

Unhappy Valley
Book One: State & Class   Book Two: Violence & Ethnicity
BRUCE BERMAN & JOHN LONSDALE

The Mau Mau War in Perspective
FRANK FUREDI

Squatters & the Roots of Mau Mau 1905–63
TABITHA KANOGO

Penetration & Protest in Tanzania
The Impact of the World Economy on the Pare 1860–1960
ISARIA N. KIMAMBO

The Second Economy in Tanzania
T.L. MALIYAMKONO & M.S.D. BAGACHWA

Siaya
DAVID WILLIAM COHEN & E.S. ATIENO ODHIAMBO

Changing Uganda
HOLGER BERNT HANSEN & MICHAEL TWADDLE (eds)

Uganda Now
HOLGER BERNT HANSEN & MICHAEL TWADDLE (eds)

Decolonization & Independence in Kenya 1940–88*
B.A. OGOT & WILLIAM OCHIENG' (eds)

Slaves, Spices & Ivory in Zanzibar
Integration of an East African Commercial Empire into the World Economy
ABDUL SHERIFF

Zanzibar Under Colonial Rule
ABDUL SHERIFF & ED FERGUSON (eds)

Being Maasai
Ethnicity & Identity in East Africa
THOMAS SPEAR & RICHARD WALLER (eds)

Economic & Social Origins of Mau Mau 1945–53
DAVID THROUP

Kakungulu & the Creation of Uganda 1868–1928
MICHAEL TWADDLE

* forthcoming

Education
in the Development
of Tanzania

1919–90

Lene Buchert

James Currey
LONDON

Mkuki na Nyota
DAR ES SALAAM

Ohio University Press
ATHENS

James Currey Ltd
54b Thornhill Square
Islington
London N1 1BE

Mkuki na Nyota Publishers
P.O. Box 4246 Dar es Salaam

Ohio University Press
Scott Quadrangle
Athens, Ohio 45701

1 2 3 4 5 98 97 96 95 94

British Library Cataloguing in Publication Data
Buchert, Lene
  Education in the Development of Tanzania,
  1919-90. – (Eastern African Studies)
  I. Title II. Series
  370.9678

ISBN 0-85255-704-3 (Paper)
ISBN 0-85255-709-4 (Cloth)

Library of Congress Cataloging-in-Publication Data
Buchert, Lene
Education in the development of Tanzania 1919-90/ Lene Buchert.
    p.   cm. -- (Eastern African Studies (London, England)
    Includes bibliographical references and index.
    ISBN 0-8214-1083-0 (Cloth) ISBN 0-8214-1084-9 (Paper)
    1. Education--Tanzania--History--20th century. 2. Education-
-social aspects--Tanzania--History--20th century. 3. Education and
state--Tanzania--History--20th century.   I. Title. II. Series.
LA1841.B83 1994
370'.9678--dc20   93-50745
                                                            CIP

ISBN 0-8214-1084-9 (Paper Ohio)
ISBN 0-8214-1083-0 (Cloth Ohio)

Typeset in 10/11 pt Baskerville by Opus 43, Cumbria
Printed and bound in Great Britain by Villiers Publications, London

Contents

vi

vii

List of Maps, Figures
& Tables

Maps

Figures

Tables

List of Maps, Figures & Tables

Abbreviations & Acronyms

ACAE	Advisory Committee on African Education
ACEC	Advisory Committee on Education in the Colonies
BRALUP	Bureau of Resource Assessment and Land Use Planning
CCM	Chama cha Mapinduzi
CDR	Centre for Development Research
CESO	Centre for the Study of Education in Developing Countries
EEC	European Economic Community
ERP	Economic Recovery Programme
ESAP	Economic and Social Action Programme
FEP	Foundation for Education with Production
GDP	gross domestic product
GNP	gross national product
HMSO	His/Her Majesty's Stationery Office
IBRD	International Bank for Reconstruction and Development
IDR	Institute of Development Research
IDS	Institute of Development Studies
IIEP	International Institute for Educational Plannning
ILO	International Labour Organisation
IMF	International Monetary Fund
MTUU	Mpango wa Tanzania/UNICEF/UNESCO
NEC	National Executive Committee
NUTA	National Union of Tanganyika Workers
SAP	Structural Adjustment Programme
SAPES	Southern Africa Political Economy Series
SAUSSC	Southern African Universities Social Science Conference
SIDA	Swedish International Development Authority
TANU	Tanganyika African National Union
TIRDEP	Tanzania Integrated Rural Development Programme
TNA	Tanzania National Archives
UN	United Nations
UNDP	United Nations Development Programme
UNESCO	United Nations Educational, Scientific and Cultural Organisation
UNICEF	United Nations International Children's Emergency Fund
USAID	United States Agency for International Development
UWT	Umoja wa Wanawake wa Tanzania

Preface

This book is the result of a long and continuing personal struggle with the understanding of the function of education in society, how it can be analysed historically, what are adequate approaches, and what can be learned from specific historical experiences. The core was presented as a PhD dissertation to the University of London in October 1991. The choice of Tanzania as a case study was due to a fascination with the fact that, more than in other countries, education was selected by Tanzanian policy-makers as a determining variable to create a certain kind of society. This took place at a time when much university teaching and social science research adhered to Marxist thinking, which declared or was interpreted to declare the economic base as determining societal development 'in the final instance'. Is it possible to control the educational process to such an extent that creating 'socialist man', in combination with other measures, will result in the creation of 'socialist society', however defined? And, if so, what does this tell us about the relative importance of the socio-economic and politico-ideological structures in society during specific historical periods?

This underlying question can only be addressed by placing education in its specific context and relating its functions in society to both the socio-economic and the politico-ideological dimensions. A high degree of interaction in the use of different social science disciplines was, therefore, needed in this analysis in order to expand traditional historical approaches and the perspectives of much writing on education. This interdisciplinarity is reflected in the book in the incorporation of theoretical understandings of society to guide the selection of historical data, in the combination of traditional historical 'source criticism' with anthropologically-based oral interviews, and in the use of economics and politics as important frameworks within which to understand the relative success and failure of education to achieve wider societal goals.

The backbone of the book, however, remains the use of history as applied to education. Specialists in some of the other disciplines which are touched upon, e.g. agricultural economics, anthropology and political science, will look in vain for the subtleness and sophistication of analysis that each individual discipline would demand and deserve if the study was more focused in time and space or was more specifically related to only one discipline. My hope is, however, that the book is sufficiently balanced to allow readers to gain the perspective needed to understand the relative importance of a range of societal dimensions for educational development, and that it is judged as valuable to provide a new starting point for other analyses that are more focused in nature, or that apply this more general approach to studies of education in societal contexts other than Tanzania.

Originating as it did from my PhD work, the financial support and intellectual stimulation for the book are of long standing. Different phases of the work on the dissertation were supported by different agencies, including the British Council, the Scandinavian Institute of African Studies, the Danish Research Council for the Humanities, the Danish Social Science Research Council, the Danish Research Academy and the Danish Council for Development Research. The final research work for the book and its publication were supported jointly by the Danish Research Council for the Humanities, the Danish Social Science Research Council and the Danish Council for Development Research. I am indebted to all of these agencies for the long term interest in my work which has been expressed in this continuous financial support. Thanks are also due to the Johns Hopkins University Press in Baltimore and the Foreign and Commonwealth Office in London for permission to reprint two of the maps in this book. Furthermore, the Centre for Educational Studies in Developing Countries (CESO) in The Hague kindly gave their permission to use as the basis for one chapter in this book data contained in an article published by them.

The attachment to the University of London gave me access to expertise and materials that are still scarce resources in my home environment. Dr Trevor Coombe and Dr Dennis Dean of the University of London provided the psychological and professional support that was needed to undertake and complete the dissertation. Other valuable contributions and help were given by Prof. Abel Ishumi, University of Dar es Salaam, Juhani Koponen, Research Fellow at the University of Helsinki, Dr Martin McLean, University of London, and John Anderson, Principal of the College of St Mark and St John in Plymouth. Upon my return to Denmark, I was fortunate to gain attachment to the Centre for Development Research in Copenhagen. Several colleagues commented critically and constructively on my PhD work, in particular Poul Ove Pedersen, an Area Research Director, Dr Phil Raikes, Senior

Researcher, and Prof. Karen Tranberg Hansen, (then) Visiting Fellow from the Northwestern University in Chicago, USA. Prof. Herb Kells, formerly of Rutgers University, has followed the work from its first draft as a PhD dissertation to its final version as a book with never-ending enthusiasm, questioning and support.

Much of the work could not have been undertaken without the help of staff in libraries and archives in both Europe and Tanzania. As important were the time, assistance and interest of central, regional and district educational officials in Tanzania, and of village officials and villagers in the communities selected as case studies and, finally, of my interpreters. The field experiences were the highlight of the work, during which national issues could be explored in the living reality of the people for whom policies were designed. My official nomination as a member of the Kwamsisi village moved me to dedicate this book to the hopes for a better future expressed by the Kwamsisi villagers, and in particular to the children of Kwamsisi, whose spirit enlivens its cover.

Copenhagen, Denmark

One

Introduction

In this study of education in the development of Tanzania[1] from the time it became a British mandate until today (1919–90), the function of education is related in important ways to the wider social, economic and political development of the territory. The focus of the analysis is the congruence or lack of it between the formulated educational purposes, goals and policies and their degree of implementation, and, again, their relationship to changing purposes, goals and policies of the overall development process in Tanzania. In order to achieve maximum understanding of the role of education, the analysis is undertaken both at the macro (national) level related to the creation and development of the national educational system, and at the micro (institutional) level related to the function of selected educational programmes in specific local contexts in the territory.

Underlying Understandings and Methods

Underlying the analysis is an understanding of Tanzanian society during the entire period as a predominantly non-capitalist agricultural country existing at the periphery of the world economic system. While national and sub-national agents, factors and circumstances have always been important in the direction of the Tanzanian development process, the international environment has intervened to a substantial extent in national policy formulation and implementation and the general development since the pre-colonial period. The relative power, influence and impact of the international environment, the state and civil society have been expressed in fundamental tensions between the three. These tensions resulted partly from conflicting goals for and expectations of the development process, and partly from a distortion of the goals in the implementation process due to disagreement by or lack of incorporation in decision-making processes of specific individuals and social groups, and because of other unforeseen and intervening factors.

Since the pre-colonial period, there have been different understandings of what should be the predominant development strategy in Tanzania. This has involved a struggle between adherents of capitalist and of non-capitalist economic development. The polity has been more or less dominant in shaping the direction of economic development and has allocated over time different relative roles in society for education in support of the overall process. In this book, the analysis of education in society explores whether education was used to follow or lead societal development, whether mass or elite education was to be the primary focus of investment, and whether education was to promote primarily social as opposed to economic or even political goals. It also includes an analysis of the extent to which designed policies corresponded with the expectations from and use of education by individual clients, particular social groups and specific educational agencies.

In order to guide the investigation of these long-term and complex development patterns, a broad framework of analysis was designed which combines elements from different research traditions, disciplines and contemporary development discussions. The central concerns of the historian, namely with time and space, are reflected both in the adaptation of Fernand Braudel's three-dimensional time-scale and in the application of aspects of the development debate which allows for an understanding of Tanzanian society in its global context. The central concerns of the educational analyst are reflected in the attempt to make education visible as a variable in societal development with its functions related to social, economic and political purposes.

The French *Annales* historian Fernand Braudel developed his three-dimensional time-scale in order to study the historical complexity of development and change. Whereas studies of historical development often imply the rooting of a historical sequence in unilinear time, i.e. a single time-scale characterised by continuity of development, Braudel's three-dimensional scale allows for a combined analysis of structures and events along cyclical patterns. Braudel distinguished between the long-term impact of the fundamental conditions of material life, states of mind and the natural environment; the medium-term impact of forms of social, economic and political organisation; and the short-term impact of individuals and historical events.[2] This perspective is adapted in this book, for instance, with the long-term analysis of agriculture as a 'fundamental condition of material life', the medium-term analysis of social and economic policies underlying the development of educational institutions, and the short-term analysis of intervening internal and

2

What about "short term states of mind"?

external events and the identification of key individuals or singular institutions in the development of Tanzania.

The understanding of the nature and dynamics of Tanzanian society is based on the early perspectives of the dominant development theories seen in relation to the contemporary debates concerning the relative role of the economy and the polity, of agents and structures, and of the importance of the sub-national level in national development. The core notion derived from these perspectives and pursued in the book is the need for analysis of the dynamic interaction between the polity and the economy. Another focus is the attention to indigenous explanatory factors at the sub-national level which interact with exogenous factors in the international community and indigenous factors at the national level.

Education as a societal variable is seen in this book as related both to the economic and political structures of society and to the underlying value and cultural patterns. Through the transfer of knowledge, skills and attitudes, educational institutions are considered as agents with the potential to stimulate development and change of Braudel's long-term fundamental conditions of material life, states of mind and the impact of the natural environment, the medium-term social, economic and political organisations, and the short-term role of individuals and historical events. Furthermore, it is believed that, for individuals and specific social groups, education can simultaneously function as a means of social mobility when it combines with access to particular socio-economic or politically influential roles and a means of social control, when individuals or social groups are sorted out or have limited access to certain levels or specific contents of education which are a pre-condition to economic and political influence.

The historical investigation of Tanzanian education and development at the national level is based on an analysis of primary official, semi-official and unofficial historical sources supplemented by secondary literature. The major part of the primary historical evidence was collected in the National Archives in Dar es Salaam and the Public Records Office in Kew Gardens near London. For the contemporary period, many of the basic statistical materials and policy documents were secured from government and other official publications. The investigation of the selected educational institutions and programmes at the micro level relied on primary historical evidence in two cases, and on oral data and statistics collected on site in the other two cases.

Both quantitative and qualitative measures were used in the long-term analysis of the function of education in the development of Tanzania. With respect to the basic statistical materials upon which quantitative patterns and trends were based, a variety of sources were included in order to achieve as high a reliability as possible. While this method did not discard the relative unreliability of the individual figures, it did assist in the establishment of the more reliable development trends which were of primary interest in the study. An underlying assumption was that changing trends might be fairly reliable when coinciding with and reflecting changing formulated policies.

The qualitative measures were also questionable, partly because of the relatively small samples taken and the subjective nature of the data. In addition, the aspect of the analysis which seeks to analyse the relative effect of education in societal development can mostly be established only as a correlational relationship because the combined quantitative and qualitative measures are insufficient to determine a cause–effect relationship. They can, however, give some indication of the probable contribution of education to fulfilling national development goals and, hopefully, also point to issues which could be addressed in future analyses, and to ways in which scientific concepts and tools could be further refined.

Research Themes and Structure of the Book

A central theme of the book is the analysis of the disparities between the formulation and implementation of educational policies in the context of the wider socio-economic and political development process. This analysis includes internal conflicts in the policy process at the national and sub-national levels, as well as the relative influence of external factors, such as the international community, during specific time periods. It also includes the changing relative emphases over time in the overall purposes of education (socio-cultural, politico-ideological and economic), in the focus on specific levels of education (for example, basic mass compared with higher elite education), and in the contents of education (for example, vocational compared with academic education).

This overall theme explains the periodisation of the book. During the British administration period, 1919–61, there was a clear shift in the underlying principles for British rule and the implemented broader development and educational policies after the Second World War. In the post-independence era, the independent Tanzanian government in 1967 redirected the inherited development and educational policies in the form of a locally-designed development strategy. From the early 1980s, this strategy was strongly modified although many of the underlying goals are still being officially defended. The major contest during the identified general periods was between modernisation or capitalist development in some form, on the one hand, and locally defined Tanzanian socialist development, on the other. The specific policies which were designed to meet the overall goals were further changing in sub-periods within the general periods.

4

Introduction

The pursuance of either capitalist or socialist development put a different emphasis on the relative importance of socio-economic, politico-ideological and socio-cultural goals for education. This relative importance was reflected in the provision of education for specific social groups, in different contents of the curriculum at the different levels of the educational system, and in the priority of investment in education for the few as opposed to the many. Across the long historical period, it is, therefore, possible to point to similarities and differences in the formulated and implemented educational policies and in their relative importance for wider societal development.

Central to the analysis is the understanding of the national policy of Education for Self-Reliance which was formulated in support of the formulated strategy of Socialism and Self-Reliance in 1967. In contrast to much writing on the subject, Education for Self-Reliance is here presented as a multi-dimensional philosophy and policy which can be distinguished both from the concept and policy of Education for Adaptation which was implemented during the British administration in Tanganyika and in numerous other dependencies, and from the concept and strategy of Education for All which was formulated at an international conference in Jomtien, Thailand in March 1990. The core similarities and differences between the three concepts appear from the analysis of the national educational system, from some of the selected case studies of educational institutions and programmes, and from the concluding discussion of the implications of the undertaken historical investigation of education in Tanzania in the context of Education for All.

The book is structured in four major periods during which important changes were made in the declared development goals and in the use of education to reach those goals. The first major period is treated in Chapter 2, where the function of education is related to the socio-economic and political development in Tanganyika during 1919–45. This is followed in Chapter 3 by a case study of the agricultural training centre established at Nyakato near Bukoba in 1932. This centre typified British educational thinking at the micro level. The analysis draws attention to both generic and specific factors influencing British educational policy-making. The second major period is identified in Chapter 4, in which education is related to the changing economic and political purposes for the British presence in Tanganyika during 1946–61. This is followed in Chapter 5 by a case study of the Singida mass literacy and education programme initiated in 1958 under the increased influence of the international community. The third major period appears in Chapter 6, in which the formulation and implementation of Education for Self-Reliance is seen in the context of the formulation and implementation of the strategy of Socialism and

5

Self-Reliance during 1967–81. Some of the key factors influencing the implementation of the policy at the nationwide level are further pursued in Chapter 7 at the local, institutional level in relation to case studies of the community school experiments in Kwamsisi and Kwalukonge. Finally, in Chapter 8, the redirection of Socialism and Self-Reliance into structural adjustment policies during 1982–90 is analysed with specific reference to the functioning of adult literacy programmes in three selected sites of Dodoma region.

In the concluding chapter, some of the lessons of the historical experiences of Tanzania are discussed in the context of the current international strategy of Education for All. While much has been said about the deficiencies of Education for Self-Reliance, not enough has perhaps been argued concerning some of its advantages compared with other strategies, such as Education for All or the dominant educational policies during the pre-independence period, Education for Adaptation and Education for Modernisation. The historical investigation, thereby, provides a valuable perspective on important current issues concerning, for instance, the purported 'vocational school fallacy', the current contest between quality and equality in education, the nature of devolution of responsibility for educational provision, and the cooperation in international educational development between national governments and international donor agencies. It can, hopefully, also bring forth additional ideas for their solution to national governments and the international community.

Notes

1. The study considers only today's mainland Tanzania. The area formed part of German East Africa until after the First World War, when it became a British Mandate area under the name of Tanganyika. Tanganyika in 1964 amalgamated with Zanzibar and became the United Republic of Tanzania. The terms German East Africa, Tanganyika and Tanzania are applied in the study during the relevant historical periods.
2. Braudel 1967, 1969.

Two

Education for Indirect Rule,
Peasant Production & Western Civilisation
1919–46

One of the major impacts of the British, and before that the German, presence in Tanganyika was the introduction of new political and socio-economic principles of organisation into the existing indigenous societies in order to link them more strongly with the international economy. The underlying philosophy and policy of the British administration in the interwar period were those of adaptation which emphasised a blending of local and Western patterns, values and institutions. The policy was gradually more strongly supported by educational facilities for the local populations established by the British administration in competition and cooperation with the already functioning educational agencies in the area. The adopted policy of Education for Adaptation is here presented in the context of the wider political and socio-economic circumstances which determined its initial content, direction and use by the British administration.

The Political and Socio-Economic Setting

The hand-over of part of German East Africa to Britain as a mandate area after the First World War led to international supervision of British rule in what was named Tanganyika. This supervision was initially undertaken by the League of Nations and, after the Second World War, by the United Nations. In the mandate agreement of 1922, the British administration was accorded full legislative, executive and judicial power. It was to be responsible for law and order in the area, to secure the rights and interests of the local population vis-a-vis those of British and other member states of the League of Nations, and to promote the 'material, moral and social progress' of the local population.[1]

The interpretation of this mandate by the British administration was consistent with the then prevailing British philosophy of adaptation, according to which British rule was to preserve in the traditional societies and cultures what were considered by the British authorities to be 'sound and healthy elements',[2] and to blend these with selected modern Western influences. The philosophy can be interpreted as one which both attempted to recreate traditional institutions and culture from a Western perspective, and to slow down an overall Westernisation process. The philosophy was reflected in the adopted policies for political, socio-economic and educational development. The characteristics and relative importance of each of these spheres were modified during 1919–46, particularly under the impact of the international depression, which affected Tanganyika in the early 1930s.

The Indirect Rule System

An immediate interest of the British administration was to set up a political system through which the area could be ruled. Until 1922, the British administration adopted the previous German system of direct rule. The German government declared German East Africa a protectorate in 1885 and, by 1891, established a formal administration with a governor at its head. The colony was divided into districts and administrative centres were set up inland along the pre-colonial caravan routes, though particularly in settled regions. District officers were responsible for law and order and for collecting the hut-and-poll tax introduced in 1898. They had a high degree of power and autonomy mainly due to lack of communication with the headquarters, and sought alliances with accommodating African leaders, particularly during the 1890s. The cooperation was based on mutual needs for political and military support. Where such cooperation was not achieved or where it collapsed, the Germans appointed akidas and jumbes – Arab or Swahili civil servants from the coast – to act as local administrators (to, among other things, collect taxes and try cases).[3]

After the mandate agreement of 1922 and in a context where native[4] interests had been declared to be 'paramount' in cases of conflict with immigrant communities, in particular white settler or Indian interests,[5] an active British policy of indirect rule was pursued. For Tanganyika, the principle of the paramountcy of native interests must be seen in relation to the territory's mandatory status, which implied external supervision of British rule at a time when there were still risks that the area might be handed back to the Germans, and when developments in the Indian sub-continent created fears concerning the possible consequences of the colonial experience. Tanganyika became, therefore, particularly after the appointment of Lord Cameron[6] as governor in

1925, a prime site for the system of indirect rule, which was established over virtually the whole territory by 1931.

The system of indirect rule involved the integration of the indigenous political systems into the central British administrative structure. The indigenous societies were from the pre-colonial period characterised by differences in political organisation which seemed to be related to the predominant economic forms: agriculture, pastoralism and hunting–gathering as well as some combination of the three. Banana-based agricultural societies seemed to have had the highest level of social differentiation and highly centralised political institutions organised around the chief or the clan. Grain-based agricultural and pastoral societies were more fragmented and seemed not to have developed central political organisations. In all of these societies stratification was based on age and sex. Due to their possession of 'symbolic' (ritual) and economic powers, chiefs or elders controlled the redistribution of wealth following a principle of reciprocity which was based on mutual rights and obligations.[7]

With the system of indirect rule, native administrations were run by identified or created tribal chiefs and village headmen. They comprised the native treasury which collected taxes, the native courts with judicial power, and the native authority with legislative and executive powers. They were supervised by the district or provincial officers of the British administration who could issue orders and otherwise intervene in native affairs. The provincial and district officers were linked with the secretariat in Dar es Salaam and responsible to the local governor who was ultimately responsible to the Secretary of State in London.[8]

In London, the Colonial Office was advisory to the Secretary of State who was responsible to the cabinet and ultimately to parliament. In Dar es Salaam, the governor acted through an Executive Council, which in 1926, was supplemented by a Legislative Council. Each council contained representatives of the main interest groups in the area, essentially those of agriculture, commerce and the missionary organisations. They also included the heads of British government departments, who constituted a majority during the whole period. There was no direct African representation until 1945. In London, the Secretary of State had the power to legislate for the colonies. Once local legislative structures had been developed, the great bulk of legislation was produced locally in a context where the governor controlled the votes of the official majority and the Secretary of State had the power of veto.[9]

The Formation of Peasant Societies

The Colonial Development and Welfare Acts stated the fundamental economic principles underlying British rule in all dependencies. Until the

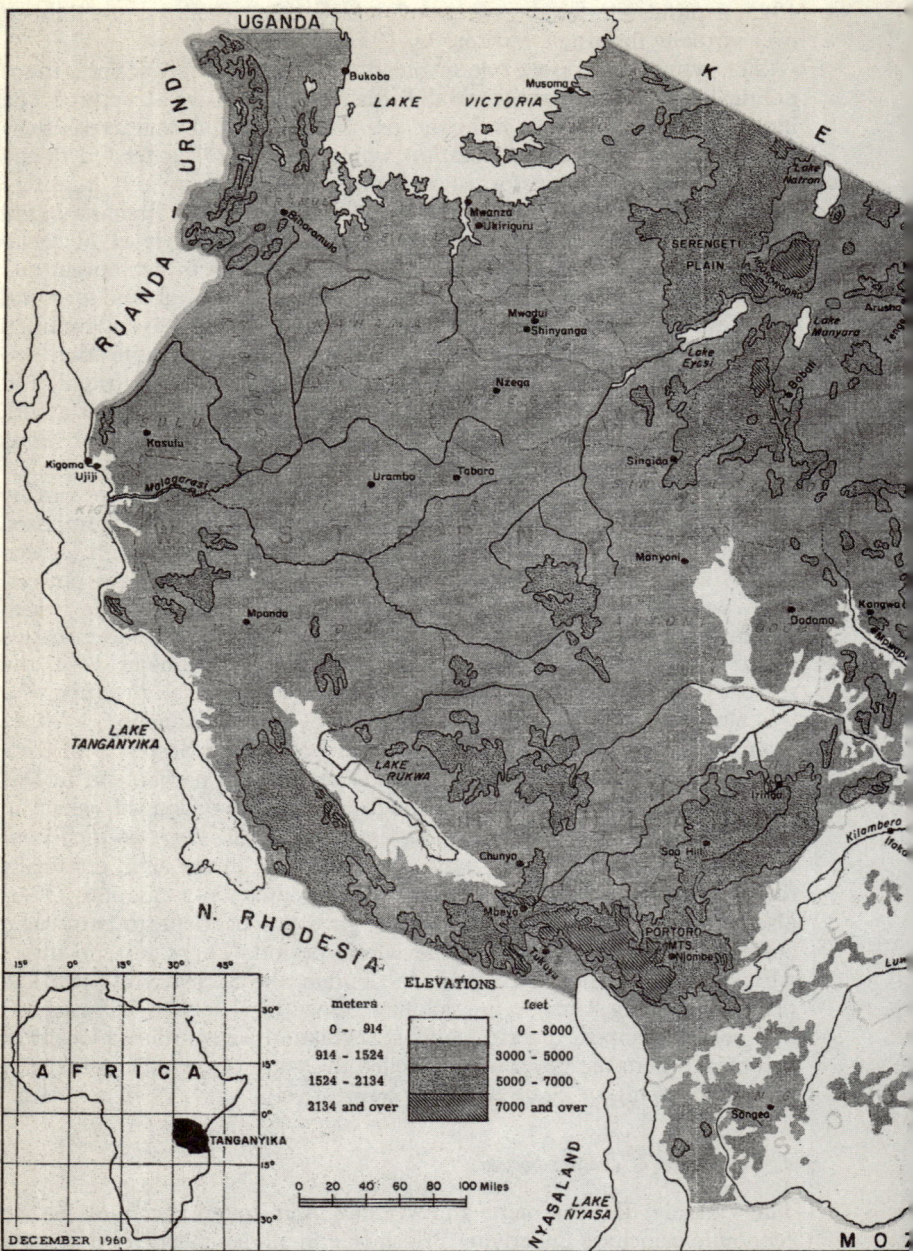

10

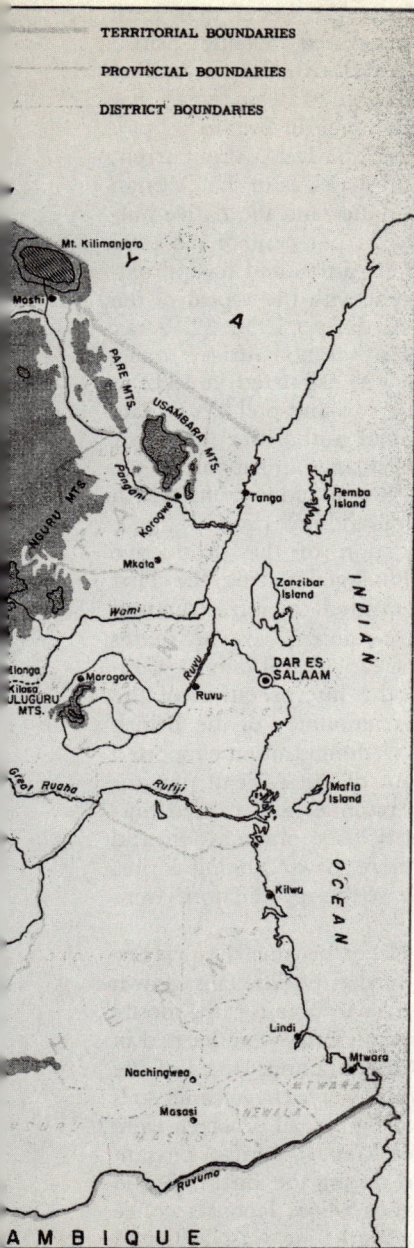

Map 1
Tanganyika

Source: *The Economic Development of Tanganyika*, The Johns Hopkins University Press, 1961.

11

Second World War, British policies rested on the belief that local development should be based upon locally generated revenue. British interest in access to particular raw materials and an enlarged market could, however, encourage British investments in strategic areas that would support agricultural and industrial development in Britain.[10]

British financial policy aimed at balanced budgets, the current revenue deriving mostly from local taxation and duties as in the German period. During 1926–27 to 1930–31, customs duties and the native hut-and-poll tax constituted in all approximately 73 per cent of the total revenue, while the native hut-and-poll tax alone amounted to approximately 35 per cent. From 1932, and concurrent with the repeal of the non-African education cess which was levied during 1930–32, a tax representing 1 per cent on the taxable income of the non-African (male) population was introduced. The total amount was estimated in 1932 at £19,000 or around 4 per cent of the native hut-and-poll tax.[11] The system of indirect rule provided the traditional authorities (chiefs or native councils) with an independent source of finance in support of the development of local services, such as roads and education, which constituted approximately 25 per cent of the hut-and-poll tax.[12]

Public expenditure aimed at the restoration of the productive potential of the area, which was severely damaged during the First World War. During 1926–32, it was concentrated on infrastructural development which partially replaced the pre-colonial caravan routes and porters and, from 1932, on an increase of agricultural output. Consistent with the adaptation philosophy and the interpretation of the principle of 'paramountcy' to indicate the paramountcy of the British administration over settler interests, the British administration supported African peasant production. The development of the African peasant sector increased the ties with the Western economies and caused outside attempts at changing the underlying principles, organisation and methods of local production patterns. Furthermore, new economic forms, in particular plantation industry and white settler production, were introduced.

Thus, the banana- and grain-producing societies became the primary areas for African peasant production which turned traditionally grown products into crops for the world market in order to obtain cash, mostly to meet the demands of taxation. Banana-based societies were located in the particularly well-endowed and populous mountainous areas of the north-western and north-eastern highlands with their rich volcanic soils and also along the shore of Lakes Victoria and Nyasa, all of which were characterised by high and reliable rainfalls (see Map 1). African peasant cash crop production of coffee was reinforced during the British period among the Haya in the north-western highlands where Robusta coffee was traditionally intercropped with bananas. Marketing was facilitated along the British-built railway to Uganda, which was completed in 1901. Arabica coffee, on the other hand, was introduced among the Chagga on Kilimanjaro. It was marketed by way of the German-constructed railway line from Tanga along the Pangani valley to Kilimanjaro – which was commenced in 1891. Cotton production was concentrated among the Sukuma on the western plateau and was marketed internationally along the central railway line which reached Lake Tanganyika at Kigoma from Dar es Salaam in 1914. Cashew nuts were added to the groundnut production for export and cotton and coffee also spread to the southern highlands. Marketing, especially of cotton, was facilitated by an extension of the central railway line from Tabora to Mwanza on Lake Victoria in 1928.[13]

The German-established sisal plantation industry was extended along the central railway line to the Morogoro district and was taken over by different European owners: mostly British, who constituted 60 per cent, Greeks 14 per cent and Asians 10 per cent at independence in 1961.[14] Plantations had already been established on the mainland in the pre-colonial period as food-producing entities for the caravans and cities.[15] Production was, then, undertaken by slave labourers who were allocated their own plots of land on the plantation to meet their subsistence needs. In contrast, the plantations established during the German and British periods were large-scale, capital-intensive industrial enterprises located along the northern railway line, on the coast and in the Usambaras. They had far-reaching effects on the local societies since they relied on active policies of land alienation and introduced Africans to wage-labour along 'capitalist' lines. Wage-labour was recruited provisionally from the surrounding local areas until the local peasantry managed to take up cash crop production or food crop production for the plantations and the coastal towns to meet their cash needs. At that time, migrant wage labour was provided through active policies, especially from the former porter- and slave-producing areas, i.e. the western plateau, the south and the south-east. This migrant wage-labour remained attached to its home communities, which covered the basic subsistence needs of the wider family as well as those of the labourer when he was not working in the plantations.[16] New plantation crops were introduced during the British period, particularly tea in the southern highlands and sugar in the north-eastern highlands, but they remained relatively insignificant compared with sisal.

Like the plantations, white settler production relied on land alienation and African wage-labour. It was located particularly on the lower slopes of Mt Kilimanjaro and Mt Meru as well as in the southern highlands and concentrated on products such as rubber, maize and coffee. The northern railway was extended from Mombo to Arusha in 1912 in support of white settler production but, significantly, a railway line was never planned in the southern highlands. White settler production was generally smaller in scale than the plantation industry and relied on mechanised production techniques and intensive cultivation. The white settler community remained small in size during the German period, approximately 880 in 1913.[17] Despite concessions during the British period it numbered only 9,345 in 1938.[18] Like the Germans, the British did not favour a railway line to the southern highlands. White settler production was instead facilitated by road development and motor transport, partly supported by the traditional authorities.[19]

At the end of the German period in 1913, African and foreign producers contributed relatively equally to agricultural exports in terms of value. This relative balance was modified, first, with the dominance of the African peasant sector in the early 1920s (constituting 61 per cent of total value in 1923) and, again, in the late 1920s with the boom in the plantation industry (increasing by 20 per cent in terms of value during 1923–29). While forced peasant production during the depression was reflected in an increased proportion of total value (49 per cent of the total in 1935), it was sisal which became the single most important export product after the Second World War (accounting for 61 per cent of total value in 1946).[20]

Cash crop production was a contributory factor to the regional differentiation which was discernible at the end of the German period. It intensified during the British period, when the specialisation among different geographical areas in cash crops, food crops and labour supply took place. In addition to this regional differentiation and specialisation, the traditional stratification along age and gender lines was supplemented during the German and British periods by emerging racial and socio-economic divisions based on relative cash incomes. This was related particularly to the relative dominance of Asians and Europeans in the small modern sector. The economic activities that secured the international exchange economy, such as banking, financing and import/export services, rested on and benefited first German and then British and other European interests. Retail trade, which followed in the wake of the international exchange and moved inland with the German and British administrations, was monopolised by the growing Asian community. Arab low- and middle-level civil servants were gradually replaced by Africans, whereas German and, later, British officials took over at the higher level.[21]

The establishment of the indirect rule system and the development of peasant production were supported by a variety of educational measures. They were based on increased control by the British administration of educational policy and provision of education in the formal system, specific experimental schemes run or supported by the British administration, and non-formal education programmes particularly aiming at increased production and productivity in agriculture. In all three areas, British educational interests interacted with those of other established interests and social groups who responded differentially according to their own expectations and felt needs. The following analysis concerns the involvement of the British administration in the formal educational system, whereas the subsequent chapter analyses a specific educational scheme which was set up in one of the cash crop-producing areas in support of peasant production.

The Role of Formal Education in Political and Socio-Economic Development

Formal Western-type education was introduced into what became Tanganyika by missionary organisations of different denominations which had established themselves in the territory since the 1840s. It supplemented traditional forms of education, through which knowledge about the prevailing norms and practices of the indigenous societies was passed on by elders to new generations. The purposes of the traditional educational activities were to transmit a common culture and the prevailing gender-based division of labour. Education, thus, simultaneously fulfilled a culturally cohesive and a socio-economically differentiating role.

The educational activities undertaken by the missionary organisations introduced competing values into the indigenous societies as the primary objective was to 'civilise' and Christianise the 'heathen' populations. The missionary activities expanded geographically under the protection of the formal German administration in the 1890s. Although the predominant religious aim was maintained, education also came to include secular purposes, in the forms of an academic curriculum and vocational activities. The secular orientation became more important after 1900, when the German administration became involved in the formulation of educational policy for the area and began to support mission schools financially.[22]

The German administration's interest in education derived from its growing needs for middle layers of administrative personnel that could provide a proper level of communication, and for technical personnel that could secure economic development in the territory. The first government school was established in Tanga in 1892. It was followed by others which were set up on the coast and, after 1897, in the interior, where the mission schools were mainly concentrated. The education in government schools was non-religious and, unlike the mission schools, did not directly attempt to assimilate the local populations to Western values. Due to the location of the schools on the coast and to a policy which emphasised Kiswahili as the language of communication in the area, the government schools, in fact, initially supported the spread of Islam, as the recruited students were mostly Arabs or Indians, who became employed as akidas in the district offices. From 1896, (African) headmen were obliged by the German administration to send their sons to the Tanga school. From 1899, when the written Kiswahili script changed from Arabic to Latin the headmen and sons of headmen were also trained in mission schools. These measures diminished the relative Arab influence and were, at the end of the German period, also reinforced by the deliberate adoption by the missionary organisations of education as an active means of curtailing the influence of Islam.[23]

The spread of formal education in the area was slow during the period due to the scepticism of, if not resistance from, the local populations. The missionary societies initially recruited many of their converts from marginalised social groups (for instance slaves), whereas the students of the government schools came from the Arab and Indian communities rather than the African. In the course of the period, however, education became a means for Africans to change their position in the traditional societies, which was otherwise based on ascriptive criteria. For some, education led to occupations in the middle position between the colonial administration and the local rulers, while, for others, it became a way to escape from the forced labour demands of the German administration related to, for instance, the construction of railways and the plantation industry.[24]

The quality of education varied in both the government and the mission systems and the terms 'school' and 'student' did not involve common characteristics or clearcut categories and definitions. Any attempt to quantify the educational activities during the period is, therefore, highly questionable. For the year 1913, the German administration listed nine government main schools (in the cities and mission stations) with 2,394 pupils, 89 government branch schools (in the surrounding African communities) with 3,706 pupils and six government artisans' schools with 166 pupils. The total number of pupils in missionary schools was indicated as 108,551.[25]

Most of this educational groundwork was seriously damaged during the First World War. It was restored during the British period as missionary societies resumed their activities and as both the British administration and the native authorities began to participate in the provision of education for the local communities. The formulated objectives for education, however, changed. In contrast to the German educational policy, the British policy emphasised both political and economic goals for the educational system, which led to a higher degree of intervention in the local circumstances. The policies were formulated in a number of documents issued by the Colonial Office in London addressing the educational needs of the indigenous populations in all British dependencies. They were adopted and adapted locally in the different dependencies under the impact of local interests and changing local circumstances.

The Policy of Education for Adaptation

The policy which determined educational development in Tanganyika until the Second World War was that of adaptation. It was announced in 1925 in the first and probably most influential policy paper of the Colonial Office Advisory Committee on Education, *Education Policy in British Tropical Africa.*[26] Under the impact of the depression, it was extended in the *Memorandum on the Education of African Communities* in 1935 and in a report on *Higher Education in East Africa* in 1937. The stated aim of education was to

> render the individual more efficient in his or her condition of life ...
> to promote the advancement of the community as a whole through
> the improvement of agriculture, the development of native industries,
> the improvement of health, the training of the people in the manage-
> ment of their own affairs, and the inculcation of true ideals of citizen-
> ship and service ... The first task of education [was] to raise the
> standard alike of character and efficiency of the bulk of the people,
> but provision [was] also to be made for the training of those who
> [were] required to fill posts in the administrative and technical
> services, as well as of those who as chiefs [would] occupy positions of
> exceptional trust and responsibility. As resources permit, the door of
> advancement, through higher education ... must be increasingly
> opened for those who by character, ability and temperament show
> themselves fitted to profit by such education.[27]

The well-being of a country was considered to rest as much on the character of the people as on their increasing intellectual and technical ability and their social progress. The teaching of religion and moral instruction must therefore be accorded equal standing with secular subjects in the 'formation of habits of industry, of truthfulness, of manliness, of readiness for social service and of disciplined co-operation' which was the foundation of character.[28] It was stressed that better education of girls and women was urgently required which, again, demanded urgent training of female teachers. The education of females was seen in the context of their traditional domestic role as wives and mothers. Educated females would ensure that 'clever boys, for whom higher education is expedient [could] look forward to educated mates'. Female education was also seen to have a positive impact on infant mortality, general hygiene, public health, child welfare, and the care of the home and the domestic economy.[29]

The educational system which was envisaged to fulfil the stated purposes was to comprise elementary education for both boys and girls; secondary or intermediate education, including more than one type of school and several types of curricula; technical and vocational education; institutions which might reach university rank and which would offer professional and vocational higher education; and adult education for men and women.[30]

The strong emphasis on vocational agricultural education, health, community development and self-help was inspired by recommendations to the Colonial Office Advisory Committee by the Phelps–Stokes Commission which undertook two study tours to Africa in the 1920s, the second one in 1924 to East, Central and South Africa. It had the secretary of the Advisory Committee, Hanns Vischer, as a member. The Commission recommended for the African context what was practised in some institutions in some American southern states, namely an education which adapted the black population to its likely place in the occupational structure and reinforced the traditional female reproductive role. For Africa, it implied emphasis on the development of the rural sector and the improvement of the socio-economic conditions of the mass of the population. For women and girls, the adaptation of education implied 'health and hygiene related to the life of womanhood and especially to the care of children; agriculture and gardening for food; the home and its responsibilities for the preparation of food, for restful sleep, for clothing, and for the full round of family life; recreation for childhood, youth and adults; [and] character development'. Ultimately, it was stressed, 'women must share the inspiration of all education ... Her leadership in Africa is as basic as that of womanhood in Europe and America'.[31] The Commission also expressed scepticism about the narrowly proselytising purposes of much missionary education on the one hand, and the consequences of educating 'black Englishmen' on the other.[32]

From the mid-1930s, doubts were expressed among authoritative British officials concerning the benefits of the system of indirect rule and the philosophy of adaptation. It was recognised that much of the traditional structure of authority and customs of African societies had been profoundly and differentially altered by the colonial experience, and that advantages could possibly be gained by speeding up a Westernisation process which would link the local economies more effectively with the metropole. This led to a more pronounced emphasis on development and research, Western institutions and self-government.[33]

The point of departure for the foreseen higher interaction between African and European cultures and civilisations still discredited the dynamics of African society: it was an interaction between 'the African theory of traditionalism and the European theory of progress'. The task for the British administration was to 'interpret to the youth of Africa the higher values of the present world and to assist Africans in a difficult process of adjustment so that they shall be able to live without strain in the composite conditions which have been created'.[34]

The purposes for education were expanded by the British in the light of the growing experience of the ideas contained in the 1925 memorandum. It was stressed that the school could make its most effective contribution only if it was part of a comprehensive programme directed to the improvement of all aspects of life in the community. Education of the young had to go hand in hand with education of adults, and education of males hand in hand with that of females. While the simultaneous education of young and adults was to prevent increasing social gaps, the education of females was, as in the earlier period, directly related to the matrimonial needs of males. General primary or elementary education and advanced higher training were considered to be complementary, and the development of education and the material base of society to be mutually reinforcing.[35]

The earlier emphasis on health and agriculture was retained and could best be achieved, it was argued, by the general education of Africans, since reading and writing skills were likely to lead to material progress and to a sound and prosperous rural population. While 'the education of the child must be based upon the facts of that rural life in which he will participate',[36] it was important not to ignore 'that small but growing group of Africans who by patience and industry [were] now ready to acquire a higher culture'.[37] The school needed, on the one hand, to be related as closely as possible to the institutions and traditions of the society of which it was part. On the other hand,

> it [was] the task of the school to further social progress by interpreting the changes which [were] taking place in African society, by communicating the new knowledge and skill which [were] necessary to improve the life of the community, by supplying new motives and incentives to take the place of those which [had] ceased to be adequate, by re-creating continuously the sense of social obligation, and by fostering an intelligent interest in environment which will heighten for individual and community the enjoyment of life.[38]

There was an expressed need for a clear recognition of the connection between economic policy and educational policy. Educational programmes had to be limited largely by the capacity of the people to bear the cost and were to provide as wide a scope as possible for local initiative and responsibility. Native authorities were, therefore, to be related as closely as possible with community development programmes.[39] In order to promote economic development, qualified African experts must be trained who had been exposed to Western knowledge and scientific principles. These Western elements had to interlock with African practice in order to fashion an indigenous culture which represented a synthesis of both.[40]

The Adoption of Education for Adaptation in Tanganyika

In the dependencies, the governor could adopt and adjust the metropolitan recommendations to the local situation subject to the approval of the Secretary of State for the Colonies. In Tanganyika, the educational policy-making process was influenced by the different interest groups in the area, including the missionary organisations and the native authorities. In contrast to the announced metropolitan statements, the provision of education in Tanganyika concerned both African and non-African communities. Of the non-African communities, the European and Indian groups were particularly influential in economic and political life despite their paucity in number. From the very early years of British rule, they were, as will be discussed below, successful in achieving support for the education of their children at the expense of the African population.

The British administration in Tanganyika formally acknowledged its responsibility for the education of Africans at its first education conference in Dar es Salaam in 1925. The meeting assembled the missionary, commercial and industrial interests in the territory but had a very limited African representation. On this occasion, the British administration welcomed the 1925 memorandum on *Education Policy in British Tropical Africa* as the charter for future educational activities and committed itself to the principle of Education for Adaptation. The land was considered to be the African's natural vocation and agricultural education was seen as a means of preventing the production of educated unemployed – the overriding concern of the government at the time, 'the source of most of the world's social ills'.[41] Formal cooperation concerning education was established between the administration and the missionary and commercial interests. This cooperation was gradually extended to the native authorities. In accordance with the 1925 memorandum, the central administration became responsible for the formulation of educational policies. It was to supervise all educational institutions, to set up educational advisory bodies and to establish a grants-in-aid scheme for non-government institutions which fulfilled government standards.[42]

In a similar way to the Colonial Office Advisory Committee, the advisory bodies set up in Tanganyika acted as channels for views on and demands for education. Missionary influence was strong both in the Advisory Committee on Education in the Colonies in London and in the local Advisory Committee on African Education (ACAE) which was formed in 1926. Missionaries were considered to represent African interests as well as their own, and direct African representation was always restricted. Besides the ACAE, separate local advisory committees for European and Indian education were nominated in 1929. They were chaired by the Director of Education but were otherwise dominated by direct representation of the two groups who were granted executive power in 1948. This executive influence involved: the planning and organisation of education for their respective communities; the construction, maintenance and inspection of schools; the preparation of annual budgets, which were presented to the Director of Education; and control over their respective educational funds.[43]

The central mechanisms of the grants-in-aid scheme were the number of qualified teachers and of registered and attending students. At different times grants-in-aid were given for specific purposes, such as the provision of industrial tool kits. The scheme led to controversies, especially between the British administration and the missionary societies concerning the use of the local vernaculars, Kiswahili or English as the medium or subject of instruction, and the relative balance between religious and secular subjects in the curriculum.

In the late 1920s, the British administration seems to have focused on its staffing needs rather than the provision of agricultural education for Africans, as the Education Ordinance of 1927 and the Education Regulations of 1928 favoured technical and vocational education and instruction in Kiswahili and English, despite the adoption of Education for Adaptation as the guiding principle.[44] This practice was reversed after the depression when the grants-in-aid scheme of 1933 favoured elementary education for Africans in the vernacular.[45]

The reversal followed the report and recommendations of a government financial mission to the Secretary of State for the Colonies that social services and educational expenditure in Tanganyika had to be cut as part of the fiscal strategy applied to the territory during the depression.[46] Cuts in educational expenditure were not, however, to affect non-African education. In 1931, the British administration declared that non-African communities affected by the abolition of the educational cess levied during 1930–32 would be entitled to a greater part of the allocation from the territorial revenue.[47]

As the economy regained strength, the concern expressed by the British administration, after reconfirming the basic principle of the 1925 charter of education, was that Africans were not in a position to compete successfully in the more remunerative employment markets of

Table 2.1   Source of Expenditure on African, European and Indian Education in Tanganyika 1930/31–1945. £ 000

Source	1930/31			1936			1945		
	African	European	Indian	African	European	Indian	African	European	Indian
Territorial revenue	97,691	5,261	8,350	62,670	9,877	12,072	151,000[a]	30,000[a]	43,500[ab]
Education tax	n/a	426	986	n/a	–	–	n/a	–	–
Balance in educational funds	n/a	–	–	n/a	–	3,043	n/a	–	–
Native authorities	9,093	n/a	n/a	7,898	n/a	n/a	27,500	n/a	n/a
Grand total	106,784	5,687	9,336	70,568	9,877	15,115	178,500	30,000	43,500

n/a   Not applicable.
Notes: Contributions from missionary societies are unavailable for the indicated period.
    a   Approximate net expenditures.
    b   Including special grant of £5,730.

Sources: United Kingdom, *Report for the year 1932:* 67, *1937:* 123, *1947:* 269; Department of Education, *Annual Report 1945:* 2.

the territory, which were dominated by Europeans and Asians. Educational unemployment was no longer considered to be an immediate danger since the absorptive capacity of the economy was regarded as being vast enough for educated Africans to be employed along with Europeans and Asians. The government acknowledged at the same time its responsibility for the education of the non-African communities.[48]

The Provision of Education

In the interwar period, all funding of education by the British administration from the recurrent revenue was based on direct and indirect taxation of the African population as discussed above. The total allocation to education was relatively low, although it was increasing from below 1 per cent of the total recurrent expenditures during 1919–25 to around 5 per cent during 1930–45.[49] In addition, education was financed from private contributions from the missionary organisations, taxation retained by the native authorities, taxation of the European and Indian communities during 1930–32, and private contributions from the various communities.[50]

Education was provided in racially separate educational systems, in different categories of schools run by different agencies, and according to different curricula. Since the education conference in Dar es Salaam in 1925, it was the declared policy of the British administration to support expanded educational facilities for the African population. With respect to the immigrant communities, the British administration gave some financial assistance even before 1925. This assistance continued after the imposition of the educational tax on the (male) European and Indian communities in 1930. During the interwar period, the British administration also gained increased control of African education, including that provided by the other educational agencies in the territory.

While the overwhelming part of total educational expenditure from the education department was spent on African education, its relative share dropped in the interwar period from 88 per cent of total expenditure in 1930/31 to 67 per cent in 1945 (Table 2.1). African education was instead increasingly financed by the native authorities whose share rose from 8 to 15 per cent during 1930/31–1945. Missionary organisations gradually lost their independent influence as they became dependent on the grants-in-aid scheme from the British administration.[51]

In contrast, the relative spending by the British administration on European education increased from 5 to 13 per cent and on Indian education from 7 to 19 per cent during 1930/31–1945 (Table 2.1). The relative contribution of the education tax to total educational expenditures amounted to 7 per cent for European and 10 per cent for Indian

Table 2.2 African Education in Tanganyika by Category 1931–46: Schools and Enrolment

Category	1931 Enrolment				1946 Enrolment			
	Schools	Male	Female	Total	Schools	Male	Female	Total
Government								
Village schools	44	2,668	3	2,671	–	–	–	–
Primary education (stds I–IV, V–VI)	–	–	–	–	53	6,554	1,353	7,907
Girls' schools	3	n/a	143	143	–	–	–	–
Central schools	8a	1,766a	–	1,766a	–	–	–	–
Secondary education (stds VII–XII)	–	–	–	–	7	667	–	667
Technical, vocational, teacher training	–	–	–	–	17b	551	79	630b
Post-secondary education	–	–	–	–	1c	21	–	21
Sub-total	55	4,434	146	4,580	78	7,793	1,432	9,225
Native authority								
Village schools	39	3,071	–	3,071	–	–	–	–
Primary education (stds I–IV, V–VI)	–	–	–	–	189	18,015	2,333	20,348
Secondary education (stds I–IV, V–VI)	–	–	–	–	1	28	–	28
Sub-total	39	3,071	–	3,071	190	18,043	2,333	20,376

Table 2.2 cont.   *African Education in Tangayika by Category 1931–46: Schools and Enrolment*

Category	Schools	Male	Female	Total	Schools	Male	Female	Total
Mission assisted								
Village schools	149	8,878	4,398	13,276	–	–	–	–
Primary education (stds I–IV, V–VI)	–	–	–	–	647	52,321	21,524	73,845
Central schools	16[a]	1,766[a]	–	1,766[a]	–	–	–	–
Secondary education (stds VII–XII)	–	–	–	–	15	717	34	751
Technical, vocational, teacher training	–	–	–	–	34[b]	996	278	1,274
Sub-total	165	10,644	4,398	15,042	696	54,034	21,836	75,870
Mission unassisted								
Village schools	3,175[d]	90,688[d]	53,310[d]	143,998[d]	–	–	–	–
Primary education (stds I–IV, V–VI)	–	–	–	–	198	8,517	4,562	13,079
Central schools	5[a]	832[a]	–	832[a]	–	–	–	–
Sub-total	3,180	91,520	53,310	144,830	198	8,517	4,562	13,079
Grand total	3,439	109,669	57,854	167,523	1,162	88,387	30,163	118,550

n/a Not applicable.
Notes: a Including vocational education.
    b Including teacher training, some attached to secondary schools, stds. VII and VIII doing academic work.
    c Makerere College.
    d Including bush schools.

Sources: Department of Education, *Annual Report 1931:* 62–65, *1946:* 32–33.

education in 1930/31. The balance in the educational funds was exhausted in 1934 in the European system and in 1937 in the Indian system when education was subsequently financed by the British administration.[52]

During the early interwar period, most education in the African system was provided by missionary societies in unassisted village schools and 'bush' schools. This category constituted approximately 90 per cent of all schools with 82 per cent of all enrolment in 1931 (Table 2.2). During 1931–46, many of the mission unassisted village schools were absorbed in the government-controlled system because of their reliance on grants-in-aid. The relative enrolment in the mission assisted schools increased from 10 to 64 per cent of all students during this period. Furthermore, native authorities also became more responsible for the provision of education, increasing their relative share from 2 to 17 per cent of total enrolment. The government-run system remained small in size, enrolment increasing from only 3 to 8 per cent during the period.

Most of the African education provided was at the elementary level. Only approximately 3 per cent of all students participated in education beyond the primary level during 1931–46. Of these the number of females was miniscule (approximately 340 in 1946). Female enrolment was concentrated in the mission unassisted and mission assisted systems. During 1931–46, females constituted approximately one third of total enrolment in the unassisted system and, despite increasing numbers, approximately one quarter of the total in the mission assisted system. In the native authority and government-run systems the number of enrolled females was even lower. It was approximately 10 per cent of total enrolment in native authority schools in 1946 and increased from approximately 3 to 15 per cent in the government system during 1931–46.

Missionary societies generally supported elementary education for Africans as understood in more cultural or religious terms than stipulated by the British administration. Education beyond the elementary level was provided by missionary societies primarily to create staff for expanded mission, including educational, activities. In the village schools, the three Rs and other subjects, such as religion, geography, biology, history, Kiswahili and agricultural activities were taught in the local vernacular in sub-standards I and II and in standards I and II. The bush schools were mainly religious centres which brought literacy skills to converts as a result of the teaching of Christianity. As the bush schools developed into mission assisted village schools, they had, however, to conform to the centrally decided curriculum and other educational policies. This affected, in particular, the relative importance of religion in the curriculum and the use of the vernacular as the medium of instruction.[53]

During the interwar period, teaching beyond standard II was undertaken in mission unassisted, mission assisted and government primary and central schools. In standards III and IV, the teaching was in Kiswahili and included English as a subject, in addition to the previously mentioned subjects taught in the village schools. In standards V and VI, English was the medium of instruction and the curriculum was academic. Vocational training, including teacher training (level II (Kiswahili)), different trades and clerical training, was also offered. Some central and special schools had further education for standards VII and VIII, including teacher training (level I (English)), trade and clerical training as well as technical and administrative training. The central schools, of which Tabora[54] was the most prestigious, gave preference of entry to the expected future rulers: the sons of chiefs and headmen. Besides fulfilling positions in the indirect rule system, the boys were expected to be able to compete with Indians for lower clerical positions in the central administration and the commercial firms.

Native authorities and chiefs demanded government or government-supported educational facilities to avoid proselytisation or mission control, and as a means of developing cash crop production or providing low- and middle-level clerical staff for the native and British administrations. Both cash crop production and clerical work were likely means of increased influence and prestige. Demands for a literary and industrial education for Africans alongside agricultural education were also expressed during the 1920s and 1930s by the African representatives in the ACAE.[55] Literary and industrial education, particularly knowledge of English, was the most important foundation for African access to the modern sector of the economy and the central political institutions. The small participation in education beyond the primary level (3 per cent of total enrolment) indicates the lack of success in forcing this issue.

Europeans and Indians sought to establish educational facilities in the territory to substitute for those of their home countries and to provide a similar academic curriculum. For them, education, particularly post-elementary education, was also a means to gain access to the modern sector of the economy or to retain and enhance their communities' relative position in it. During the interwar period, both the European and the Indian educational systems offered six years of primary education (Tables 2.3 and 2.4). One government school in the Indian system offered six years of secondary education. While the European system primarily consisted of government-assisted or government schools, many of the private unassisted schools in the Indian system were, in fact, assisted from the education tax fund.

Approximately half of the students were enrolled in the private assisted institutions in the Indian system, whereas they constituted less than one-third in the European system. There was a relatively equal distribution of males and females in the European system. In the Indian

Table 2.3 *European Education in Tanganyika by Category 1931-46: Schools and Enrolment*

Category	1931				1946			
		Enrolment				Enrolment		
	Schools	Male	Female	Total	Schools	Male	Female	Total
Government								
Primary education (stds I-IV)	2	47	38	85[a]	4	218	194	412
Private assisted								
Primary education (stds I-IV)	11[b]	236	202	438[b]	6	94	108	202
Secondary education (stds VI-XII)	[c]				–	9	10	19[d]
Sub-total	11[b]	236	202	438[b]	6	103	118	221
Private unassisted								
Primary education (stds I-VI)	n/a	n/a	n/a	n/a	n/a		n/a	
Grand total	13	283	240	523	10	321	312	633

n/a   Not available.
Notes: a In addition 40 children were assisted by correspondence course.
   b Including Kindergarten, and mixed (including Goan) schools.
   c No secondary school facilities but parents were assisted in sending their children to Kenya.
   d There were no secondary schools for European children in Tanganyika but in 1946 children studied up to standard IX at two schools and up to standard VII at one school. In all 159 boys and girls attended secondary education in Kenya subsidised by the British administration. Others were assisted in Southern Rhodesia and South Africa.

Sources: Department of Education, *Annual Report 1931:* 67–68, *1946:* 30.

Table 2.4 Indian Education in Tanganyika by Category 1931–46: Schools and Enrolment

| | 1931 | | | | 1946 | | | |
| | | Enrolment | | | | Enrolment | | |
Category	Schools	Male	Female	Total	Schools	Male	Female	Total
Government								
Primary education (stds I–VI)	2	209	80	289	2	912	268	1,180
Secondary education (stds VII–XII)	1	184	7	191	1	431	69	500
Sub-total	3	393	87	480	3	1,343	337	1,680
Private assisted (Aga Khan and others)								
Primary education (stds I–VI)	11	715[a]	505[a]	1,220[a]	48	3,043	3,054	6,097
Secondary education (stds VII–XII)					28	630	417	1,047
Sub-total	11	715[a]	505[a]	1,220[a]	76	3,673	3,471	7,144
Private unassisted								
Primary education (stds I–VI)	31[b]	n/a	n/a	855[b]	n/a	n/a	n/a	n/a
Grand total	45	1,108	592	2,555	79	5,016	3,808	8,824

n/a Not available.
Notes: a 1932 figures as 1931 figures were not available.
　　　　 b 31 of the schools were assisted from the education fund.

Sources: Department of Education, *Annual Report 1931*: 62–71, *1932*: 72–73, *1946*: 31.

system, males and females were relatively equally distributed in the private assisted system, whereas there was a higher male participation rate in the government-run system. During 1931–46, female participation in secondary education increased from approximately 4 to 14 per cent of the total. The contents of the curriculum corresponded with those of the communities' home countries and were strictly academic. Vocational subjects were never included, Kiswahili was taught only in Indian schools and not until 1958, and English was taught already at the primary level in schools which used another medium of instruction in the early years (such as Urdu or German).[56]

Education for Adaptation as a Mechanism of Social Control: Concluding Remarks

All categories of educational institutions were concentrated in the centres of African cash crop production, plantation or white settler production and the centres for trade, administration and service industries (see Map 2). This location meant that schools were within easy reach of the small European and Indian populations, whereas only approximately two-thirds of the African population, in theory, had access to all kinds of education. Some unassisted and village or native authority schools also existed in the more remote areas which continued to operate outside formal government control, maintained traditional forms of organisation and were exposed to traditional education and/or minimal instruction in the three Rs in the vernacular, mainly for proselytisation purposes. These areas were likely to have stayed relatively socially cohesive, since functional and institutional specialisation and differentiation were low and as there were no strongly competing value systems. The areas incorporated into the exchange economy, on the other hand, witnessed conflicting forces and contrasting purposes as they combined several different economic forms of organisation, had a higher degree of political control and were exposed to competing value systems through educational institutions which focused on different norms and skills for different purposes.

The stated policy of Education for Adaptation applied only to the African population and was provided for males rather than females. It aimed at the provision of basic reading, writing and accounting skills in support of the indirect rule system, the transfer of vocational agricultural skills to develop peasant agriculture and the transmission of Western civic values and Christianity to 'civilise' and mute certain traditional values and customs. During the interwar period, the emphasis on teaching for 'civilisation' in mission unassisted schools was replaced by teaching of secular skills according to the interpreted political and

Map 2 (Overleaf)
Educational Facilities in Tanganyika 1947
Northern and Central parts of the country

The original map used colour to indicate the division between
Protestant and Catholic mission stations and schools

Source: Report by His Majesty's Government
on the Administration of Tanganyika
for the year 1947. HMSO London 1948

UGANDA

LAKE VICTORIA

KISUMU

KISII

L. EDWARD

MASAKA

MBARARA

R. KAGERA

MUSOMA

R. MARA

RUCHURU

KABALE

BUKOBA

B

A

A

B

R. GRUMETI

RUANDA

KIGALI

LAKE KIVU

BIHARAMULO

GEITA

MWANZA

A

B

P R O V I N C E

R. RUVUVU

URUNDI

USUMBURA

KITEGA

R. Moyowosi

MOSONDO

R. Nkonga

SHINYANGA

KAHAMA

R. Manonga

SEKENKE

A

R. Ntiagasoi

R. Igombe

NZEGA

SINGIDA

A

2

A

BELGIAN CONGO

KASULU

KIGOMA

2

A

B

TABORA

(A)

B

W E S T E R N

RIVER UGALLA

ITIGI

MANYONI

R. Kizig

ALBERTVILLE

LAKE TANGANYIKA

B

R. Kaluma

R. Rungwa

R. Njombe

S O U T H

SUMBAWANGA

Map 2 (Overleaf)

Educational Facilities in Tanganyika 1947
Southern and Central parts of the country

The original map used colour to indicate the division between
Protestant and Catholic mission stations and schools

Source: Report by His Majesty's Government
on the Administration of Tanganyika
for the year 1947. HMSO London 1948

REFERENCE

Principal Mission Stations with European Staffs, PROTESTANT............■

"   "   "   "   "   ROMAN CATHOLIC............■

Other Missions or Schools, PROTESTANT............▲

"   "   "   -   ROMAN CATHOLIC............▲

Government Secondary and/or Teacher Training Schools for African Boys......●A

"   "   Boarding   Schools   "   "   "   "   Girls.........●B

Village and Native Authority Schools............○

Schools for European Children............●C

"   "   -   Indian............●

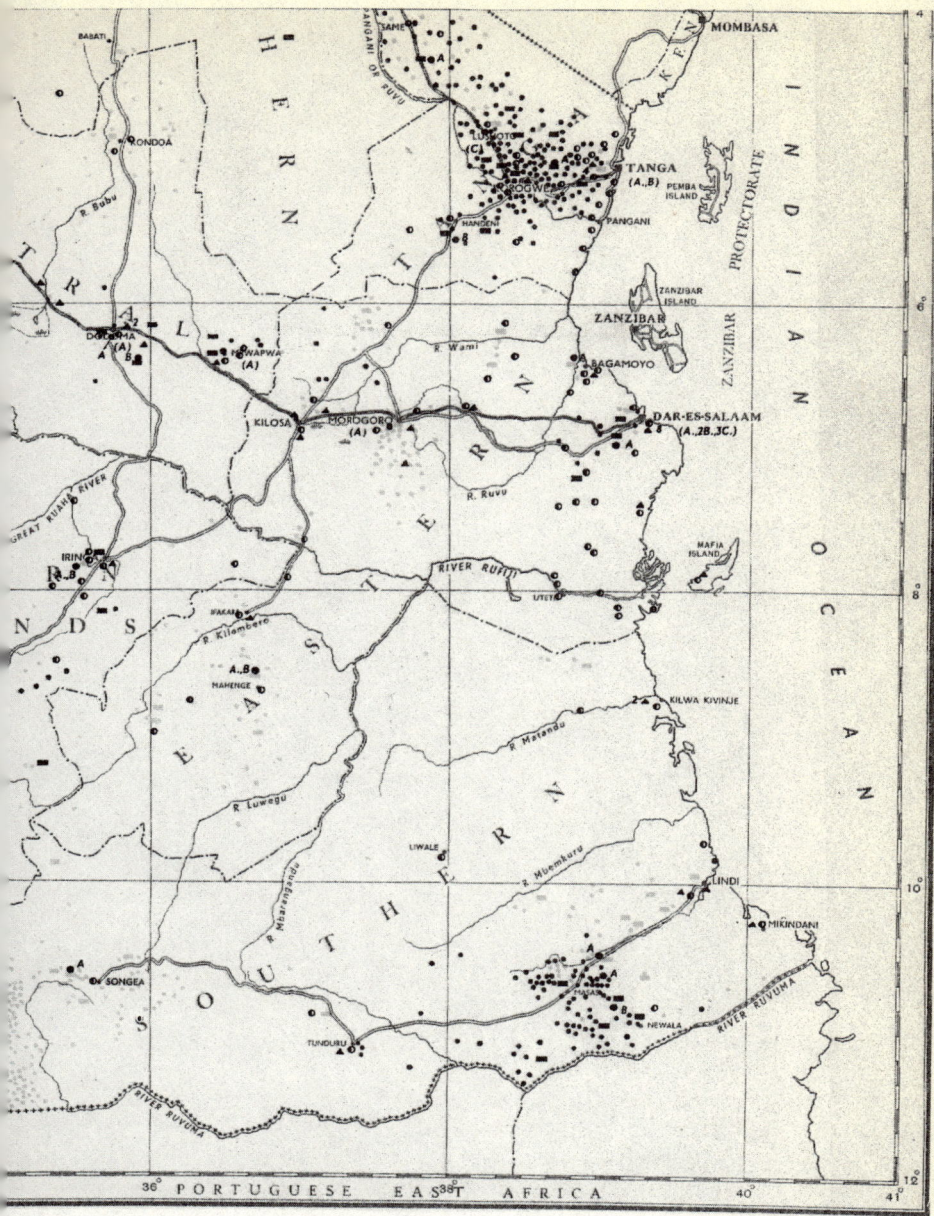

MOMBASA

BABATI

KONDOA

R. Bubu

SAME

A

LUSHOTO
(C)

KOROGWE

TANGA
(A.,B)

PEMBA
ISLAND

HANGENI

PANGANI

ZANZIBAR
ISLAND

ZANZIBAR

DODOMA
(A)
A_2
(A)
A_1
B_1

MPWAPWA
(A)

R. Wami

BAGAMOYO

KILOSA

MOROGORO
(A)

DAR-ES-SALAAM
(A.,2B.,3C.)

R. Ruvu

MAFIA
ISLAND

IRINGA
A,B

RIVER RUFIJI

UTETE

GREAT RUAHA RIVER

IFAKARA

R. Kilombero

A.,B
MAHENGE

KILWA KIVINJE

R. Matandu

R. Luwegu

LIWALE

R. Mbemkuru

R. Mbwemkuru

LINDI

MIKINDANI

A

SONGEA

MASASI

A
B

NEWALA

RIVER RUVUMA

TUNDURU

RIVER RUVUMA

PORTUGUESE   EAST   AFRICA

INDIAN   OCEAN

PROTECTORATE

KENYA

NORTHERN

CENTRAL

EASTERN

SOUTHERN

R LANDS

36°   38°   40°   41°

4   6   8   10   12

economic mission of adaptation. This was reflected in increased control by the British administration of the mission schools and in more direct participation and funding of the government-run system during 1931–46.

African access to the kind of literary and industrial knowledge which would lead to alternative opportunities and which was argued for by the African representatives in the ACAE remained small. This was the case for both males and females. This knowledge was instead provided for the European and Indian populations, who, based on further education abroad, could maintain or enhance their access to the modern sector of the economy and their participation in the central political institutions while also preserving the underlying value systems of their cultures of origin.

As a concept, Education for Adaptation had strong political implications. The British administration relied for its implementation on the native authorities and the missionary societies, and, thereby, preserved the traditional political structure and a local community-oriented education that disregarded the socio-economic dynamics of the African peasant sector. Except in some innovative and short-lived cases, the education of traditional rulers never implied attempts at integrating the local political institutions and structure into the central political system or at readjusting the colonial structure to fit more properly with the traditional African political system. Instead the two systems were understood as separate or complementary parts of the machinery of administration, whose duties 'should never conflict, and should overlap as little as possible'.[57]

Innovative projects in support of the development of local African rulers, such as the Malangali project which was proposed in 1927 by William Bryant Mumford[58] as an anthropological, primarily cultural experiment in the adaptation philosophy, aiming at the preservation of the tribe and the natural evolution of indigenous traditions and customs, were closed down because of suspicion and negative attitudes by British officials and because of lack of consistency in educational policy-making. Similarly, the knowledge and skills provided through Education for Adaptation, at most, improved the basic agricultural techniques, but did not lead to higher technological levels. Even innovative efforts aimed at improved production and productivity of the peasant sector were not sustained. As will appear from the following analysis of the Nyakato agricultural training centre in the West Lake Province, which was typical of other innovations during indirect rule, such efforts were affected by conflicts in interpretation and implementation of educational policies among British officials, by their lack of consistency with and agreement on the underlying purposes of education, and their lack of consideration of local needs and wishes.

Notes

1. League of Nations 1922: Article 3.
2. United Kingdom 1925: 4.
3. Iliffe 1972: 8–9, 1979: 88–122; Temu 1980: 100–101.
4. 'Native' was the official term used during this period concerning the indigenous population which represented different ethnic groups. The term is applied here in accordance with the prevalent official use. It is otherwise replaced by 'African'.
5. United Kingdom 1923.
6. Lord Cameron replaced Sir Horace Byatt and was governor of Tanganyika during 1925–31. He was transferred from Nigeria where he had held different positions since 1908, including colonial secretary (1912), secretary to the central government (1914) and chief secretary (1921–24). His partnership in Nigeria with Lord Lugard, the architect of the indirect rule system, made him a firm believer in its application to Tanganyika.
7. See, for example, Kjekshus 1977: 26–69; Koponen 1988: 219–236, 241–257.
8. Hailey 1938: 434–443; Iliffe 1979: 318–341.
9. Brett 1973: 56–58. See also Hailey 1938; Morris–Hale 1969.
10. United Kingdom 1929.
11. United Kingdom 1932: 16–34.
12. Brett 1973: 228.
13. Iliffe 1979: 274–276, 286–291; Rodney 1980.
14. Ruthenberg 1964: 13–15.
15. Koponen 1988: 64, 92–93.
16. Iliffe 1971, 1979; Rodney 1980.
17. Rodney 1980: 136.
18. Brett 1973: 221.
19. IBRD 1961: 22; Brett 1973: 227–228; Iliffe 1979: 141–151; Rodney 1980: 132–234.
20. These calculations are based on figures in the annual reports of the Department of Agriculture. See also Brett 1973: 222 and Coulson 1982: 44.
21. Iliffe 1979: *passim*; IBRD 1961: 12; Rodney 1980.
22. Oliver 1965; Wright 1976.
23. Koponen n.d.
24. Ploeg 1977.
25. Koponen n.d.
26. The committee was set up in 1923. From 1929, it was named the Advisory Committee on Education in the Colonies (ACEC).
27. United Kingdom 1925: 4.
28. United Kingdom 1925: 5.
29. United Kingdom 1925: 8.
30. United Kingdom 1925: 8.
31. Lewis 1962: 210.
32. Lewis 1962. See also King 1971.

33. Hailey 1938, 1942.
34. United Kingdom 1937: 10.
35. United Kingdom 1935: 2–3, 1937: 14–16.
36. United Kingdom 1937: 11.
37. United Kingdom 1937: 12.
38. United Kingdom 1935: 2.
39. United Kingdom 1935: 6–7, 16–20.
40. United Kingdom 1937: 8–10, 13–16.
41. *Report of the Education Conference 1925*: 5–6.
42. *Report of the Education Conference 1925*: 3–13.
43. Department of Education, *Annual Report 1925*: 65, *1929*: 53, *1947*: 1, *1948*: 2–3.
44. See, for example, United Kingdom, *Report for the year 1925*: 65–66, *1927*: 60, *1935*: 102; Department of Education, *Annual Report 1927*: 60.
45. United Kingdom, *Report for the year 1932*: 65–70, *1933*: 65, App. X, *1934*: 87.
46. United Kingdom 1932: 62–67.
47. Department of Education, *Annual Report 1931*: 3.
48. *Memorandum on African Education in Tanganyika* 1933; *Memorandum on Education in Tanganyika* 1934.
49. United Kingdom, *Report for the year(s) 1922–38, 1947*: public finance.
50. Official figures on private contributions from the missionary societies and the individual communities are generally unavailable for the interwar period. Besides, official figures were not presented in a systematic way until the British administration became more involved in educational provision from 1930/31. During the British period, the methods of enumeration and presentation changed and figures are, therefore, not always comparable. The official statistical materials were less reliable in the interwar period than after the Second World War. Figures in the annual reports of the education department have, therefore, been compared with other official and unofficial figures. This is also the case with the presented figures on schools and enrolment. While this method has increased the relative reliability of the presented trends, it has not solved the fundamental problem of the underlying materials.
51. United Kingdom, *Report for the year(s) 1932*: 67, *1947*: 269.
52. United Kingdom, *Report for the year(s) 1932*: 67, *1947*: 269.
53. Department of Education, *Annual Reports 1923–46*: *passim*; United Kingdom, *Reports for the years 1919–38*: *passim*.
54. Tabora was opened in 1925 and run on the principles of the English public school. The boys were divided into groups according to geography and administrative district. Each group elected a boy as head chief and one or more boys as sub-chiefs. School orders were passed through the elected chief who passed them on to his group and was responsible for adherence to the orders by the group. The boys were taught English, geography, mathematics, book-keeping, accounting, tribal history and British history.
55. *Proceedings of the Tanganyika Advisory Committee on African Education 1929*: 17, *1933*: 20; Oliver 1952; Austen 1968: 135–138, 176–178, *passim*; Wright 1971: 178, *passim*; Lawuo 1984.

56. Department of Education, *Annual Reports 1923–59*: *passim*; United Kingdom, *Report for the year(s) 1919–38*: *passim*.
57. Lugard 1965: 203.
58. Mumford was education officer in Bukoba and headmaster of Bukoba central school during 1923–25 and headmaster of Dar es Salaam central school in 1925. He did his PhD in Canada on the Malangali experiment which was closed down after his resignation in 1933.

Three

The Adaptation
of Peasant Production
The Case of Nyakato

Nyakato was an innovative agricultural training centre which operated under the Department of Agriculture during 1933-39. Both before and after this time it was a formal educational institution under the control of the Department of Education. The changing status of the school related to wider changes of British educational policy, in particular the extent to which it was believed that the curriculum must be related to the future agricultural occupation of the students. The teaching of agriculture in schools in the Tanganyika territory was often met with scepticism by the local populations and there was also mutual scepticism between the agricultural and educational departments concerning their respective capacities and responsibilities to teach scientific agriculture. In the particular case of Nyakato, these conflicts in combination with wider politico-economic circumstances, determined the rise and fall of the centre as an agricultural experiment.

The Establishment of Nyakato as an
Agricultural Training Centre

Nyakato was located in the heart of the coffee growing area of the Bukoba district in the West Lake Province (see Map 3). The district had a highly successful commercial production of coffee, the proportion of which was the highest in the province, and a long tradition of organised education. As indicated earlier, coffee was traditionally grown together with bananas by the royal clans, but was also produced commercially by the common peasantry by 1904. Throughout the 1920s and during the depression in the 1930s, coffee production kept expanding, reaching a record high in 1935 of 10,881 tons which was not achieved again until 1970.[1]

35

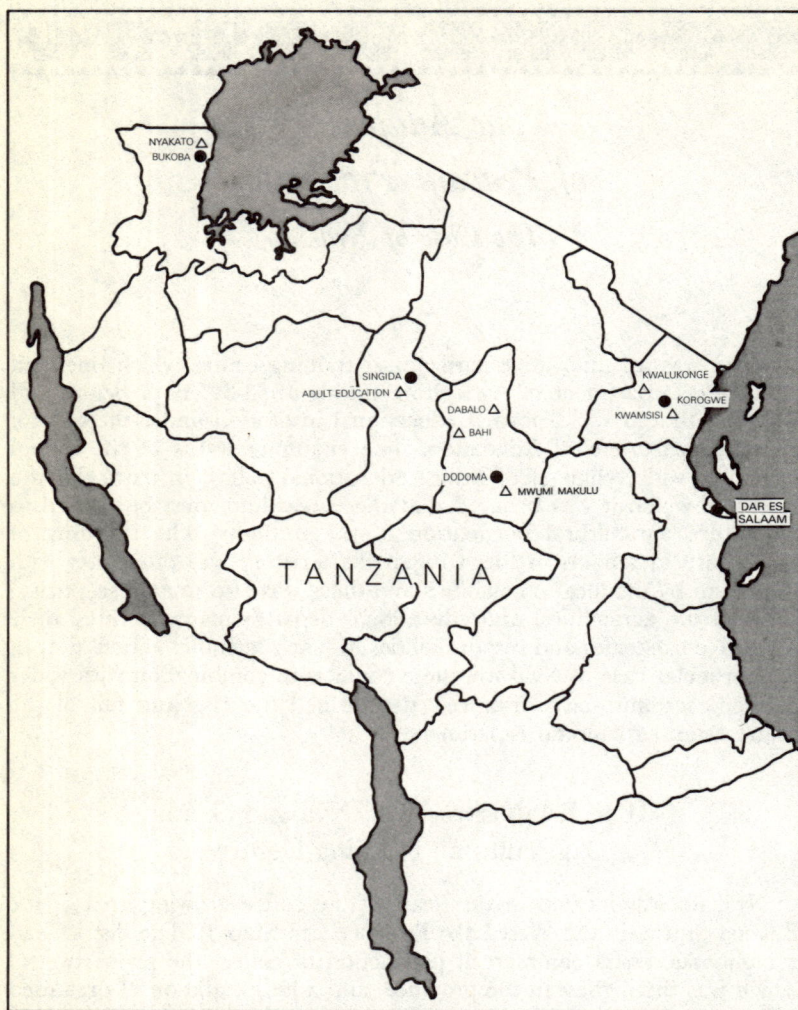

Map 3   Location of Case Institutions and Programmes

One of the effects of the indirect rule system in Bukoba, however, was a declining responsibility of the chiefs for the agricultural and educational activities which were previously under their control. The chiefs could no longer profit directly from all increases in the agricultural productivity of their subjects, although the exercise of the legislative powers did provide them with a theoretical means of control. Similarly, the traditional educational institution under the bakama,[2] the muteko (band of children), was prohibited by decree in 1916. School facilities of the native authorities, which continued to expand until the depression in the 1930s, were subject to the inspection of government education officers, and the growing missionary sector also became increasingly dependent on subsidies from the central authorities.[3]

The muteko institution was important both for social cohesion and for the selection of commoners for the courts of the bakama and the sub-chiefs. The muteko system aimed at education in the correct attitudes to authority, involving both ritual and military training. At regular intervals during the age of 12–15, boys selected by a mukungu (a man of high social standing) spent defined periods at a mukama's residence. The boys belonged to rival companies (groups) and the education aimed, among other things, at identifying the most competitive boys who were, eventually, retained at the mukama's residence. Depending on their age the boys were taught, for instance, ceremonial procedures, warfare skills, cultivation and the art of building houses and fences. Young women were apparently also brought to the courts through the less organised buzana institution which, according to missionaries, largely served sexual purposes for the bakama.[4]

The muteko and buzana institutions were officially prohibited in 1916, although the growth of mission schools throughout the district had diminished their power before that time. In 1923, chiefs also lost the responsibility for the provision of district schools, including the feeding and clothing of the children who attended them, which they had otherwise maintained since the abandonment of the muteko system. This responsibility was reinstituted in 1927 through contributions to education via the native treasury. There were at the time eleven schools in the district: one central school in Bukoba township; nine village schools in each county of the district except for Kianja which had two; and one village school at Biharamulo. In all, 933 boys were under instruction, of whom 110 were in the central school in Bukoba township.[5]

In 1929, the Bukoba township central school was moved to new premises at Nyakato, the funding for which was provided on a shared basis by the native authorities and the central administration. It faced initial difficulties in terms of non-attendance and criticism of educational quality, as academic teaching of the boys by the superintendent of education was initially restricted and the boys instead participated in finalising construction work on the school.[6] The Director of Education, Rivers-Smith, in 1930 indicated in a letter to the Chief Secretary that he always expected Bukoba to 'become the first province to present difficulties' with respect to the absorption of educated boys unless they could be 'induced to turn their attention to improved and extended agricultural activities'.[7]

While this view was supported by the district agricultural officer, who argued that 'it was through schools and particularly central schools that improved methods could be taught',[8] the Reverend Father Rivard of the White Fathers Mission expressed concern about shamba (school field) work because this kind of work was traditionally done by women.[9] In the territory as a whole until 1931, only elementary schools aimed consciously to any extent towards the production of farmers through the teaching of agriculture in the school gardens. In 1928, when syllabuses in agriculture and husbandry were drawn up and when it was arranged that the agricultural department was to train a small number of teachers in agriculture at its farm near Morogoro, there was still no agricultural syllabus for the central schools and the subject was not examined in central schools until 1932.[10]

The change of Nyakato's status into an agricultural training centre under the Department of Agriculture was related to the impact of the depression. Despite the modest and inexpensive provision of social services in Tanganyika supplied during 1925–31, Sir Sydney Armitage-Smith in his 1932 report to the Secretary of State on the economic situation in Tanganyika singled out government central schools as one mechanism to reduce educational expenditure. The Bukoba central school was among those selected for termination.[11]

In response to the recommendation, the Director of Education in 1932 informed the headmaster of Nyakato that 'owing to the financial position it was necessary to close [the school] as [a] central school and suggesting that [it] should become [a] farm school'.[12] Provincial officials welcomed the idea of establishing a school which could help improve the dominant agricultural coffee industry and the general prosperity of the area. While they pointed to the support of the chiefs as a crucial factor if such an experiment was to be successful, the fact that Nyakato was located on bad agricultural land which had never been cultivated by the local population seemed not to be an important issue. In 1927, even before the Bukoba township central school was moved to Nyakato, it was realised by the coffee officer and the agricultural officer in agreement with the then headmaster that, while the deficient soils did not represent insuperable difficulties, undertaking scientific agriculture at Nyakato would depend on manuring, donations of cattle and water facilities.[13]

The Functioning of Nyakato 1933–39

Nyakato started as an agricultural training centre in 1933. The conversion implied that the Department of Education withdrew, except for inspection, from educational activities in the area, leaving the more advanced type of education to be provided by the missionary organisations or to be achieved in the government school in Tabora. These consequences were not discussed with the local population, who were instead informed by the Chief Secretary of the new purpose of Nyakato as a matter of fact, and which they would soon realise was in their best interest.[14]

The overall purpose of the school was to contribute to improved coffee cultivation methods by teaching the theory and practice of coffee cultivation to youth and adults in the area. The emphasis was on the effective transfer of skills to students who, it was believed, could act as agents of change in their communities, either by being employed as agricultural instructors with the native and British administrations or by setting positive examples when applying the new production methods on their own plots.[15] This purpose of the school and the intended employment of the students must be understood in the context of growing pressure among British officials to ensure that coffee production methods were improved in order, in their view, to prevent diseases from striking the coffee trees. It resulted in the formulation of orders in 1928 by the British administration which were to be imposed on the peasantry around Lake Victoria by the native authorities. They were followed by new legislation in 1930 and 1935 concerning the cultivation and preparation of coffee and in 1937 by rules which provided for inspection and enforced improvement of the quality of the coffee.[16]

Neither chiefs nor parents initially gave the training centre their strong support and only a few sons of chiefs, sub-chiefs and headmen were included as students. The senior agricultural lecturer at Nyakato questioned whether 'any pupil of a desirable type with the ability to read and write Swahili could be persuaded to enter the institution without the promise of continued academic teaching'.[17] This concern was shared by the district officer and the acting provincial officer who both argued in favour of the inclusion of general subjects in the curriculum for Nyakato.[18]

The agricultural course at Nyakato was originally designed by the agricultural lecturer in charge of Nyakato, Mr Haarer, as a two-year course for boys from either native administration or mission schools who had completed the two sub-standards and standards I and II. According to demand and for a limited number of students, further standards were added in specific years, namely during 1933–34 standards III and IV, in

1935 standard V, in 1935 and 1937 standard VI, and in 1938 standard VII. The higher standards were established according to the wishes of the chiefs at a later time when more of their sons attended the school. The total number of students increased from 19 in 1933 to 68 in 1939, the average being 40 in the interim period. According to British officials, the students were not the best students in the area, who preferred the higher level academic teaching in missionary central schools or in the government school in Tabora. The agricultural lecturer at Nyakato did, however, point to some exceptional students being enrolled in the course, and the number who failed each year was limited. As the applications for entry into the school were increasing, a more substantial selection procedure was established which involved the agricultural lecturer in charge of Nyakato and the schools from which the students applied.[19]

The syllabus combined academic subjects with practical work. The relative emphasis between the two was roughly 10 hours per week of academic subjects unrelated to agriculture, 2½ hours per week of classroom teaching of agriculture and 10½ hours per week of practical agricultural work. The pure academic subjects included arithmetic, Kiswahili, geography and general knowledge. English was only taught as an out-of-school activity in the later years of the centre's existence. The agriculture-oriented academic teaching was concentrated on the theory of agricultural practices, botany and soils with specific reference to coffee cultivation. Practical activities were undertaken, for instance, on demonstration plots and on self-contained plots reserved for the students. Industrial activities, especially carpentry, were similarly related to the production of tools needed for coffee production. The school also functioned as an adult education centre, providing a six months' course in improved coffee farming for a limited number of nearby adult male farmers.[20]

A central element in the teaching of improved coffee cultivation to the students and adult farmers was soil fertilisation experiments. Coffee was traditionally grown in and among the banana groves where the soil was mulched, aerated and fertilised and where the heavy rainfall enabled coffee to grow vigorously. The intercropping in banana groves was due both to land shortage and to the nature of the husbandry system on the very poor and infertile soils which were severely lacking in plant nutrients.[21] According to the agricultural officer at Nyakato, the local population had not increased its mulch or its manure since the interplanting of the vast number of coffee trees, and both the banana and the coffee crop suffered accordingly. Since there was pressure on the good land in the coffee belt and as it was necessary to plant bananas two to three years in advance of planting coffee, the experiments at Nyakato attempted to show how coffee farming on already existing and new plots could be improved by applying a compost made of local grass and cow dung. While fertilisation experiments at Nyakato yielded positive results after two years of work, there seems to have been no consideration or discussion by the British officials of the possible implications of a more widespread use of these techniques in the local area. The realisation that students had to be given cattle to follow up the experiments on their own plots after leaving the school was not seen in a context of how an increased number of cattle, and of banana stems to create the mulch, would inevitably put further pressure on the grazing land and could interfere in the traditional subsistence production.[22]

During 1933–35, there was a continuous expansion of the different kinds of activities which were to constitute the school as an agricultural centre. Besides the development of demonstration plots for coffee growing, they included, for instance, the construction of cattle kraals (cattle being provided by the native authorities and the British administration for breeding purposes and to obtain cow dung for the soil fertilisation experiments); the establishment of coffee nurseries (where experiments with different kinds of coffee plants were undertaken); the planting of trees and elephant grass (as an anti-soil erosion measure and to provide grass for the soil fertilisation experiments); the inclusion of the Bukoba native authority agricultural sub-station on the school's premises (for teaching and experimental purposes); and the construction of a hydram (to provide water for irrigation). This work was undertaken as an inter-departmental effort of the British administration, involving the agricultural, the veterinary and the forestry departments in cooperation with the local native authorities.[23]

During 1936–39, the teaching of coffee growing in theory and practice was consolidated and some of the less promising experimental work was given up (for instance, the use of the hydram and the planting of different kinds of grasses). The centre continued to attract many visits from government officials, chiefs, sultans and other interested parties from within and outside the province. Annual rallies at the school were used as occasions to promote the Nyakato cultivation methods in the wider community and, specifically, to persuade parents to allow their sons to apply the acquired knowledge on parental plots upon their return from school. The practical teaching began to include field trips to plots outside the school where innovative methods were practised, among others, by ex-Nyakato students. Negotiations were, moreover, undertaken with the British administration and the native authorities concerning a settlement scheme for Nyakato students on new land after the completion of their course.[24]

The Reaction to Nyakato

As measured by the increasing number of students, the added higher grades, the many visits from outside, and the level of activities under-taken in active cooperation between national and local authorities, Nyakato seems to have been a rewarding experience. The enthusiasm for the place was recorded by the acting provincial commissioner, who, in 1935, informed the Chief Secretary that Nyakato 'had been extremely popular with the chiefs and the local people'[25] and that a request for a similar centre had been made by the Chagga.[26] The district officer in 1933 viewed the progress of the centre as being excellent, it 'has the beginnings of a real agricultural centre',[27] and the provincial commis-sioner saw the future prosperity of the province in an extensive agri-cultural training.[28]

In 1937, however, the government inspector of schools in the Lake Province, G.N. Eeles, claimed that Nyakato was fulfilling 'no useful purpose'[29] and discussions were ongoing within the British administration concerning the failure of the experiment. It was argued that Nyakato had failed in its purpose since the majority of the students did not settle as peasant farmers applying the new labour-intensive methods, after they had completed their course. The students reflected, it was implied, the attitudes of the wider environment that had grown rich too easily using traditional coffee cultivation methods and had an expressed distaste for manual labour.[30] The school was subsequently to revert to the Depart-ment of Education in accordance with the 'wishes of the Bukoba people'.[31]

The judgement that Nyakato had failed as an agricultural experiment was, thus, apparently made in the light of an overriding need to see a cause–effect relationship between the training and employment of students. It seemed not to have involved any detailed assessment of the many different experiments, the reasons for their failures and successes, or whether more sustained inputs from the British administration in cooperation with the local community could have resulted in the improvement of their viability. Similarly, the lack of rain in some years and the fact that the soils were naturally deficient were used as argu-ments to close down the experiment rather than to evaluate the achieve-ments in consideration of the less than favourable circumstances.

The African Association of Bukoba and individual chiefs did in 1935 and again in 1938 plead for the reestablishment of a government central school in Bukoba, having been encouraged by the government schools inspector. The claim was that knowledge of English was imperative to the teaching of technical agriculture, and that English teaching in central schools outside their home district uprooted the boys socially and culturally.[32] This argument, in fact, supported the view of the agricul-tural officer at Nyakato that, with regard to elementary botany and plant physiology, it was impossible to expect the local students to reach the standards of students in England, because of their imperfect knowledge of Kiswahili and unfamiliarity with the concepts in English.[33]

The fact that students of Nyakato in 1935 voiced a protest against the agricultural lecturer in charge of Nyakato because, it was claimed, he had replaced academic teaching by pure manual labour can hardly be interpreted as an expression of an innate attitude against manual labour. Rather it seemed to be a reaction against unfulfilled expectations and promises of the school as a scientific agricultural centre and was, possibly, also related to the fact that most manual labour was traditionally done by women. It is noteworthy that the protest was supported by the district and provincial offices with a subsequent discharge of the lecturer in question from the school.[34]

The wider employment prospects of the students were, more probably, determined by the creation of new opportunities to which the British administration contributed little. The negotiations concerning the settlement scheme for graduates, which the chiefs were ready to establish and support with capital and land and which the Department of Agriculture also favoured, were still ongoing when the British administration instead decided to close down Nyakato as an agricultural centre because of unresolved issues related to various aspects of the scheme. In addition, the British administration provided few, if any, opportunities for the students as agricultural instructors through the Department of Agriculture and native administrations.[35]

It is important to realise that the request from the chiefs for a government central school was not made in preference to the continuation of Nyakato, but was discussed as a possible addition to already existing educational facilities in 1935. Parents were strongly concerned that their children had to leave their home district to receive education in English in Tabora, and the African Association expressed willingness to contribute more to total educational expenditures by means of the hut-and-poll tax. While the government inspector was of the opinion that parents in Bukoba were no more willing to pay for their children's education than was any other African, the actual total educational expenditures in Bukoba were lower than the national average despite the relative prosperity of the area and the substantial interest in education.[36]

The context within which the pleas from the African Association and individual chiefs were made was one of increasing tension with the British administration over interventions in coffee production. The quasi-political African Association, which aimed at the welfare of the African population, was dominated by individuals who saw modern education and improved farming as beneficial to the indigenous people and who saw the chiefs as standing in the way of progress. Even though the Association represented the most effective link for the British administration with the peasantry, the administration did not support its request in 1934 to gain an increasing share of the lucrative coffee trade which was controlled by Asian businessmen. The resulting local tensions were further intensified when, in 1937, new coffee rules were introduced. The rules, which were implemented by the chiefs, aimed at preventing diseases from affecting the coffee trees and allowed inspectors to uproot what they considered to be sick trees. The interference in the traditional intercropping system prevented the use of old banana stems for mulching and, therefore, represented a serious threat to both the carefully developed soil fertility and the peasantry's subsistence crops. Their implementation was met with severe resistance from the peasantry and from leaders of the African Association and had implications for the future cooperation between the chiefs and the British administration.[37]

The local reaction to the new coffee rules in 1937 was to the British administration confirmation of the difficulty in promoting improved agriculture largely due to a perceived conservatism and laziness among the peasantry. In 1938, the government inspector of schools in the Lake Province argued for the establishment of an English-teaching school in the province as an urgent necessity in view of the recommendations of the commission on *Higher Education in East Africa* in 1937, which saw a need for an extension of the junior secondary scheme (beyond vernacular standard VI) in order to create candidates for higher training in, amongst others, agriculture, veterinary science and forestry. At this time, the Department of Agriculture was already planning to also establish a 'new Nyakato' on better soils at Kingolwira near Morogoro for the eastern part of the country. From the perspective of the British administration, reconverting Nyakato into a government central school, supported if necessary by native administration rather than education department funds, could be made at a negligible cost compared with the construction of new buildings at a time when some of its functions could be taken over by Kingolwira, when it would possibly be interpreted by the chiefs as a positive gesture in a tense political situation, and when the belief in changing the practices of coffee production had severely withered. In 1939 it was planned, in principle, that Nyakato should revert to the Department of Education as a government secondary school. It became a junior secondary school under native administration due to the impact of the Second World War.[38]

Technical Innovation of Peasant Production: Concluding Remarks

As an innovative experiment, Nyakato was short-lived and its effect on the local agricultural community was likely to have been small. No sustained educational policy brought continuity to the institution and no follow-up programmes for students, in the form of employment and higher-level courses, were established. The teaching of the new skills could possibly have made a difference to individual farmers provided they were supported by initial capital investments. Extensive application of the methods could, however, also have resulted in overgrazing of the scarce land resources and disturbances of the traditional intercropping patterns.

Like the national educational system, Nyakato was influenced by the continuously changing priorities of the British administration in view of the wider politico-economic context. While decisions to change the status of Nyakato were made with reference to the apparent wishes of the local population, there seems to have been no profound assessment either of Nyakato as an initial site for agricultural experiments or of its actual achievements as an agricultural centre. As was the case in the development of the national educational system throughout its formation during the British period, short-term needs and pressures took precedence over long-term measures and strategies.

The understanding of the wishes of the local population and the wider Bukoba peasant society by the British administration, as reflected in its treatment of conflicts at Nyakato, was restrictive. No attempt seems to have been made to meet the needs for truly scientific agricultural teaching which combined academic English teaching with advanced agricultural knowledge and training. Similarly, peasant reactions to enforced agricultural change were explained by perceptions of laziness and distaste for manual labour. The fact that the new agricultural methods demanded hard work without assured economic benefit, a perfectly rational ground for rejection of the methods, seemed not to have been considered. Furthermore, there seemed to have been little or no understanding of the fact that the new methods could disrupt certain cultural patterns, including the social division of labour, and social institutions related to issues of autonomy and settlement. If there was an expressed suspicion of the motives behind the technical innovations from the local community, it was probably related to their non-incorporation in decision-making at a time when unwanted interference in coffee production was already taking place.

While many of the underlying issues relating to Nyakato remained unresolved and influenced discussions even beyond the presence of the British administration in Tanganyika, others were dealt with more directly in the changing circumstances after the Second World War. The British attempts at adaptation were replaced by attempts at modernisation, which demanded new and improved knowledge and skills among the local population in order for the British administration to support its targeted efforts to model society more directly according to Western (British) patterns. The formal educational system was expanded and redirected to fulfil new needs, the struggle between the different communities in the area to gain access to the new opportunities became more severe, and the understanding of the need for community development took another turn as the African community became more politically vocal, as the international community came to play a more influential role, and as the British administration tried to adjust to a new political struggle for survival.

Notes

1. Hyden 1980: 50; Raikes 1976: 6.
2. Bakama (chiefs) is the plural of mukama in the Kihaya language.
3. Austen 1968: 174–178.
4. Primitive Native Educational System (Muteko). Bukoba district, TNA Acc. 215/26/Part I; Austen 1968: 144.
5. Notes on Bukoba Schools for the half-year ended 30/6/28, TNA Acc. 215/26/Part I; TNA SMP 10514/Vol. I.
6. TNA SMP 10514/Vol. I; Quarterly Report on the Government Schools in Bukoba Province for the Quarter Ended September 30th, 1930, TNA Acc. 215/26/Part II.
7. Letter dated 30th July 1930, TNA SMP 19141.
8. Minutes of the Fourth Meeting of the Mwanza Provincial Education Committee, 21 May 1930, TNA Acc. 215/E.1/44.
9. Minutes of the Fourth Meeting of the Provincial Education Commission of Bukoba Province, TNA SMP 19141.
10. Thompson 1965: 214–216.
11. United Kingdom 1932: 62–67.
12. Conversation at Mwanza 1 September 1932 between the Provincial Commissioner, the Senior Agricultural Officer and the Secretary for Native Affairs, TNA SMP 19972.
13. Report on the General Situation at Nyakato from the Headmaster to the Provincial Commissioner, Bukoba, 17 January 1927, TNA Acc. 215/26/Part I; Conversation at Mwanza 1 September 1932, TNA SMP 19972.
14. Conversation at Mwanza 1 September 1932, TNA SMP 19972; Letter 1 November 1932 from the Chief Secretary to the Native Administration Office, TNA Acc. 215/617/Vol. I.
15. Letter 27 November 1935 from the Acting Provincial Commissioner to the Provincial Commissioner, TNA Acc. 215/827A/Vol. I; Minute 1936 to the Chief Secretary, TNA SMP 23765; Letter 13 January 1937 from the Provincial Commissioner to the Chief Secretary, TNA SMP 23765.
16. Cliffe and Saul 1972: 17–18; Hyden 1980: 50–51.
17. Letter 6 September 1928 from the Provincial Commissioner to the Chief Secretary, TNA SMP 10514/Vol. I; Letter 13 February 1933 from the Agricultural Lecturer, Nyakato to the Senior Agricultural Officer, Mwanza, TNA Acc. 215/617/Vol. I.

18. Letter 27 November 1935 from the Acting Provincial Commissioner, Lake Province to the Provincial Commissioner, Lake Province, TNA Acc. 215/827A/Vol. I; Letter 6 January 1936 from the District Office, Bukoba to the Provincial Commissioner, Lake Province, TNA Acc. 215/827A/Vol. I.
19. Quarterly Report on the Government Schools in Bukoba Province for the Quarter Ended September 30th, 1930, TNA Acc. 215/26/Part II; Minute to the Chief Secretary 2.4.36, TNA SMP 10514/Vol. I; Native Administration Schools in the Bukoba Province 1937, TNA Acc. 215/827A/Vol. I; Monthly Reports Nyakato 1933–39, TNA Acc. 215/617/Vol. I/Vol. II/Vol. III.
20. Monthly Reports Nyakato 1933–39, TNA Acc. 215/617/Vol. I/Vol. II/Vol. III.
21. Raikes 1976: 2.
22. Report on the General Situation at Nyakato 17 January 1927, TNA Acc. 215/26/Part I; Monthly Report Nyakato November 1933, TNA Acc. 215/617/Vol. I; Letter 25 March 1935 from the Director of Agriculture to the Chief Secretary, TNA SMP 23271/Vol. I; Minute 1936 to the Chief Secretary, TNA SMP 23765.
23. Monthly Reports Nyakato 1933–35, TNA Acc. 215/617/Vol. I/Vol. II.
24. Monthly Reports Nyakato 1936–39, TNA Acc. 215/617/Vol. III.
25. Confidential letter 14 February 1935 from the Acting Provincial Commissioner, Lake Province to the Chief Secretary, TNA SMP 10514/Vol. I.
26. Letter 16 December 1935 from the Director of Agriculture to the Chief Secretary, TNA SMP 23437/Vol. I.
27. Letter 22 September 1933 from the District Officer, Bukoba to the Provincial Commissioner, Lake Province, TNA Acc. 215/617/Vol. I.
28. Letter 2.3.1936 from the Provincial Commissioner, Mwanza, TNA SMP 24523.
29. Native Administration Schools in the Bukoba District, 1937, TNA Acc. 215/827A/Vol. II.
30. Memorandum 6.5.36 from the Director of Education to the Provincial Commissioner, TNA Acc. 215/617/Vol. II; Memorandum 10/5/36 on Nyakato Ex-Pupils, TNA Acc. 215/617/Vol. III; Annual Report Nyakato 1936, TNA Acc. 215/617/Vol. II; Minute 24.8.38 to the Chief Secretary, TNA SMP 23271/Vol. I.
31. Education in the Lake Province, TNA Acc. 215/827A/Vol. III.
32. Letter 27 January 1935 from the African Association of Bukoba to the Government Inspector of Schools, TNA SMP 10514/Vol. I; Letter 17 September 1935 from the Native Administration Office to the Government Inspector of Schools, TNA SMP 10514/Vol. I; Address Presented to the Governor from the Bakama of Bukoba, June 1938, TNA SMP 23271/Vol. I.
33. Monthly Report Nyakato May 1933, TNA Acc. 215/617/Vol. I.
34. Letter 15 May 1935 from Nyakato Pupils to the District Office, TNA SMP 23271/Vol. I; Confidential letter 19 April 1935 from the Acting Provincial Commissioner to the Chief Secretary, TNA SMP 23271/Vol. I; Letter 6 June 1935 from the Acting Provincial Commissioner to the Chief Secretary, TNA SMP 23271/Vol. I.
35. Memorandum on Nyakato Ex-Pupils 16/5/36, TNA Acc. 215/617/Vol. III; Letter 13 January 1937 from the Provincial Commissioner to the Chief

Secretary, TNA SMP 23765; Letter 24 February 1937 from the Chief Secretary to the Provincial Commissioner, TNA SMP 23765; other correspondence during 1937 between the Provincial Commissioner and the Chief Secretary, TNA SMP 23765.

36. Letter 27 January 1935 from the African Association to the Government Inspector of Schools, TNA SMP 10514/Vol. I; Confidential letter 14 February 1935 from the Acting Provincial Commissioner to the Chief Secretary, TNA SMP 10514/Vol. I; Letter 7 October 1935 from the Director of Education to the Chief Secretary, TNA SMP 10514/Vol. I; Native Administration Schools in Bukoba District, TNA Acc. 215/827A/Vol. II.

37. Hyden 1980: 50–52; Austen 1968: 216–232.

38. Quarterly Report on the Government Schools in Bukoba Province for the Quarter Ended September 30th, 1930, TNA Acc. 215/26/Part II; TNA SMP 23271/Vol. I/Vol. II; Letter 28 June 1937 from the Director of Education to the Chief Secretary, TNA SMP 25083/Vol. I; Letter 17 August 1937 from the Director of Agriculture to the Chief Secretary, TNA SMP 25083/Vol. I; Letter 9 February 1938 from the Director of Agriculture to the Secretariat, TNA SMP 25083/Vol. I; Annual Report of the Government Inspector of Schools 1938, TNA Acc. 215/827A/Vol. III; Minute 21/4/38, TNA Acc. 215/617/Vol. III; Minute 13.2.40 to the Chief Secretary, TNA SMP 23271/Vol. II; Minute 2.9.41 from the Director of Agriculture to the Chief Secretary, TNA SMP 23271/Vol. II; Various correspondence during 1941 and 1942 to the Chief Secretary, TNA SMP 22337/Vol. II.

Four

Education for Self-Government, Capitalist Development & Citizenship
1947–61

The focus on Western modernisation for the British colonies after the Second World War implied an attempt to establish a development process similar to that of Britain, by which industrialisation based on capitalist agriculture and the expansion of a modern urban sector were given priority over the development of the traditional rural sector. This economic development process was to be supported in the colonies by a socialisation into Western political traditions and the introduction of Western political institutions, with the aim of establishing political self-government in due time. While policy statements indicated a strong emphasis on the priority of self-government, it was, in reality, economic aims which were heavily pursued. This was reflected in the adopted educational policies, as modernisation competed with and, in certain areas, took prominence over adaptation in order to secure the transfer of the full range of skills and norms for the envisaged development process.

The New Metropolitan Goals
for Education and Development

The overall metropolitan aims for development in the colonies after the Second World War appeared from a number of policy papers for education during the period. They were, first, foreshadowed in the Advisory Committee's 1943 memorandum on *Mass Education in African Society*, which, in addition to the earlier emphasis on the need for socio-economic development in the colonies, introduced the issue of political self-government as being of central importance. The goal of the British government in the colonies, it was stated, was to secure '(1) the improvement of the health and living conditions of the people; (2) the

49

improvement of their well-being in the economic sphere; [and] (3) the development of political institutions and political power until the day arrives when the people can become effectively self-governing'.[1] One of the most essential and urgent measures needed for the accomplishment of this task, it was argued, was the widespread development of education:

> the general health, well-being and prosperity of the mass of the people can only be secured and maintained if the whole mass of the people has a real share in education and has some understanding of its meaning and purpose ... without such general share in education and such understanding, true democracy cannot function and the rising hope of self-government will inevitably suffer frustration.[2]

The committee pointed to the need for more systematic and energetic measures for the education of the mass of the community alongside the plans for school education. Since Africans themselves must be the main agents in improving African life, the training of all the Africans who were to take a share in the work was imperative, it was argued. Therefore, plans for universal schooling of both sexes must not continue to disregard the education of the adolescent and the adult.

Such social adjustment was becoming more important as the pace of social and political change accelerated. Mass education was to provide the needed changing attitudes which would allow the development of social and civic responsibility, by emphasising: (i) more complicated techniques, for instance, concerning agricultural processes; (ii) citizenship in the form of a mature grasp of public issues and knowledge of the factors influencing decision-making; and (iii) the play of economic forces upon life and welfare. Mass education would, thus, secure true democracy by providing understanding of the forces of change in society and at the same time call out the ability and will to share in the direction and control of these very forces.[3]

The purpose of mass education for a democratic state was further pursued in the Advisory Committee's 1948 memorandum on *Education for Citizenship in Africa*. The central purpose of the British administration was here based on a statement of the Secretary of State, Mr A Creech Jones, 'to develop the Colonies and all their resources so as to enable their peoples speedily and substantially to improve their economic and social conditions, and, as soon as may be, to attain responsible self-government'.[4] It was considered to be natural and desirable that peoples under British administration should aspire to the evolutionary democracy which Britain had marked out. Responsible self-government of the colonial peoples by the people and for the people was, therefore, the declared aim which all economic and social development and, especially, education should have in view. Colonial peoples could not, however, it was argued, be given an education which fitted them for citizenship in a democratic state unless the political and economic organisation of the state developed in such a way as to enable democracy to flourish in it. For its successful maintenance, democracy demanded both peculiar habits of mind and habits of action as 'democracy is not merely a matter of political institutions, but of the spirit in which they are worked; ... must arise from within, and cannot be imposed ... from without; [and] can only be judged by being seen in action'.[5] It was, therefore,

> not enough to train patient and skilful and reliable farmers, artisans, clerks, and minor-grade employees; [or] even to train professional men, technicians, and men capable of assuming responsibility in managerial and administrative positions. We have to go further and train men and women as responsible citizens of a free country. Constitutional advance, culminating in responsible self-government, is a necessary consequence of advances in general education.[6]

Education for citizenship must, it was argued, take account of the social customs and institutions in native society. The fact that indigenous political institutions existed in contact with Western civilisation created an urgent need to educate the colonial peoples to appreciate the instability of the situation and to control the future development of their own political institutions. Old institutions had, therefore, to be made effective for new purposes. New ideas could be put into practice, it was believed, for instance by turning local governments into training sites for the national government in view of the expected African participation in future national policy-making. Local government efforts were also to be extended through other institutions, such as cooperative societies, local education committees and local welfare and development committees.[7]

Education for citizenship was to be taught in the school through particular academic subjects of the curriculum, for instance language, geography and history, science, arithmetic and domestic subjects. With respect to domestic subjects, there was specific mention of the importance of extending women's interests outside of the home not only to marketing and food supply, but to all the local services: sanitation, water and electricity, health and education. It was important that women learned to cooperate with the wider community in the use of these services and realised their particular responsibility in certain areas, such as hygiene, it was stated. Citizenship was also to be taught in out-of-class activities through experience gained with the methods of organisation and discipline in non-academic clubs and other activities, such as the scout and youth movements. Among illiterate and literate adults, mass education was to concern itself not only with literacy or with the acquisition of new skills or new habits, such as better agriculture or hygiene, but also with the development of a heightened social consciousness.[8]

In addition to the importance of popular education to create political awareness, participation and improved living circumstances at the local level, university education was stressed in 1945 in the *Report of the Commission on Higher Education in the Colonies* as indispensable to national self-government. It was the universities that could produce the 'men and women with the standards of public service and capacity for leadership which self-rule requires ... and offer the best means to [promote] the formation of political institutions on a national basis'.[9] While popular instruction was considered to be most urgent, there were higher rewards from investing in higher education, it was argued.

Universities were stressed as centres for teaching, research and extra-mural activities, in particular adult education. University education must

> give the colonial citizens an opportunity for self-development [in order to fit them] for the management of their own concerns; to train themselves for their future responsibilities by gaining the expert knowledge necessary for the service of their own communities; and finally to prepare them to take their place among those who are contributing to the intellectual life and scientific progress of man.[10]

Education in agriculture was singled out as the area which could contribute significantly to progress in the economic field. It had, however, to combine the teaching in practice of the principles of improved farming to cultivators through extra-mural activities with the training of 'men who are qualified to apply the principles of modern scientific agriculture to the special circumstances prevailing in the colonies, or to conduct research, both of the fundamental and "applied" type into the problems which colonial agriculture presents'.[11] The specification of 'men' stood in contrast to the general principle adopted in the report that access to higher education must be based on academic achievement and be irrespective of class, wealth, race, sex and creed.[12] It, thereby, indirectly reflected and supported the views of some of the previous documents that education was to improve the reproductive capacity of women related to improved food production, not to scientific agriculture.

The Political and Economic Circumstances in Tanganyika

The changed emphases of British rule were also a reflection of the terms of the trusteeship agreement of the United Nations in 1946. It was here underlined that the administration was to promote the 'political, economic, social and educational advancement' of the local population,[13] and to develop free political institutions, and participation by the local population in local and national political decision-making processes.[14] In effect, however, in colonies and dependencies with settler interests, the interwar principle of the 'paramountcy of native interests' was substituted by that of 'multiracialism' or the parity of interests between the local and immigrant communities.[15] Even in the mandated territory of Tanganyika with a small immigrant population, the European and Indian communities constituting only about half of the immigrant population and 0.2 and 0.9 per cent, respectively, of the total population at the end of the British period,[16] the principle of 'multiracialism' involved changes in the political structure. The Executive Council in 1948 became subordinate to the Legislative Council. Unofficial representation in the central councils was in 1955 to be distributed according to racial parity instead of relative representation of population in the territory, and the immigrant communities were simultaneously to be incorporated into the district councils.[17]

These restricted political opportunities for the African population were in addition to their continued limited access to opportunities in the expanding modern sector of the economy. Of the 8.7 million African population in 1957, less than 0.5 million were in paid employment, of whom around 199,000 were working on agricultural estates earning approximately 38 per cent of all wages paid to Africans. During 1948–57, more than 60 per cent of the Asians, who numbered around 100,000, continued to monopolise wholesale and retail trade. Others established themselves as capitalist owners of plantations or were engaged in public and other services. Of the approximate 20,000 gainfully employed Europeans, about half were in the public and other services primarily as administrators and technicians. Approximately 20 per cent were employed in agriculture, forestry and fishing, and a small number were owners or managers of agricultural estates or engaged in commerce and industry. At independence, Europeans and Asians together constituted around 87 per cent (Africans 13 per cent) of the highest-level graduate professionals, senior administrators and senior managers in industry and commerce. They formed in all 70 per cent (Africans 30 per cent) of the next level of technicians, sub-professional grades, executive grades in the civil service, middle management in industry and commerce and teachers with secondary education but without a university degree.[18]

After the Second World War, British investments were allowed to stimulate local production and efficiency, as improved social and economic conditions were, by then, seen to improve the general position of the dependencies in international trade and so would increase British returns from the areas.[19] The modernisation or development policies led to substantial contributions to the finance of the territory in the form of grants under the Colonial Development and Welfare Acts as well as the growth of export earnings. Import duties continued to be the principal source of income, and income tax began to constitute a new major component of revenue. The relative importance of the native hut-and-poll tax fell steadily from 15 per cent of the total incomes in 1946 to about 9 per cent in the early 1950s. It has, however, been estimated that well over half of the import duties were raised on consumer necessities and, therefore, paid mostly by the African population.[20] In addition, the African peasant farmers contributed to the administration's taxable incomes through the direct and indirect regulation of their production and producer prices.[21]

Income tax, which was introduced in 1940, fell on companies and the small group of individuals that enjoyed high incomes, i.e. almost exclusively non-Africans, whose number in 1958 has been estimated at about 124,000 according to the Minister of Finance. In 1946 and during the 1950s, income tax accounted for 10 per cent of the total revenue which corresponded to the relative contribution of the native hut-and-poll tax in the 1950s. The non-African poll tax remained insignificant, in 1946 constituting about 1 per cent of the total revenue and keeping the same low proportionate level of the native hut-and-poll tax in the early 1950s as before the Second World War. White settler and plantation production was not taxed, except for export taxes which were only significant during the sisal boom in 1950–52. Compared with the non-African communities, the African population, therefore, contributed by far the largest proportion of the current territorial revenue through taxation.[22]

Most of the pre-war policies were continued in the immediate post-war years, including enforced agricultural production of food and cash crops among African farmers. There were extensive investments in so-called development schemes in different parts of the country (see Table 4.1). The schemes represented far-reaching reforms in the agricultural and economic spheres and also aimed at achieving higher social standards through mass education efforts (see Chapter 5). They were intended to increase agricultural production by alleviating what were considered to be the negative effects on the land of 'traditional' production patterns and techniques, population pressure and cattle. Regulations were imposed through administrative ordinances and implemented by the local authorities under the supervision of officers from the agricultural department, as was the case with coffee production in Bukoba (see Chapter 3) and Kilimanjaro in the 1920s and 1930s, and cotton in Sukumaland in the 1930s. The regulations fell into three categories: anti-erosion measures (such as compulsory tie-ridging and terracing, destocking and control of grazing) as in Uluguru, Mbulu, Usambara and Pare; improved methods of cultivation (such as destruction of old cotton plants and mulching of coffee) and of animal husbandry (such as cattle-dipping) as in Sukumaland and Bukoba; and prevention of famine (compulsory production of some famine crop such as cassava or groundnuts) as in Usambara, Sukumaland and the coastal strip.[23]

Table 4.1 Major Development Schemes by Location in Tanganyika in 1952: Area and People Involved

Location of scheme	Approximate area covered by its operations in sq. miles	Number of inhabitants affected in individual area
Sukumaland	20,000	1,115,000
Uluguru	500	50,000
Usambara	8,500	220,000
Bukoba	6,000	300,000
Masailand	23,000	57,000
Mbulu	6,000	150,000
North Mara	1,500	110,000
Pare	3,000	85,000
Total	68,500	2,087,000

Source: United Kingdom, *Report for the year 1952*: 203.

By the mid-1950s it was clear that the direct enforcement of regulations was counterproductive. Measures were, therefore, undertaken instead via agricultural extension work. This concentrated resources on relatively rich farmers and/or villages that could be expected to increase their marketed production by the use of machinery and fertiliser and by hiring labour. Parts of the southern and north-eastern highlands, the best known being Ismani and Mbulu, became key areas for the development of rural elites due to these efforts. In Ismani, land was cleared for maize production. High yields in the early 1950s enabled some of the first farmers to purchase tractors and weed farms of 100 hectares or more using hired migrant labour.[24] In Mbulu by the end of the 1960s, about 150 African farmers were cultivating large areas of wheat and providing an efficient hire service for about 4,000 households in the area, most of whom grew wheat.[25]

In addition, efforts were made among small-scale farmers to expand the modern sector by using the principle of 'persistent persuasion', i.e. by appealing to the peasants' self-interest in cash crops as a means of increased cash and social status. Demonstration farms were set up for this purpose in order to popularise simple innovations and to expand the application of modern farming techniques to both food and cash crop production. Other schemes were failed attempts at large-scale, mechanised production of beef and groundnuts by European farmers and relatively unsuccessful measures of introducing plantation crops among African farmers.[26]

In total, the area provided by land alienation for the plantation and estate agriculture amounted to 2.5 or 3 million acres between 1956 and

1958, having been below 2 million acres in 1949.[27] The number of personal and corporate holders was around 1,500. It has been estimated that 29 per cent of the alienated area was not in use in 1961. The total area corresponded to about 1 per cent of Tanganyika's land area and 10 per cent of the arable land, frequently that of higher grade soil.[28] In comparison, the total land area under African cultivation has been estimated at 4½ million acres in 1956.[29]

Despite the overall importance of the sisal plantation industry (amounting to 63 per cent of total output and 41 per cent of value in 1954), the African peasant sector did not lose its relative share of total production in terms of output and value. The United Nations estimated that in 1954 African farms accounted for 75 per cent of the total agricultural product, 65 per cent of the produce offered for sale and 55 per cent of the exports.[30] It has been been estimated that 40 per cent of the total agricultural production in 1958 did not enter the market economy.[31] In terms of value, African export production accounted for approximately 43 per cent of the total value in 1954.[32]

The emphasis of the British authorities on export and cash crop production strengthened the regional and social differentiation process of the interwar period. At the end of the British period, the central railway line virtually divided a richer north from a poorer south, with some areas within the north and the south being better off than others. Furthermore, the pattern of specialisation between the cash crop producing northern highlands, the food crop producing areas situated within reach of the coastal towns and plantations, and the labour-producing areas of the south and on the western plateau further intensified.

The number of farmers engaged in the market economy increased drastically. It has been estimated that at least half of the peasants in Tanganyika were undertaking cash crop production at independence, including approximately 400,000 coffee farmers, primarily in the Kilimanjaro and Bukoba areas, 250,000–300,000 cotton farmers in Sukumaland and 60,000–80,000 pyrethrum farmers.[33] The larger part of the peasants added cash crop to subsistence production and did not innovate or change existing forms of cultivation. This was viewed as a 'rational policy' by the World Bank as the terms of trade between food and cash crops were highly variable and the margin beyond starvation narrow. Besides, specialisation would have depended on improved transport facilities and increased storage in many areas and on increased efficiency in food production.[34]

The location and nature of the export crop production, including the varied labour inputs and the fluctuating terms of marketability led to increased differentiation among the African peasantry. Cashew nut growers in the southern region have been estimated to have added only around sh. 50–100 to their annual incomes in the 1950s, though against reasonably low labour inputs.[35] In comparison, in 1961 an average 3-acre coffee holding in Kilimanjaro, with reasonably low labour inputs once the coffee had been planted, was estimated to yield gross returns of sh. 1,880, the average family income being sh. 1,463. The average gross yield of cotton, which was an annual crop with much lower return to labour and highly responsive to price fluctuations, was, on the other hand, estimated in a 1963 survey of Sukumaland to yield about sh. 2,000, the average farm income being sh. 1,500.[36] African money incomes appeared to have averaged roughly sh. 120 per capita in 1957/58, high-income coffee growers in Kilimanjaro and Meru having secured around shs. 940 per capita.[37] Most peasants invested their cash income in bride-wealth, school fees, funeral expenses, cattle or commodities from the exchange economy, such as kerosene. Some also invested in the market economy *per se*, for instance in mechanised production (oxen, ploughs, tractors, coffee hullers), intensive cultivation (fertilisers, insecticides, labour) and marketing capability (motor transport, shops).[38]

The combined effect of the political and economic development process, which continued to favour non-African at the expense of African interests, was increased African pressure for self-government. Despite the stated claims by the British authorities, they measured African self-government in centuries rather than decades. African demands were channelled through the Tanganyika African National Union (TANU), which was established in 1954 as a national, territorial movement to further the interests which were earlier on represented in the local branches of the Tanganyika African Association. Their demands were supported by international organisations, such as the United Nations Educational, Scientific and Cultural Organisation (UNESCO) and the United Nations (UN). The leading figures of the movement were the selected few who managed to gain access to the formal educational system despite the continuous divisions between the African and non-African educational systems with respect to access and contents of education. The selected few joined interest with the many who had but restricted access to education and who reacted against the cooperation of the native authorities with the British administration in the implementation of agricultural and community development schemes which often represented interference in the traditional production patterns and their underlying principles.

The Purposes of Education as Stated by the British Administration

After the Second World War, the British administration in Tanganyika distinguished between ultimate and immediate objectives in its educational policy. Whereas the ultimate objective of a community 'well-equipped by the advancement of education in its widest sense to assume full responsibility for guiding and shaping the destiny of the country' corresponded with the principles of the metropolitan statements, the administration laid emphasis on the immediate objective of advancing the more backward segments of the inhabitants.[39] The underlying view was similar to that expressed in the metropolitan documents, namely that literacy would make labour and production more effective and, therefore, should be considered as a form of capital investment. Educational activities could, however, only be expanded if the general economic development process allowed for increased economic growth, for which reason investment in the directly productive sectors of society was given priority. Any higher educational expenditure was expected to be covered totally or partially by the communities concerned. With respect to the African community, emphasis was laid on self-help activities and the contributions from the native authorities. With respect to Europeans and Asians, a special education tax was to be reintroduced in 1948 to cover the planned expansion.[40]

Despite the emphasis on the immediate objective of advancing the more backward sections of the population through literacy, the planned activities by the education department largely excluded adult education and were instead concentrated on formal education of the young. Adult education instead became the responsibility of the Social Welfare Department and other departments of the administration. Until the mid-1950s, the primary aim was to ensure that as large a proportion as possible of the child population of school age would become literate, which implied a vast expansion of the school system at the primary level. The ultimate objective was more in focus from the mid-1950s. Middle level schooling, which provided agricultural and other practical skills determined by the local area, was emphasised, along with a planned increase in the number of pupils who completed the secondary course, in order to secure a constant supply of well-educated Africans with special technical and academic training. For the European and Asian communities, recommendations were made for expanded primary and secondary educational facilities as well as grants-in-aid for higher education outside the territory.[41]

The major difference between the stated purposes of education at the metropolitan level and their adoption by the British administration in Tanganyika was, therefore, the limited emphasis locally on higher education for Africans and on adult education. In the metropolitan statements, both higher and adult education were seen as necessary means to create political leaders at the national level and a participating population with political awareness at the local level, besides fulfilling purposes related to the economic structure of society. Even though local educational policies were designed in a situation where long-term plans and purposes might well have been overtaken by short-term needs, which may explain the stronger emphasis on formal education for economic development rather than political self-government, the planning of education in Tanganyika was also undertaken with obvious attention to the non-African communities. These populations continued to be in a stronger political and economic position than the Africans to influence educational decision-making. They became the preferential political partners as the emphasis on national development shifted from one of adaptation to one of modernisation.

The Provision of Education

Despite the stated emphasis on education as a capital investment, the allocation to education from the recurrent revenue continued to be relatively low. It was, however, increasing steadily from an approximate 5 per cent of the total recurrent expenditure immediately after the Second World War to an approximate 12 per cent at the end of the British period (16 per cent when including capital expenditure).[42] Both African and non-African education were also supported from a number of different funds established after the Second World War.

As appears from Table 4.2, by far the largest absolute amount of total expenditure from the education department continued to be spent on African education. Its relative proportion of the total was, however, relatively unchanged during the period, increasing from 76 per cent in 1949 to 78 per cent in 1961. Of the territorial revenue, which was based on taxation of Africans rather than non-Africans as discussed above, the African share, though somewhat increasing from 81 to 87 per cent during 1949–61, was almost unchanged compared with 1930/31 (88 per cent). This development took place despite the strong pressure for both higher and wider education which was voiced by educated civil servants, teachers and African peasants in the 1940s and 1950s and the demands of the independence movement for more education for Africans.[43] It also took place despite the sisal boom of the early 1950s. The relative funding of African education by the local authorities increased by approximately 10 per cent of the total during the period, while the relative proportion from the missionary societies, although increasing in absolute terms, declined by almost 15 per cent.

The European and Indian communities also received fairly equal proportions of the total expenditure from the education department in 1949 compared with 1961 (Table 4.2). In both cases, their relative shares were somewhat increasing between 1949 and 1956 and somewhat

Table 4.2 Source of Expenditure on African, European and Indian Education in Tanganyika 1949-1961. £000.

Source	1949 African	1949 European	1949 Indian	1956 African	1956 European	1956 Indian	1961 African	1961 European	1961 Indian
Territorial revenue	405	44	51	2,220	182	171	2,988	170	281
Other government departments	23	–	0.4	40	–	–	–	–	–
Development Plan Reserve Fund	–	–	–	–	–	–	44	–	–
Custodian of Energy Property Fund	–	–	–	137	112	162	–	–	–
Colonial Development and Welfare Fund	184	–	–	84	–	–	548	–	–
Loan funds	–	–	40	45	51	97	40	2	–
Education tax	–	30	40	–	52	104	–	98	179
School fees and staff boarding charges	–	21	9	–	117	26	–	51	63
Balance in educational fund	–	–	–	–	53	28	–	97	68
Special loan	–	–	–	–	–	–	–	7	–
Total	612	95	100.4	2,526	567	588	3,620	425	591
Local authorities	85	–	–	520	–	–	917	–	–
Voluntary agencies	151	–	–	436	–	–	413	–	–

Sources: Department of Education, *Annual Report 1949*: 88-91, *1956*: ix, xiii, xviii; Ministry of Education, *Annual Summary of the Ministry of Education* 1961: vii, xi, xv.

declining between 1956 and 1961. The European community received approximately 9 per cent of the total and 5 per cent of the territorial revenue in 1961, while the Indian community received approximately 13 per cent of the total and 8 per cent of the territorial revenue in 1961. The declared purpose that expanded educational activities for the non-African communities were to be financed by the special education tax which was reintroduced in 1948 was never fully achieved. There was, however, an increased level of self-finance by the two communities, particularly concomitant with the changed plans for education in 1956 and the African political reactions to their restricted opportunities in the mid-1950s and onwards. In all, European and Indian self-finance (via education tax, school fees and staff boarding charges, and the balance in the educational fund) constituted approximately half of the total expenditures on these communities in 1949 and 1961, but was lower in both cases in 1956, 39 and 27 per cent, respectively.

The resources spent by the British administration were differentially focused within the tripartite educational system (see Table 4.3). With respect to the African community, funding by the British administration was concentrated at the primary and middle levels with a small increase from around 60 per cent of the total expenditure in 1949 to 64 per cent in 1961. In the European and Indian systems, more resources were concentrated on secondary and post-secondary education at the end of the British period compared with earlier. In the European system, 66 per cent of the total expenditures were allocated to primary and 29 per cent to secondary education in 1949, while the comparative figures in 1961 were 54 per cent for primary and 43 per cent for secondary education. In the Indian system, support for primary education dropped from 70 to 44 per cent, whereas secondary and post-secondary education increased from 25 to 56 per cent during the same period.

After the Second World War, the educational structure of the African educational system became more closely associated with that of Britain. It was fully formalised at the end of the British period into four years of primary, four years of middle, and four or six years of secondary education (O and A level, respectively). Vocational and teacher training (level II) were offered after standard VIII (middle level), and teacher training (level I), government departmental courses and technical training after standard XII. Form VI gave access to higher education, such as at Makerere in Uganda, which was the only university college for the whole of East Africa at the time. While the curriculum was largely maintained with Kiswahili as the medium of instruction at the primary level and English at the middle level, middle schools in rural areas were taught according to an agricultural syllabus during 1952–59. This agricultural emphasis was abandoned, however, due to strong African objections to the teaching of rural skills on a differential basis.[44]

Table 4.3 Allocation of Expenditure by the Department of Education to African, European and Indian Education in Tanganyika by Level 1949–61. £000

Level	1949			1956			1961		
	African	European	Indian	African	European	Indian	African	European	Indian
Recurrent									
Primary education	416	48	61	895	226	186	⎱ 1,907	227	262
Middle education	–	–	–	374	–	–	⎰	–	–
Secondary education	151	21ª	22ª	171	173	131	324	180	307
Teacher training	44	–	–	114	–	5	151	–	8
Technical and vocational	34	–	0.4	113	–	1	163	–	–
Post-secondary education	11ª	–	–	230	–	–	269	–	–
Administration	34	4	4	240	5	7	174	9	14
Sub-total	690	73	87.4	2,137	404	330	2,988	416	591
Non-recurrent									
Capital and special	158	23	13	388	164	259	632	9	n/a
Total	848	96	100.4	2,525	568	589	3,620	425	591

n/a   Not available.

Note: a   Including overseas and regional scholarships.

Sources: Department of Education, *Annual Report 1949*: 88, *1956*: ix, xiii, xvii; Ministry of Education, *Annual Summary of the Ministry of Education 1961*: vii, xi, xv.

As displayed in Table 4.4, African education continued to be mostly provided in the missionary assisted and native authority sectors which together constituted approximately 93 per cent of all institutions in 1956 and 1961. The government sector accounted for only approximately 4 per cent of all institutions in 1961 and had declined by half of the total since the Second World War. Students were concentrated in missionary assisted and native authority institutions, although there was some minor growth (by about 7 per cent) in attendance in government and missionary unassisted institutions during the period. While 90 per cent of all students were enrolled in primary education and 8.7 per cent in middle education in 1956, middle school students increased somewhat, to approximately 11 per cent of total enrolment, in 1961. Females constituted approximately one third of the student population, amounting to 34 per cent in 1961. They were almost exclusively enrolled in primary and middle education during the period, though with some small increase at the middle compared with the primary level (93 per cent primary and 6 per cent middle) in 1961. While 2 per cent of the male student population was concentrated in secondary, technical, vocational and teacher education in 1961, the corresponding figure for females was only approximately 1 per cent.

In contrast, government institutions constituted almost one-third of the European system and increased from approximately 4 to 11 per cent of the Indian system during 1956–61 (Tables 4.5 and 4.6). Of all students in the European system, 58 per cent were enrolled in government institutions, as were an increasing number (from 23 to 33 per cent of all students) in the Indian system. In both systems the relative participation of students at the primary level was declining whereas the number enrolled in secondary education was increasing. In the European system, while 86 per cent of all students received primary education in 1956 (87 per cent of all females), the relative per centage in 1961 was 71 per cent (also for females), secondary education expanding by the relative difference. In the Indian system, an even higher per centage of all students moved from the primary to the secondary level, primary school students in 1956 constituting 72 per cent of the total (76 per cent of the females) and 60 per cent in 1961 (63 per cent of the females).

Education for Modernisation as a Mechanism of Social Differentiation: Concluding Remarks

Inherent in the British view on education were two contrasting beliefs concerning the contribution of education to societal development. Education for Adaptation advocated social improvement from the bottom of the educational pyramid, aiming at the development of the

Table 4.4 African Education in Tanganyika by Category 1956-61: Schools and Enrolment

Category	1956				1961			
		Enrolment				Enrolment		
	Schools	Male	Female	Total	Schools	Male	Female	Total
Government								
Primary education (stds I–IV)	51	7,101	3,153	10,254	64	9,217	6,355	15,572
Middle education (stds V–VIII)	23a	1,296	952	2,248	37	3,082	2,063	5,145
Secondary education (stds IX–XII)	10	1,003	121	1,124				
Secondary education (stds IX–XII, forms V–VI)					14	2,194	368	2,562
Technical, vocational, teacher training	17	1,355	169	1,524	5	1,213	171	1,384
Post-secondary education	1b	–	–	167	n/a	n/a	n/a	n/a
Sub-total	102	10,755	4,395	15,317	120	15,706	8,957	24,663
Native authority								
Primary education (stds I–IV)	660	63,208	20,854	84,062	700	72,011	34,334	106,345
Middle education (stds V–VIII)	89c	8,761	168	8,929	121	15,070	499	15,569
Sub-total	749	71,969	21,022	92,991	821	87,081	34,833	121,914

Table 4.4 cont. *African Education in Tanganyika by Category 1956–61: Schools and Enrolment*

Category	1956				1961			
	Schools	Male	Female	Total	Schools	Male	Female	Total
Mission assisted								
Primary education (stds I–IV)	1,806	156,187	79,329	235,516	1,966	180,018	107,983	288,001
Middle education (stds V–VIII)	220a	16,111	4,081	20,192	230	24,318	7,468	31,786
Secondary education (stds IX–XII)	15	1,183	81	1,264	27	2,914	493	3,407
Technical, vocational, teacher training	22	1,105	413	1,518	28	849	602	1,451
Sub-total	2,063	174,586	83,904	258,490	2,251	208,099	116,546	324,645
Mission unassisted								
Primary education (stds I–IV)	72	4,569	1,678	6,247	100	25,321	15,405	40,726
Middle education (stds V–VIII)	25c	1,052	424	1,476	20	2,420	696	3,116
Secondary education (stds IX–XII, forms V–VI)	1	20	1	21	1	51	11	62
Technical, vocational, teacher training	1	32	3	35	8	246	3	249
Sub-total	99	5,673	2,106	7,779	129	28,038	16,115	44,153
Grand total	3,013	262,983	111,427	374,577	3,321	338,924	176,451	515,375

n/a   Not available.
Notes: a   Including district schools standards V–VI and pre-secondary standards VII–VIII.
         b   Makerere College.
         c   Including district schools standards V–VI.
Sources: Department of Education, *Annual Report 1956*: i–ii. Ministry of Education, *Annual Summary of the Ministry of Education 1961*: i–ii.

65

Table 4.5 *European Education in Tanganyika by Category 1956–61: Schools and Enrolment*

Category	1956				1961			
		Enrolment				Enrolment		
	Schools	Male	Female	Total	Schools	Male	Female	Total
Government								
Primary education (stds I–VI)	8	544	560	1,104	10	512	562	1,064
Secondary education (stds VII–XII)	1	167	123	290	2	27	30	57
Technical, vocational, post-secondary and teacher training	a		a		1	21b	81b	102b
Sub-total	9	711	683	1,394	13	560	673	1,223
Private assisted								
Primary education (stds I–VI)	16	413	356	769	10	263	238	501
Secondary education (stds VII–XII)	1	18	24	42	6	331	240	571
Sub-total	17	431	380	811	16	594	478	1,072
Private unassisted								
Primary education (stds I–VI)	6	136	52	188	10	222	96	318
Secondary education (stds VII–XII)	-		-		5	33	8	41
Sub-total	6	136	52	188	15	255	104	359
Grand total	32	1,278	1,115	2,393	44	1,409	1,255	2,654

n/a   Not available.
Notes: a   Part-time and full-time classes in commercial subjects were held in Dar es Salaam. Technical courses up to professional standard could be attended at the Royal Technical College of East Africa, Nairobi.
b   Including enrolment in evening classes.
Sources: Department of Education, *Annual Report 1956*: x–xii; Ministry of Education, *Annual Summary of the Ministry of Education 1961*: viii.

Table 4.6 Indian Education in Tanganyika by Category 1956–61: Schools and Enrolment

Category	1956				1961			
		Enrolment				Enrolment		
	Schools	Male	Female	Total	Schools	Male	Female	Total
Government								
Primary education (stds I–VI)	3	1,796	705	2,501	6	2,235	1,203	3,438
Secondary education (stds VII–XII)	4	1,626	575	2,201	8	2,951	1,427	4,378
Technical, vocational, post-secondary and teacher training	a		a		2	597b	415b	1,012b
Sub-total	7	3,422	1,280	4,702	16	5,783	3,045	8,828
Private assisted								
Primary education (stds I–VI)	114	5,773	6,087	11,860	105	6,133	6,505	12,638
Secondary education (stds VII–XII)	31	1,834	1,551	3,385	28	2,432	2,695	5,127
Sub-total	145	7,607	7,638	15,245	133	8,565	9,200	17,765
Private unassisted								
Primary education (stds I–VI)	1	97	3	100	1	56	25	81
Secondary education (stds VII–XII)	-		-		-	-		
Sub-total	1	97	3	100	1	56	25	81
Grand total	153	11,126	8,921	20,047	150	14,404	12,270	26,674

n/a   Not available.
Notes: a Indian students were admitted to part-time classes in commercial subjects and tailoring in Dar es Salaam, to the Mombasa Institute of Muslim Education for trade training, to the Royal Technical College of East Africa, Nairobi for technical studies up to professional level and to teacher training colleges in Kenya.
b Including enrolment in evening classes.

Sources: Department of Education, *Annual Report 1956:* xiv–xvi; Ministry of Education, *Annual Summary of the Ministry of Education* 1961: xii.

traditional rural sector in cooperation with the rurally based African leadership, in order to blend the existing culture with new Western elements. Education for Modernisation supported economic development at the top of the educational pyramid, aiming at an expansion of the modern urban and capitalist sector and accompanied by the introduction of Western democratic political institutions in order to establish a Western national politico-economic unit.

While Education for Adaptation was provided solely for Africans, Education for Modernisation was provided disproportionately for Europeans and Indians in competition with the selected few Africans. The importance of the actual provision for the different communities related to the fact that the modern sector was small and that fluency in English was a precondition of African participation in the central political system. The lack of African access to Education for Modernisation, therefore, also limited their influence in economic and political life. When translated into actual figures, at independance the total number of employees at the two highest professional employment levels (see p. 53) was 17,142, of whom Africans constituted 4,468, Europeans 4,309 and Indians 8,365. These numbers were reflected in the small attendance of Africans at the secondary and post-secondary level. Although the overall size of the African system was immense compared with the European and Indian systems, more Indians (9,505) than Africans (6,031) received secondary education in 1961. Respectively, 80 and 95 per cent of the European and Indian age groups were enrolled in primary and secondary education in 1956, whereas African enrolment in primary and middle schools, which was virtually equal to enrolment in the whole system, represented only 8.5 per cent of the age group (even when discounting the effect of attrition).[45]

The obvious social differentiation along racial lines which resulted from the unequal provision of education was accompanied by gender inequalities in education. Despite the continuous statements at the metropolitan level concerning the need for equal educational opportunities for African boys and girls and men and women, an even smaller proportion of African females than males received any kind of schooling at independence. While there was some small increase in their relative participation during the British administration period, they far from participated in proportions equal to their European and Indian age group counterparts and were far less represented at the higher levels of the educational system than their male counterparts. With respect to the content of education, it was clearly seen as important primarily to the traditional roles of mother, housewife and provider of basic necessities. Even the strong emphasis on the need for female teachers was largely unreflected in higher female enrolment in teacher training which was relatively insignificant during the period.

The policies of Education for Modernisation and Education for Adaptation fulfilled the British administration's total need for manpower in a society with stated plans for progress. The provision of Education for Modernisation for the non-African communities and of Education for Adaptation for the African community simultaneously secured the skills and norms for a likely relative improvement of the dominant rural sector and the development of the urban and capitalist agricultural sector. For Africans, however, the lack of access to the academic knowledge and skills which Education for Modernisation provided was the most important reason for rejection of rural skills which might otherwise have been relevant to changing production outcomes and generating higher incomes in the rural sector. They could not, however, have fulfilled ambitions for political power. Such rejection has often been associated with the 'vocational school fallacy' which claims that African students and parents object to the teaching of vocational, agricultural skills because they want access to the well-paying jobs in the modern sector.[46] As important in the specific context in Tanganyika was, undoubtedly, the fact that the middle school agricultural syllabus represented the teaching of alternative skills compared both with the provided academic curriculum provided in the African urban middle schools and the purely academic curriculum in the European and Indian educational systems. For the students of the rural middle schools who naturally associated themselves with the small elite they did, in fact, belong to in the formal education system, the middle school syllabus thus represented a further tool of differentiation and restriction of access to possible opportunities compared both with urban Africans and with the European and Indian communities.

While the British educational efforts clearly concentrated on the provision of formal education for Africans and non-Africans, their announced emphases on mass education of the African population through non-formal educational programmes also received some attention after the Second World War both in the form of isolated educational programmes and as part of wider community development schemes. One such scheme was undertaken in Singida in the late 1950s, partly initiated by the United Nations International Children's Emergency Fund (UNICEF), in response to African pressure for wider educational opportunities. It combined, as will be seen in Chapter 5, the teaching of literacy with basic community development for both men and women. This and other similar schemes established or supported by the British administration can, in many ways, be considered to be the forerunners of the mass education idea, which was taken up with much more vigour by the Tanzanian authorities in part of the post-independence era as another means of securing 'relevant' education.

Notes

1. United Kingdom 1943: 4.
2. United Kingdom 1943: 4.
3. United Kingdom 1943: 5–11.
4. United Kingdom 1948: 5.
5. United Kingdom 1948: 9.
6. United Kingdom 1948: 6.
7. United Kingdom 1948: 6–15.
8. United Kingdom 1948: 18–32.
9. United Kingdom 1945: 10.
10. United Kingdom 1945: 57.
11. United Kingdom 1945: 69.
12. United Kingdom 1945: 15.
13. United Nations 1946: Article 10.
14. United Nations 1946: Article 6.
15. Coulson 1982: 109–119.
16. *Statistical Abstract 1962*: 11.
17. Temu 1969; Pratt 1976: 1–63.
18. *Report on the Census of the Non-Native Population 1948*: Table XXXVII; *Report on the Census of the Non-African Population 1952*: Table XXV, *1957*: Table 45; IBRD 1961: 12; Hunter 1963: 58.
19. Colonial Development and Welfare Act 1940.
20. Ehrlich 1964: 268.
21. United Kingdom, *Report for the year 1947*: 58, *1957*: 111; Bowles 1980: 166–175.
22. United Kingdom, *Report for the year 1947*: 58, *1957*: 111; Ehrlich 1964: 268–270.
23. Cliffe 1972: 17–18; Ruthenberg 1964: 48–58.
24. Coulson 1982: 58.
25. Raikes 1972: 20.
26. Ruthenberg 1964: 60–103; Iliffe 1971: 36–42.
27. Hyden (1980: 47) indicates 2.5 million acres in 1958, whereas Bowles (1980: 184) indicates 3 million acres in 1956.
28. Ruthenberg 1964: 15.
29. Hyden 1980: 47; Bowles 1980: 187.
30. Ruthenberg 1964: 18.
31. IBRD 1961: 26.
32. These calculations are based on the relative share of export crop production between Africans and non-Africans calculated by the United Nations (Ruthenberg 1964: 18).
33. Ruthenberg 1964: 18.
34. IBRD 1961: 26.
35. Bowles 1980: 187.

36. Ruthenberg 1964: 25–26.
37. IBRD 1961: 27. Official per capita incomes during this period are considered to be exaggerated (Beck 1963).
38. Ruthenberg 1964: 24, 28, 37; Hyden 1980: 18.
39. United Kingdom, *Report for the year 1947*: 151.
40. *Ten Year Development and Welfare Plan for Tanganyika Territory* 1946: 2, 12, 55–56; *Revised Development and Welfare Plan for Tanganyika 1950–56*, 1951: 7ff, 34–35; *Ten Year Development and Welfare Plan for Tanganyika* 1950: 4, 7, 9–13.
41. *Ten Year Plan for the Development of African Education* 1947: 7, 16–17; *Development of African Education* 1956: 1; *Five Year Plan for African Education 1957–1961*, 1958: preface, 4–28; *Report of the Special Committee on European Education 1948, 1951*; *Report of the Special Committee on Indian Education 1948, 1951*; *Non-African Education* 1955: 7–66, 83–90; *Development of Non-African Education* 1956: 1–15.
42. United Kingdom, *Report for the years 1947–1960*: public finance; *Development Plan for Tanganyika 1961/62–1963/64*: Tables VIII, IX.
43. UN Visiting Mission 1948: 144ff, 1954: 11ff.
44. Department of Education, *Annual Reports 1947–1959*: *passim*; United Kingdom, *Report for the years 1947–1960*: *passim*; Ministry of Education 1961.
45. Egerö and Henin 1973: Table 134; *Report on the Census of the Non-African Population 1957*: App. VI.
46. This thesis was put forward by Philip Foster (1966). It has become the starting point for discussions of the relationship and mix between vocational training and academic education, including the understanding of the success and failure of Education for Self-Reliance in post-independent Tanzania, as will be discussed later in the book.

Five

Mass Adult Education
& Community Development
The Case of Singida District

The mass education and community development schemes established in Tanganyika after the Second World War were, in most ways, reflections of the policy documents issued in London in the interwar period rather than later ones. The schemes generally attempted to integrate literacy skills with programmes to improve the basic living conditions of the local communities rather than to transmit citizenship skills in order to activate a political self-rule process locally and nationally. Programmes were undertaken in many of the same geographical areas as the wider agricultural development schemes (see Table 4.1) and, like the wider schemes, blended 'modern' ideas with 'traditional' patterns of life. The investment made by the British administration in the mass education and community development programmes was, however, insignificant compared with that of the wider agricultural schemes, just as the amount invested in mass education was miniscule compared with that for formal education.

The first pilot scheme for mass education and community development was set up in North Pare in 1949. It led to the initiation of five other schemes in different areas of Tanganyika in 1951. With the increased pressure on the British administration for both wider and higher educational opportunities for Africans during the 1950s, which was channelled through TANU and supported by international organisations like UNESCO and UNICEF, programmes began to mushroom. This happened even in areas with no long tradition for education and little support for formal educational activities by the British administration and other local agencies. One such case was Singida district where a literacy campaign was started in 1958, followed by community development programmes for men and women in 1959 and 1960. The nature of these activities reflected those of the North

Pare scheme despite the different local context. As in the case of Nyakato, they were generally an interpretation of local needs by the British authorities rather than the formulated needs of the local population.

From Social Welfare to Social Development 1947–61

Until around 1951, adult education under the Social Welfare Department was concentrated on the teaching of individual men and women in social welfare centres located in urban and semi-urban areas. From then on, stress was laid on the general social development of whole communities in the rural areas. The Social Welfare Department, in fact, changed its name to the Social Development Department in 1959 when it became part of the Ministry of Social and Cooperative Development which, in turn, in 1961 was named the Ministry of Local Government and Housing. The community development efforts in the rural areas were emphasised by the British authorities both because large-scale investment in person-related social welfare activities was considered to be non-productive, and because increasing social gaps between urban and rural social groups were considered to be dangerous.[1]

In 1948, there were in all 33 social welfare centres distributed across eight provinces, including the Central Province. Actual expenditure on the activities by the Social Welfare Department in 1948 amounted to only £4,417, which mostly covered overhead costs of the centres, such as fuel, light, water and wages (for cleaning staff). The centres were, generally, expected to become self-financing. The teaching involved subjects like English, Kiswahili, arithmetic, sewing and knitting, child welfare and carpentry. Classes were given to two categories of Africans: employees with schooling background, for whom the teaching provided further stimulation and learning; and uneducated men and women, who gained access to basic reading and other skills. Women were reported to be particularly enthusiastic and active both in the reading classes and in the classes oriented to the traditional female work areas.[2]

Consideration was, however, also increasingly given to developing methods of spreading community development ideas among the so-called less advanced rural peoples.[3] Community development work was encouraged in the districts through the allocation of sums of money for specific projects from a special Rural Social Development fund. This, in 1951, amounted to £100,000 which was to be spread over five years and to be used only for genuine community efforts, to which the local people contributed, for instance, with labour. In 1947, Professor C.H. Philips of the School of Oriental and African Studies in London recommended in a report to the Secretary of State for the Colonies that the British administration must initiate mass education and community development schemes among selected groups in the rural areas in order to introduce them to the fundamentals of better living. His recommendations led to the initiation in late 1949 of a pilot study of a mass literacy and community development programme in the mountainous North Pare.[4]

North Pare was selected due to its long tradition of self-help efforts in, for instance, the construction of roads and the building of schools and dispensaries. The population amounted to approximately 20,000 people. Many of the men were involved in the cash economy and had left their homesteads in charge of their wives. While the central sections of the hill area had large numbers of schools, elementary education being available for almost 80 per cent of the children of school age, the rate of illiteracy in the area was much higher for women than for men.[5]

The North Pare literacy campaign was initially undertaken in the central part of the hills, but began to spread to the peoples living on the mountain slopes, down into the plains, and eventually into the South Pare mountains. It was based on a survey undertaken in 1949 by a team selected by the Social Welfare Department. Local committees were formed and enrolment also began to take place, but the actual teaching had to await the final production of literacy primers in 1950. At this time, the initial strong enthusiasm for the campaign had somewhat waned. Suspicion was expressed by the educated in North Pare concerning the underlying motives for the campaign and the reasons for investment in the teaching of the aged rather than improving the quality of the schooling for children. By the end of 1951, an estimated 1,500 people, who were mostly women and girls, were involved in the campaign which came to a conclusion toward the end of 1954. The learners were taught in groups of up to 80 participants by six trained Africans, three of whom were local men teaching in their home parishes. Testing also began in this year and in all 143 literacy certificates were issued. This first stage was followed by a second-stage school where, in addition to further practice in reading and writing, talks on hygiene and agriculture were given. Plans were also made to organise the women into self-running women's handicraft clubs and to run a health campaign. A district newspaper was printed as the most important follow-up literature.[6]

When enthusiasm for the literacy campaign was at its height, the scheme was enlarged in order to assist broader community development tasks. This broader campaign largely came to an end in 1953. The efforts were concentrated on what the British administration considered to be one of the major problems of the hills – and a well-known concern in the wider development schemes – the need for better land usage related to erosion and congestion. Specialist officers of the district team, who were joined by agricultural officers from the central administration, specified the following interrelated targets: the fostering of stall-feeding of cattle to protect and limit the use of the grazing land; the planting of barrier hedges of elephant grass both to provide extra fodder and to prevent loss of soil; and the planting of trees to protect the hill tops and individual land. Courses in these anti-erosion measures were designed for teachers, and the literacy groups were used as platforms for conveying them. Demonstrations were made to the women, and some men, of methods of planting elephant grass and trees. They were carried out in practice assisted by voluntarily established village committees. It was reported that women, in particular, willingly accepted elephant grass as an anti-erosion measure, probably because it lightened their work burden considerably. The agricultural department, however, developed second thoughts concerning the soundness of the experiments. It began, for instance in South Pare in 1953 and 1954, to advocate instead the readoption of the indigenous measures of dry stone walls on the contour, although with little success.[7]

The concrete achievements of the scheme were measured in

> a thousand or so new literates and several thousand given the rudiments of reading and writing; some 40 water points improved; a flourishing district newspaper established; a few thousand yards of elephant grass or stone walls on the contours; 35 women's clubs started; [and] an impetus to the traditional community making of roads and buildings and to tree planting.[8]

Even though these results could be regarded as modest, the scheme was termed successful by the British administration for several reasons. Firstly, in contrast to the forced terracing in the wider development scheme undertaken in Pare in 1956,[9] the North Pare community development measures were generally not met with resistance by the local population. Furthermore, the adopted approach through literacy groups made it possible to incorporate the women who were otherwise not reached by the barazas and other formal public meetings.[10]

The scheme was also interpreted as confirming the underlying notion that through the teaching of literacy in large groups of learners, it was possible to enhance a community spirit which could support the introduction of new ideas and self-help efforts in order to improve the local living conditions. This key notion was further pursued in the schemes which spread to other parts of the territory, including Singida in the Central Province. The Singida programme can be interpreted as equally successful as the North Pare scheme in terms of the numerical involvement of the local population in literacy groups and the number of village improvement projects undertaken. It was not, however, initially selected by the local population as a priority activity and, while having an instant effect on social life, did not involve substantial medium- and long-term improvement of the harsh conditions in the area.

The Socio-Economic Characteristics of Singida District

Compared with some of the other areas in Tanganyika, such as Bukoba and Arusha, where mass education and community development efforts were implemented (based on the North Pare experiences), the context of the Singida scheme was one of severe living conditions and low educational standards. The district is located in an area with difficult climatic conditions and relatively poor soils (see Map 3). Unreliable rains create a regular pattern of famine and the population exists at subsistence level. According to the 1957 population census, there were 161,531 people, of whom approximately 90,000 were adults (over 16 years of age), 38,810 being men and 51,551 women. The literacy rate was estimated at 5 per cent in 1958, compared with approximately 10 per cent for the territory as a whole. At the end of the British period, there were a limited number of schools: approximately 80 primary schools, six boys' middle schools and no girls' middle schools. Few boys and only one girl had entered secondary school during the British period, the girl having to leave her home district to attend middle school.[11]

The dominant ethnic group, the Turu, to whom the literacy campaign was primarily directed, numbered approximately 150,000 people. The Turu combined agricultural and pastoral activities. The fertility of the fields was maintained by manuring and surplus grain was sold for cash which was apparently reinvested in cattle. Most of the cash income, which averaged only sh.120 per year, came from the sale of cattle for meat. Almost all adult men, in particular the young ones, were migrant labourers at various periods of their lives in the coffee plantations in Arusha and in the sisal plantations in Tanga. Before independence, the important agricultural crops were millet, sorghum and different kinds of vegetables (for instance cowpeas, pumpkins, groundnuts and sweet potatoes) which mostly served as food crops. They were supplemented later on with maize, beans, bananas and sugarcane.[12]

The establishment of the districtwide literacy and community development programmes took into consideration the traditional social organisation of the Turu with respect to the geographical location of the literacy and community development groups. Attempts were also made to build on traditional and imposed criteria of authority in the implementation of the schemes. The Turu lived in scattered residential groups of 6–30 homesteads, which were organised over a large area of land in about 300 'villages' of about 300–1,000 adults each. The scattered pattern of residence was partly due to scarcity of water and of land for cultivation and grazing. The 'villages' were subdivided into several thousand 'hamlets' of about 100 adults each. The most common housing was the traditional long, low mud-and-wattle buildings with flat mud roofs and no windows.[13]

The prime loyalty of the Turu was to their immediate residential unit – lineage, age and gender being applied as criteria of differentiation. The Turu never had traditional chiefs. Formal status was instead graded according to age, and each 'hamlet' was advised by its own group of elders in cases of disputes, the elders taking the lead in formal sanctions. Male members of all 'hamlets' were considered to be equal to each other as their ancestors were brothers. The adult women formed a separate group among themselves as many of them were outsiders and as their families maintained certain claims on them. Their status was largely measured by the number of their children, particularly sons, as fertility was seen as the final approval of the ancestor. The whole group of women in a 'village' was united through their children to their husbands' families and to each other, while maintaining important roles within their lineage as daughters, mothers and sisters. Influential older women settled disputes among the women.[14]

Very close cooperation was expected between all men in the 'hamlet' and was extended to the 'village' with respect to certain ceremonies and activities like weeding, harvesting, herding and well-digging. Considerable tension and competition between and within different 'hamlets', however, remained which also affected the degree of co-operation in and fulfilment of the education and community programmes. These tensions partly existed because the Turu inheritance law – in combination with the scarcity of land and the reluctance among the people to move away from the ancestral home – introduced status differentials between otherwise 'equal' brothers. Inheritance of land, which was scarce and individually owned, and cattle, which were the primary wealth and the means of obtaining wives, depended on whether brothers were the senior, middle or junior son of one wife, or the son of senior or junior wives of one man. These status differentials also expressed themselves in terms of who could participate and how and when in the literacy and community development groups.[15]

Another set of tensions arose from the use of administrative chiefs as co-implementers of education and village development schemes which were designed for, rather than by, the local population. As in the remaining part of the territory, central political institutions had been superimposed by the external political powers upon the decentralised system of traditional social organisation. Jumbes, appointed by the German administration as local administrators responsible to the district officers, had been selected by the British administration as administrative chiefs and sub-chiefs when the system of indirect rule was introduced during the 1920s. After the Second World War, the British administration tried to involve the chiefs more closely with the district administration in order to enhance the modernisation effort among the local people, including the literacy and village improvement schemes introduced during 1958–60. While the post of chief and sub-chief gradually became hereditary within a large lineage group and brought with it new kinds of opportunities to the lineage members, the administrative chief never succeeded in obtaining real power outside his immediate clan area due to the loyalty to the residential unit. Like their German predecessors, chiefs encountered extreme difficulty in implementing externally designed social change which largely had to be enforced through rules, and of which the effect was highly localised. This lack of legitimacy led to their easy replacement by elected representatives in the district councils in 1962 and, during the implementation of the literacy and community development campaign, to the use of enforcement by the chiefs to secure local participation in the schemes.[16]

The Organisation of the Literacy Campaign 1958–62

At the end of 1957, social development assistants working directly under district committees were stationed in 16 out of the 54 rural districts of the territory, including at Singida. In November 1958, a social development officer was posted to Singida to take over control of a districtwide literacy campaign in Kiswahili which was started by the district committee under the aegis of the local authority. The start of this campaign followed the plans of the most influential of the local missionary societies, the Augustana Lutheran Mission, to launch a literacy campaign in Singida in the local languages and Kiswahili in 1958.[17]

When the districtwide literacy campaign began in 1958, Singida district was divided into six chiefdoms (Ikungi, Ihanja, Mgori, Ilongero, Mungaa and Singida) with a hierarchy of sub-chiefs and a large number of 'village' headmen. The campaign was organised through a semi-permanent decentralised structure and aimed at the voluntary establishment of literacy groups from below in all of the six chiefdoms of the district. Each chiefdom had its own chiefdom committee which included members of the chiefdom council as well as other representatives, for instance teachers and elected representatives from each literacy group in the chiefdom. 'Village' committees were responsible for organising self-governing local literacy groups within the traditional 'village' centres.[18]

The Singida campaign was coordinated by an advisory district literacy committee under the aegis of the local authority. The committee was initially under the chairmanship of the district commissioner and included local chiefs, prominent citizens, and representatives of the missionary organisations and, later on, TANU. It was reconstituted in 1960 when four members from the new Turu council were elected and the chairman of the council's social development committee was also appointed chairman of the district literacy committee. The campaign was supervised by staff from the Social Development Department, consisting of the social development officer, one senior social development assistant, two social development assistants and seven council employees (two of whom were women).[19]

The campaign in Kiswahili supplemented the adult literacy efforts in the vernacular undertaken by the missionary organisations in the area. An attempted integration of the literacy efforts of the Augustana Lutheran Mission into the campaign failed and the district literacy committee under the chairmanship of the district commissioner instead began to coordinate the mutual efforts. In contrast to the campaign run by the central and local authorities, and in accordance with disagreements over the importance of the local vernaculars expressed by a number of missionary societies with respect to the formal educational system, the Augustana Lutheran Mission considered literacy in the vernacular as a necessary first step towards literacy in Kiswahili. It also, in contrast to the districtwide campaign, adopted a permanent organisational structure with efficient supervision of the literacy classes, and used professional teachers. The teachers of the Augustana literacy classes acted as external examiners of the tests which followed the start of the teaching of Kiswahili in 1959. The scope and independent impact of the classes undertaken by the Augustana Lutheran Mission are not clear, but were likely to have been limited compared with the districtwide campaign due both to the limited number of Lutheran, compared with Catholic, adherents and to the general dominance of paganism and Islam in the area.[20]

The Singida districtwide campaign started as a pilot project in one chiefdom (Ihanja) but spread rapidly, according to local demand, initially, to the other chiefdoms of the district and, then, to the other areas of the Central Province. At the end of 1961, the province had more registered adult literacy learners than all the other nine provinces of Tanganyika combined. The bulk of the work was borne by the local authorities and the people themselves. In Singida, it relied on the joint inputs of both the local authority and the Social Development Department as well as the efforts of the learners. The local authority employed field staff, who were men born locally with, generally, six to eight years of formal education, to supervise the widespread literacy groups and to act as a link between the groups and the senior staff of the Social Development Department. The local authority also supplied the groups with blackboards and chalk bought with a grant from the Social Development Department. The learners contributed sh.2 in payment for a literacy kit (consisting of a reading primer, *Twende Tusome* ('Let's Go and Read'), its accompanying writing book and a pencil) and 50 cents per month (in cash or kind) for the employment of a voluntary local teacher, who was usually an ex-standard IV leaver. In many places, the learners constructed special buildings as the meeting place of the group. The teachers were trained locally by the staff from the Social Development Department.[21]

The Outcomes of the Campaign

As displayed in Table 5.1, the number of people enrolled in literacy groups in Singida district set up under the British administration increased dramatically during a short period of time: 14,750 in 1959 compared with 40,851 in 1962. The 1962 figure corresponded to 45 per cent of the adult population (based on the 1957 census). The number of enrolled and attending females was, like the population in general, higher than that of males, the female enrolment rate constituting 53 per cent of the adult female population compared with 34 per cent for men. The number of people attending (on a monthly basis) was, however, considerably lower, dropping from 14,444 in 1960 to 7,204 in 1962.

Table 5.1 Adult Literacy in Singida District 1959–62

Participation	September 1959	December 1960	December 1961	December 1962
Total of people enrolled	14,750	27,353	39,250	40,851
Males	6,967	10,188	12,381	13,356
Females	7,783	17,165	26,869	27,495
Total of average attendance	n/a	14,444	6,360	7,204
Males	n/a	5,220	n/a	n/a
Females	n/a	9,224	n/a	n/a
Total no. of classes	244	537	761	323
Total no. of certificates awarded during the year	320	1,080	3,313	3,480[a]

n/a   Not available.
Notes: The indicated figures, which were submitted by the literacy teachers to the district office in Singida, are questionable due to the widespread literacy groups. They serve here only as an indication of the general interest in literacy among the Turu population.
       a   September 1962 figure.

Sources: Brief Notes on Social Development and Literacy Campaign, Singida District, TNA Acc. 68/S.1/5; Literacy Campaign Report for the Month of December 1960, TNA Acc. 68/S.1/5;. Literacy Campaign Singida District, December 1961, TNA Acc. 302/LGS 1/1; Adult Literacy Groups and Adult Education Classes, Singida District, December 1962, TNA Acc. 302/LGS 1/7; Literacy Campaign Singida District, September 1962, TNA Acc. 68/S.1/5/II; Literacy Statistics Singida Region 1963, TNA Acc. 302/LGS 1/7.

The number of certificates awarded, based on a test in reading, comprehension and letter-writing was relatively small compared with the number of people enrolled (3,480 certificates in 1962 corresponded to 8.5 per cent of the registered learners). In 1962, 263 of the learners (of whom 120 were men and 143 women) who had passed the literacy test had formed 24 advanced groups, where they were taught advanced reading, arithmetic and some English.[22]

The literacy test provided no reliable basis upon which to evaluate the literacy rate of the population. The results of the tests were affected both by the effectiveness of the literacy groups based on, for example, the competence of the instructor and the availability of the literacy kits, and by the patterns of social life among the Turu. Their economic and social activities determined when testing could conveniently be held, and status differentials influenced who would sit when. Generally speaking, women and junior people would not sit for the test until their husbands or seniors had passed. Others, both women and men, refused to sit for fear of 'losing face' if they did not pass, or because of the writing test, which many found particularly difficult due to the unfamiliarity with holding a pencil. There was, generally, a higher pass rate in the reading than in the writing test. This was partly due to the fact that literacy kits were often shared among family members as one family could not afford to buy more than one kit due to extremely low cash incomes. While the reading book could easily be used by several people, the writing book could not, which, in turn, affected individual progress in writing.[23]

The comparatively low attendance rates in the literacy programme were due to severe food shortages caused by drought in 1960–61, which concentrated people's energies on cultivation. Classes were closed down in one chiefdom and meeting times were rescheduled in others. The average monthly attendance rates for the individual years, however, also showed great fluctuations during the year. This was partly related to the seasonally determined agricultural and herding activities, to migrant labour and to particular social events, such as the dry-season beer-drinking parties and the ceremonies of the women's secret society (imaa[24]) during September–October which reduced attendance to less than one third in some areas. The possibility of concentrating the literacy classes during the wet season was discussed as an alternative among the authorities, but would have been unlikely to result in higher attendance as it would have seriously interfered with the peak period of agricultural work. Attendance by men was generally more irregular than by women due to their involvement in migrant labour activities and to the continuous rivalries between different lineage groups which prevented the men from attending classes until conflicts had been resolved.[25]

The discrepancy between enrolment, attendance and awarded certificates was also related to the use of the literacy groups for purposes beyond the immediate one: to learn to read and write. While some individuals used the achievement of literacy as an alternative road to status based on non-traditional criteria, the high female participation rate (and low pass rate) has been explained by their joining the groups for social rather than literacy reasons as the groups became a forum to meet other women. It has also been suggested that the literacy classes were readily accepted by the people as relief from the tensions caused by the confinement of most daily activities within a very small area.[26]

Furthermore, many groups were not established as a voluntary effort but by the chiefs in rivalry with other lineage groups, as the number of groups was used as an expression of power. There was also a tendency among the people to gradually treat the literacy groups as a service provided by the local authority, and not as a voluntary effort assisted by the authority. Some local government officials used undue persuasion to keep classes functioning, and some chiefdom councils even began to introduce rules for their own literacy groups and, in accordance with the recognised indigenous disciplinary institution, to exact fines (njughuda[27]) from members and teachers for non-attendance and other mis-behaviour.[28] Some of these latter characteristics reflected the lack of integration of the local population in the literacy campaign on their own terms and the kind of conflicts which arose from using locally unacknowledged authorities to guide community development. Both underline the importance of deep understanding of the local setting in order to enhance the effect of introducing new ideas and efforts.

From Literacy to Community Development

As with the North Pare campaign, the principal British aim behind the Singida literacy scheme went beyond the achievement of literacy to the 'rousing of the imagination and initiative of a whole people in order to increase the pace of local development'.[29] In 1959 and 1960, the literacy groups and their organisation became the medium through which follow-up mass educational schemes in community development and women's programmes were conducted, both of which were sponsored by UNICEF.

Community development was understood by the British administration as 'a movement designed to promote better living for the whole community with the active participation and on the initiative of the community'.[30] These efforts by the central administration were to unite with those of the voluntary agencies and the local authorities in order to integrate the local communities into the life of the nation and to enable them to contribute fully to national progress. Established activities were to be based on the 'willing cooperation of a convinced public opinion'[31]

and staff of teams directing specific schemes were expected to be aware
of local conditions, opinions and needs. Financial (and human) resources
for community development at the central level expanded from the mid-
1950s, constituting in 1958/59 approximately £97,000.[32]

From the mid-1950s, local authorities, voluntary agencies and
international organisations, in particular UNICEF, also extended their
financial support. In the case of UNICEF, the scope of the activities was
widened from the training in mothercraft into adult literacy and inter-
departmental schemes of local development. The women's programme
reflected the generally increased interest of local authorities in work
among women in rural areas. This caused a change from the detailed
teaching of higher technical skills, such as dressmaking and other hand-
work, to a comparatively small number of educated women towards the
teaching of 'better living' to a large number of women with little or no
schooling.[33]

An inter-departmental 'combined operations' development team was
formed in 1959 in Singida. It consisted of a social development assistant,
a veterinary assistant, an agricultural assistant, an assistant health inspector and a woman community development assistant managed by the
social development officer on behalf of the district team. It started work
in the Ikungi chiefdom in 1959. In 1960, a UNICEF-aided women's
mass education programme was started by a mass education team of five
female social development assistants who were joined by four local
authority women employees. The team, which later divided into three
sub-teams, reinforced the parallel work of the combined operations team
in the Ihanja chiefdom.[34]

The community development work of the combined operations team
concentrated on the introduction of basic ideas for village improvement.
The key areas were agriculture, health, housebuilding and nutrition.
While the schemes relied on the initiative of the team, who discussed
their contents with the local communities, they were not necessarily
expressions of ideas developed by the local population or reflecting their
priorities. The team generally provided the necessary outside materials,
for instance concrete for construction of wells, and skilled assistance if it
was not locally available, whereas the villagers contributed with
voluntary labour and local resources.[35]

As in North Pare, the agricultural schemes concentrated on the planting of elephant grass for cattle fodder and as an anti-erosion measure,
despite the realisation gained among the British authorities that these
particular measures were not sound and, perhaps, not relevant in the
changed context. Tie-ridging of millet fields was also attempted
unsuccessfully due to resistance from the women who cultivated the
millet fields. More successful were the health and nutrition programmes,
although their impact in the area as a whole was small during the brief

period of implementation, due to the widespread location of the people. In Singida during 1963, 6 wells with pumps, 20 without covers and 30 with covers were constructed in order to protect drinking water from the cattle. The other major areas of improvement were the building of pit latrines in order to improve general health standards and the making of windows and plastering the walls in order to avoid ticks, bugs and other insects that carried sicknesses. Furthermore, the general standard of hygiene was raised by convincing the women of the need for daily sweeping of the houses and by separating the women's sleeping area from that of the farm animals. With respect to improved nutrition, programmes were introduced which aimed at securing a higher vitamin and protein content in the daily diet. They were a central part of the women's education programme and touched upon issues related to the social division of labour.[36]

The women's programme started as a pilot scheme in 1960 and was put into wider effect in 1961. It was based on a preliminary survey of the life of the Turu and the needs of the women in particular, undertaken by a woman social development officer, Marguerite Jellicoe. While the broad areas of the programme were identified beforehand by the women's team, the elements for actual teaching were specified by the local women themselves. Teaching was concentrated on improved cookery, child care and health, aiming at raising minimum standards among 3,000 women in two years. Influential leaders among the women were used to exert pressure on other women to participate and adopt the new practices.[37]

While the standard of nutrition in the district was considered to be 'higher than might be expected' by the senior social development officer,[38] the diet was still considered to be 'monotonous and limited'.[39] The standard two meals consisted of millet or maize porridge with a relish of boiled wild leaves. Ample use was made of locally available resources, for instance wild greens, roots and fruits, some of which were high in vitamin content. The teaching of improved cookery, therefore, involved the use of other vegetables, some of which were already locally grown, for instance groundnuts, pulses, onions and tomatoes, to supplement the local diet. Instructions were given to groups of women and to individuals in their homes provided water, firewood, temporary shelter and some local ingredients were supplied by the learners.[40]

Even though the programme was directed to women specifically, instructions and wider application of the new recipes could not be given without the acceptance and participation of the men. The men had to construct the temporary shelters, to approve the new recipes after having tasted the meals, and to accept the cultivation and/or use of vegetables for home consumption. While the women traditionally cultivated millet for home consumption, sometimes interplanted with pumpkins and possibly beans and groundnuts, the men grew small plots of onions, tomatoes, bananas and cabbages for sale.⁴¹ In order to extend the daily diet to include more vegetables, women, therefore, had to gain permission from the men to cultivate the new vegetables on land belonging to the men, which added to the already extensive work load of the women. Alternatively, men had to reserve part of their production for home consumption in circumstances of extremely low cash incomes, a situation which may have prevented total adaptation to the idea locally.

The issue of producing new vegetables was taken up in 1960 by the combined operations team which began to cooperate with the women's mass education team through the existing literacy groups. The team attempted to persuade the people to buy an assortment of seeds for vegetables, pulses and minor crops through resale from the local authorities. Like the teaching of literacy, however, the promotion of the new vegetables was affected by the severe food shortages caused by drought and efforts were instead directed towards the increasing of food supplies.⁴² After independence, when UNICEF doubled its assistance to the Community Development Division, community development activities continued to take place in Singida, from 1962 organised through the elected district councils.⁴³ The reported work seemed to be concentrated on immediate tasks, such as the building of more wells, rather than on the more fundamental changes involved, for instance, in the growing or control of new vegetables by women.

The lack of attention to these more fundamental issues restricted the effect of the schemes. While having some significance locally, they were concentrated in limited areas and locations and, therefore, contributed little to the solution of the more profound development problems, such as the high isolation of the communities, which was partly caused by the lack of infrastructure. Solutions to these problems would probably have brought more stimulation to the local communities and, in turn, have benefited national progress.

Mass Education for Local Development: Concluding Remarks

The mass education and community development schemes established during the British period were identified by British officials in the central administration as necessary to speed up local development and diminish the relative differences in social standards between the rural and urban areas. Even though the activities expanded in scope from the mid-1950s, they were limited compared with their emphasis in the official British rhetoric during the period. The efforts by the British administration supplemented those of missionary organisations and local authorities, with whom some kind of cooperation was generally attempted. Although the content of the schemes might differ among the three parties, their common characteristic was that they were decided by the official authorities, not by the people for whom they were designed. Local participation was instead largely defined as a continuation of the traditional self-help efforts and confined to contributions of labour and local resources.

The purpose of the mass education and community development schemes was to speed up 'improvement' or 'modernisation' in localised rural areas, such as Singida. The schemes largely aimed at gradual improvement of the social sphere, whereas there were no attempts at radical or rapid change of the economic and political spheres. The most visible outcome of the schemes was the social benefits for groups and local communities, deriving from, for instance, the increased number of wells and latrines, the growing of new kinds of vegetables and better housing. A limited number of individuals, on the other hand, did use improved literacy skills to gain access to the money economy or to become involved in local decision-making processes.

While the short-term improvements in Singida probably made life more attractive and less cumbersome, had some effect on the general health situation and created new social roles for selected individuals, they were so basic and relatively fragile that strong environmental factors, such as the periodic famines, could eliminate their impact. There was no attempt by the central authorities to secure more widespread or long-term development, for instance through improving the road system and increasing cattle production. While the lack of initiatives concerning the latter were emphasised by the British authorities as conflicting with the traditional social value system, according to which cattle were considered as social wealth rather than an economic investment, it was probably rather the guiding principle of paternalism which determined the nature of the schemes. The implementation of exactly the same kind of schemes across the country indicates that the initial local surveys were not used to identify the various alternatives or nuances needed to stimulate local development through a careful identification of its potential and an appropriate programmatic response.

The Singida schemes, and perhaps in particular the women's education programme, did reflect awareness of and sensitivity to the local social organisation and local values and the existing division of labour. The realisation that the local communities were many, organised in cooperation and competition with each other, and that any attempt at participation from the communities had to take its point of departure in the egalitarian social groups, was instrumental in forming the literacy groups through which wider development programmes could also be implemented. Other more fundamental questions concerning local identity were, however, not asked. The choice of a comprehensive literacy campaign in Kiswahili rather than the local languages reflected national rather than local communication needs. It did not involve serious attention to missionary arguments concerning the cultural and psychological need to reach literacy in the mother tongue before teaching any other language. Similarly, the issue of 'participation' never reached the stage of 'empowerment', i.e. did not imply questions of developing local initiative, local skills, local decision-making and local ownership of the established programmes.

These latter issues became of crucial importance in the formulation of the mass education schemes in Singida and in other places in the territory after the newly elected independent government designed its new educational policy in 1967. The new policy rested, as will be discussed in Chapter 6, on a different ideology for societal development which allocated a different role to mass education as a means of achieving high levels of political and economic participation in local and national development in addition to improving the social spheres of life. The problems of implementation, however, remained of overriding importance, partly influenced by changes of the surrounding circumstances. This led to serious discrepancies between stated goals and achieved reality at the local level, as will be further pursued in Chapters 7 and 8.

Notes

1. *Report on Social Welfare 1946*; Memo 7.7.48, Development of Adult Education (Prof. Philips), TNA SMP 36164.
2. *Report on Social Welfare 1946, 1947, 1948*; *Annual Report of the Social Development Department 1951*: 4.
3. *Annual Report of the Social Development Department 1951*: 38.
4. Report by Professor C.H. Philips to the Secretary of State for the Colonies on Mass Education in East Africa, TNA SMP 36164; *Annual Report of the Social Development Department 1951*: 8.
5. *Annual Report of the Social Development Department 1952*: App. D, *1953–54*: 3.
6. *Annual Report of the Social Development Department 1952*: App. D.
7. *Annual Report of the Social Development Department 1952*: App.
8. *Annual Report of the Social Development Department 1953–54*: 5.
9. Coulson 1982: 53–54.
10. *Annual Report of the Social Development Department 1953–54*: 5.
11. *Annual Report of the Social Development Department 1958*: 8; Community Development in Singida District, 30.10.1960, TNA Acc. 68/S.1/5; TNA Acc. 68/S.1/5/II: *passim*; Jellicoe 1961: 17.
12. Jellicoe 1961: 1–3, 1978: 3–19. The understanding of Turu society

presented here relies on the work of Marguerite Jellicoe who was trained as an anthropologist. She was appointed social development officer in Singida in 1959. Her intimate understanding of Turu society was undoubtedly crucial to the sensitivity with which some of the programmes were implemented in Singida, perhaps in particular the women's mass education programme, for which she undertook the initial survey.

13. Jellicoe 1962: 1–3.
14. Jellicoe 1961: 1–11, 1962: 1–2, 1978: 48–107.
15. Jellicoe 1961: 4, 1962: 1.
16. Jellicoe 1962: 2, 1978: 98–113.
17. *Annual Report of the Social Development Department 1957*: 10, *1959*: 8; Ministry of Local Government and Housing 1964: 5, 13; TNA Acc. 68/S.1/5: *passim*; TNA Acc. 68/S.1/5/II: *passim*.
18. *Annual Report of the Social Development Department 1958*: 8, *1960*: 4; Ministry of Local Government and Housing 1964: 3; Memorandum on Rural and Urban Development, Singida District, 7 July 1958, TNA Acc. 68/S.1/1; Review of the Singida Literacy Campaign, Singida District 1959, TNA Acc. 68/S.1/5; Monthly Reports Singida District 1961–1963, TNA Acc. 302/LGS 1/1.
19. *Annual Report of the Social Development Department 1959*: 4, *1960*: 3.
20. Correspondence during 1956 between the District Commissioner, Singida and the Augustana Lutheran Mission, TNA Acc. 68/S.1/1; TNA Acc. 68/S.1/5; Annual Report Singida District 1957, TNA Acc. 68/R.3/1; Memorandum on Rural and Urban Development, Singida District, 7 July 1958, TNA Acc. 68/S.1/1; District Office Singida, Monthly Report for the Month of December 1958, TNA Acc. 68/S.1/1; Letter 5 August 1959 from the Social Development Office, Singida to the Principal Social Development Officer, Tengeru, TNA Acc. 68/S.1/1; Jellicoe 1962: 16.
21. *Annual Report of the Social Development Department 1959*: 4; Literacy Campaign Report for the Month of January 1959, TNA Acc. 68/S.1/1; Brief Notes on Social Development and Literacy Campaign, Singida District, July 1959, TNA Acc. 68/S.1/5.
22. Jellicoe 1962: 6.
23. Review of the Literacy Campaign Singida District 1959, TNA Acc. 68/S.1/5; TNA Acc. 68/S.1/5: *passim*; Literacy Campaign Report for the Month of January, 1959, TNA Acc. 68/S.1/1; Jellicoe 1978: 219–228.
24. There were two complementary kinds of imaa (literally: strength or fortitude) rites: 'house' imaa and 'lion' imaa. Both were performed each year at the time of the new moon and, together, they expressed the need to preserve balance in human affairs. While 'house' imaa stressed the virtues of fertility, 'lion' imaa represented a purification of the area from the danger of strife and famine (Jellicoe 1978:16–19, *passim*).
25. TNA Acc. 68/S.1/5, 68/S.1/5/II: *passim*.
26. Jellicoe 1962: 2.
27. Njughuda represented the sanction of public opinion. Offences were reported to the elders, who, if agreeing upon the guilt of the offender, would demand an animal (e.g. a cow or a chicken) for a ritual feast as well as a fine for the injured person (Jellicoe 1978: 37–39, *passim*).

28. Literacy Campaign Report for the Month of January 1961, TNA Acc. 68/S.1/5; Jellicoe 1962: 8-12.
29. *Annual Report of the Social Development Department 1960:* 4.
30. *Annual Report of the Social Development Department 1959*: 1.
31. *Annual Report of the Social Development Department 1959*: 1.
32. *Annual Report of the Social Development Department 1959*: 1.
33. *Annual Report of the Social Development Department 1960*: 6.
34. *Annual Report of the Social Development Department 1959*: 4, *1960*: 6-7.
35. Community Development in Singida District, TNA Acc. 68/S.1/5; The 'Combined Operations' and UNICEF Teams Ihanja & Ikungi, Report for August 1960, TNA Acc. 68/S.1/5.
36. Community Development and Welfare, TNA Acc. 68/S.1/5/II; Monthly Reports Singida District 1961–1963, TNA Acc. 302/LGS 1/1; Outline for 1963 Annual Report Community Development Division, 30th December, 1963, TNA Acc. 302/LGS 1/7.
37. Memorandum on the Community Development and UNICEF Teams, Singida, TNA Acc. 68/S.1/5; UNICEF Team Mass Education Campaign, Monthly Reports 1960, TNA Acc. 302/LGS 1/1; Monthly Reports – Work among Women in Singida district 1963, TNA Acc. 302/LGS 1/7; Jellicoe 1961.
38. Jellicoe 1961: 4.
39. *Annual Report of the Social Development Department 1960*: 7.
40. Jellicoe 1962: 32–36.
41. Jellicoe 1962: 12–13.
42. *Annual Report of the Social Development Department 1960*: 6-7.
43. Ministry of Local Government and Housing 1964: 3.

Six

Education for Socialism,
Self-Reliance & Social Commitment
1962–81

The new focus for the development process in Tanzania after independence was formulated as the strategy of Socialism and Self-Reliance in
1967. Central to this strategy was the independently formulated
Education for Self-Reliance policy of the same year. With the new
national development strategy, renewed attention was focused on the
rural sector of the economy. The overall purposes for Tanzanian
development were partly reformulated in reaction to the social
differentiation which the modernisation efforts after the Second World
War, continuing largely unchanged in the immediate independence
years, brought with them. The new goals centred on equality and participation by the mass of the population in local and national development efforts as the basis for the construction of a socialist society.
Education was considered to be crucial to achieve these ends, although
the educational system had to be restructured and reoriented to meet
the new ends. While the formulated development strategy and the
educational policy in many ways represented a break with the goals and
reality of the inherited society in the early years of independence, their
implementation did not create the envisaged society in Tanzania.
Internal and external factors and barriers intervened in and influenced
the process, which was probably never implemented in the spirit of the
original formulations, and some of the stipulated purposes were already
redefined by the mid-1970s.

The Goals and Strategy for National Development

The redefinition in 1967 of the central purposes of development was a
reaction to some of the characteristics of the development in the years
immediately after independence, in particular limited growth, the sharp

reduction of foreign funds and the interpreted 'temptations' of capitalism. The new goals, therefore, centred on equality and participation as the keys to an inward-looking development process in contrast to the outward-looking process which had been pursued particularly since the Second World War. Equality and participation were considered to be the modern equivalents of the patterns of reciprocity and redistribution which were practised in the pre-colonial societies and which survived as social characteristics of the peasant household during the German and British periods. Their centrality underlined the importance to the Tanzania leadership of its African heritage which they recommended as the foundation for the socialist and self-reliant society of the future. As formulated in the ujamaa (literally: familyhood) philosophy, they replaced the belief of the British administration in the creation of rational market-oriented behaviour and economic incentives to stimulate economic development by a moral obligation of the Tanzanian population to work hard for the common good of all.

Socialism was understood to include a development both of material resources, and of socialist institutions, socialist attitudes and a socialist way of life. Although claiming in 1962 that 'the basic difference between a socialist society and a capitalist society does not lie in their methods of producing wealth, but in the way wealth is distributed',[1] the nationalisation of the 'commanding heights of the economy', including the principal financial, manufacturing and trading institutions, was announced in the Arusha Declaration in 1967. Plantations were to be taken over by the state and large-scale capitalist farms turned into state farms over time. These planned nationalisations could affect the relative position of the formerly influential non-African communities, particularly in the plantation industry, in white settler agriculture and in the Asian-dominated financial and trading sector. The accumulation and distribution of wealth by the state were intended rather to promote social equality among the African population in terms of socio-economic, rural–urban and rural–rural differences. Social amenities (dispensaries, water facilities, schools) were to be advanced in the rural areas as a means of promoting development among the mass of the population. Wage and salary levels were to be adjusted in accordance with the rural incomes of the peasantry, implying a readjustment of the high- and middle-level earnings in the modern sector, and the accumulation of private wealth by leaders in party and government was no longer permitted.[2]

Socialism was considered to be an 'attitude of mind' which was present in the traditional ujamaa household units and which could be re-created and elevated to a national characteristic through proper mobilisation of the peasants and workers and by developing a responsive leadership. Education was considered to be the crucial means to obtain both. Mass education was given priority in the educational system as the most important way to incorporate present and future generations in the development process by raising their level of political awareness and by improving their agricultural skills. Through education, leaders were to internalise the new political philosophy in order to act as an additional channel of 'consciousness-raising' of the peasantry. The leaders were to encourage the increased involvement of the peasantry in the development process by means of hard work and political participation through the TANU institutions which had become dominant in political life.[3]

The mobilisation of the rural masses was also the key to the establishment of a self-reliant nation, in which maximum utilisation would be made of the rich local resources, i.e. land and labour, and where the need for foreign assistance and investment would subsequently diminish. The basis of the strategy was the wide expansion of communal village production units, consisting of communities of people who were living and working together, from village settlement schemes into ujamaa villages. The communities would be interlocked so that they also worked for the common good of the nation as a whole.[4]

The formulated ujamaa strategy affected the principles and characteristics of both the capitalist and the peasant sectors. The central idea was to extend the system of mutual obligations and rights of the individual peasant household to the village level and, subsequently, through the individual administrative layers to the level of the nation-state. This implied, on the one hand, the elimination of the capitalist features of labour exploitation and capitalisation which, together with the planned nationalisations of large-scale capitalist agricultural enterprises, would eliminate the dominant characteristics of the capitalist mode of production.[5]

The extension of the principles of reciprocity and redistribution to the larger village unit also implied the replacement of the traditional peasant household autonomy by democratic communal decision-making in village councils. Traditional individual ownership of land was to be replaced by communal ownership of land by the communal village production unit. Communal activities, which were traditionally limited to specific tasks (e.g. housebuilding) at specific times during the agricultural season, were now to be the central focus and to include agricultural cultivation as the major activity. The peasant mode of production was to change gradually from individual to cooperative to communal farming. The village institutions were to take over the responsibility for the planning of production and for the redistribution of the economic returns. This included the planning of communal projects, such as poultry farms or village shops. The application of intermediate technology and some labour specialisation were the envisaged means for improving production and productivity among the peasant farmers. The hiring of labour was specifically prohibited.[6]

Even though the ultimate aim of the philosophy of ujamaa was a societal transformation process which was enacted from the basic village unit to the level of the nation-state, the specific focus of the philosophy was localised and narrow. It did not include more far-reaching changes, for instance, of the gender division of labour, which traditionally allocated the responsibility for food production to women and for cash crop production to men. Neither did the qualitative improvement of the production factors of land and labour specify, for instance, environmental control, the development of storage and transport facilities or the careful management of the production process, including the development and transfer of improved production skills. There was no specific indication of how the communal production units could become the basis of an expanded local–regional–national specialisation and exchange, or how they could develop other sectors of the economy and, thereby, contribute to national economic integration of the heterogeneous Tanzanian economy and society.[7]

From Manpower Development to Education for Self-Reliance

The kind of mass education activities which were important for the strategy of Socialism and Self-Reliance represented a reorientation of the educational efforts which were pursued in the years immediately after independence. During this period, Education for Manpower Development was stressed in order to fulfil expressed goals of increased economic growth and to meet the demands for an Africanisation of the middle- and high-level posts as a manifestation of politico-economic independence. The wider framework for the manpower planning approach was the human capital theory which was developed particularly by American economists in the late 1950s and the early 1960s. Manpower development dominated international thinking on education all over the world at the time, including in the international organisations, such as UNESCO. In 1963, UNESCO conducted surveys for the planning of education in Tanganyika, based on the recommendations of educational goals for the African continent as a whole, originally stipulated at a UNESCO-arranged conference for African states in Addis Ababa in 1961.[8]

Like Education for Modernisation, manpower development rested on the assumption that formal education was crucial to improve the productive capacity of a country's population and, therefore, to speed up an economic development process aiming at rapid industrialisation and an increased economic growth rate. More specifically, the concept stressed the link between the output of the educational system and the projected high- and middle-level manpower requirements in society. Education was considered to be an economic investment destined for consumption by other economic sectors, in particular the modern sector of society. It reinforced the development of skills related to science and technical subjects rather than the arts.[9] In contrast to Education for Modernisation, as it was formulated in the Colonial Office memoranda, manpower development expressed little or no concern with the wider social and political purposes of education, indicating a disregard for the value of non-economic education and for alternative private demands for education.

The shift in 1967 with the formulation of Education for Self-Reliance implied an emphasis on the socio-cultural and political purposes of education in addition to economic ones. Education for Self-Reliance, therefore, bore more immediate resemblance to the Education for Adaptation prevalent before independence than to either Education for Modernisation or Education for Manpower Development. Like Education for Adaptation, as formulated in the Colonial Office memoranda, Education for Self-Reliance was to promote mass education in order to improve production and productivity of the rural sector and to incorporate the broad population in policy-making processes. However, in contrast to Education for Adaptation, both as formulated at the metropolitan level and as adopted and implemented by the British administration in Tanganyika, Education for Self-Reliance introduced as an overriding purpose the need to restore social commitment and cooperative endeavour at every level of the educational system in order to construct a state which was rooted in the interpreted principles of the country's past, instead of being modelled on the experience of Britain.

Education for Liberation and Participation

Education was considered by the then President Nyerere, who was the crucial thinker behind the educational philosophy, to be the primary road to achieving freedom and development in the newly defined society. The object was human development as opposed to the creation of wealth. A free person was considered to be capable both of understanding and of meeting his or her own personal needs. Individuals would feel free to make strategic decisions concerning their personal life and well-being and to carry them into effect. All people were to live in human dignity and equality. This implied, on the one hand, the elimination of domination and exploitation by one person over another and, on the other, each person's equal responsibility to work and contribute to society to the limit of his or her ability. Amassing wealth was regarded as secondary to these moral principles of human dignity and equality and was only acceptable as a service to society in general. It was, then, essential to develop the minds and understanding of the people in order to create the wider social consciousness which was needed for the individual to become the master of his or her own development.[10]

Educational institutions, together with the home environment, were considered to be the crucial channel to form the attitude of mind which would bring service to the many instead of privilege to the few. Imparting knowledge or learning for its own sake was therefore no longer justified. Knowledge had to be relevant to the society which was being constructed and had, above all, to be accompanied by the social attitudes which would be conducive to the development of all people. The more education a person received, the higher was his or her expected responsibility to society.[11]

Education for Self-Reliance was closely related to the understanding of Tanzania as a 'poor, undeveloped, and agricultural economy'.[12] In order to justify the relatively high spending of government revenues on education, its vocational and social aspects must, therefore, become relevant to the predominantly rural economy, i.e. to the improvement of the lives of the people in the rural areas. It could no longer be thought of 'as a training for the skills required to earn high salaries in the modern sector of the economy'.[13] The crucial purpose of education was to prepare the young for work in a rural society and all citizens for participation in a free and democratic society. This aim was to be achieved by the inculcation of a strong sense of commitment to the total community through the promotion of cooperative endeavour and the creation of an acceptance of the values appropriate for the future. Education was to develop certain important characteristics in the individual, such as an enquiring mind, an ability to learn from others in a critical fashion, and a basic confidence as a free and equal member of society. The promotion of such characteristics and commitment was to be facilitated by integrating the schools with their surrounding communities, thus turning them into both economic and educational institutions. The active participation of students in village life and of village members in school life was interpreted as a reconstruction for the modern context of the pre-colonial African way of transmitting both mental and manual skills in an integrated fashion. It was considered to be the basis for achieving both a higher degree of self-finance for the schools and of raising awareness of the skills and attitudes needed for the village economy.[14]

Similar experiments were undertaken in other parts of the world at the time (e.g. China and Cuba), which may well have acted as an additional source of inspiration. The general views on education were also much in line with radical critics of the effect of colonial education and the colonial experience on the colonised mind, and the need for 'consciousness-raising' to gain true liberation from such conditions.[15] Thus, the principles of freedom, human dignity and equality were interpreted in relation to the human potential as a revolutionary force in the development process. While injustice and peace were considered to be incompatible in the long run, man had, it was believed, the power to decide and act against any oppressive conditions and restrictions of his freedom at any given and decisive point of history.[16] Education had to

> liberate the African from the mentality of slavery and colonialism by making him aware of himself as an equal member of the human race, with the rights and duties of his humanity. It [had] to liberate him from the habit of submitting to circumstances which reduce[d] his dignity as if they were immutable. And it ha[d] to liberate him from the shackles of technical ignorance so that he [could] make and use the tools of organisation and creation for the development of himself and his fellow men.[17]

In essence, then, Education for Manpower Development and Education for Self-Reliance contrasted an education for the few with an education for the many in accordance with the stipulated wider alternative development strategies. An important difference in the underlying thinking was that modernisation and capitalist-oriented economic development was believed to require a refinement and application of still more advanced levels of technology, whereas African Socialism and Self-Reliance relied on the individual's moral obligation to work hard in the interest of the many. While Education for Manpower Development, consequently, focused particularly on the development of science, technology and vocational skills for a limited administrative and technocratic elite, Education for Self-Reliance stressed the promotion of social commitment and social consciousness among the mass of the population.

This distinction could be seen as a parallel to the pre-independence situation, which, similarly, contrasted an education for the few at the top of the educational pyramid (Education for Modernisation) with an education for the many at the base of the educational pyramid (Education for Adaptation) in order to achieve wider desired societal goals. An important difference was that educational policies after independence were intended to support those economic policies which aimed at reducing and preventing further social and economic divisions, the presence of which was partly caused by the educational policies implemented before independence.

The Political and Socio-Economic Development

In the immediate post-independence years, the independent government was primarily concerned with a reorganisation of the inherited political–administrative system in order that it would reflect the country's independent status and adequately promote political stability and national cohesion. Economic development, on the other hand, largely continued along the lines of the British-established modernisation policies until the formulation of Socialism and Self-Reliance in 1967. The implementation of the new development strategy took different directions, with some major changes occurring in the mid-1970s and, again, in the early 1980s. The planned and implemented educational policies were attuned to these broader, periodic changes in the overall strategy.

With respect to the political–administrative system, the inherited Westminster-style pluralist democratic system was replaced in 1965 with a one-party state which established TANU as the sole party in power. There was a formal division of labour between the National Executive Committee (NEC) of TANU that formulated policies and the National Assembly that implemented policies until 1967, when the NEC had assumed the key role in both policy formulation and implementation. As head of both government and party, the president – who was during 1961–85 J.K. Nyerere – was highly instrumental as an independent policy-maker and as a mediator between party and government.[18]

A TANU authority structure was also gradually established at the sub-national level which, although aiming at increased popular participation, instead heightened party control of development. In 1962, the official powers and responsibilities of the chiefs were passed on to elected district councils, which were supervised by regional TANU commissioners and the Minister of Local Government. From 1964, the central government was linked through party officials to all administrative levels: the region, district, division and ward and the hundred-cell down to the ten-cell unit. Village, ward and district development committees co-ordinated the development activities of the central government departments.[19]

With respect to foreign policy, a strategy of 'positive non-alignment' was presented before the General Assembly of the United Nations immediately after independence. It was designed to preserve political independence by diversifying the interaction with the international community across political blocs and political ideologies and to promote the maximum use of local, as opposed to foreign, ideas and resources as a means of sustaining economic independence.[20] While practical manifestations of the principle occurred, particularly in the 1960s (see note 27) and 1970s, it did not eliminate the external influence on the national policy processes which accompanied the escalating foreign assistance to Tanzania, particularly from the mid-1970s.

From Modernisation to Socio-Economic Transformation

By far the larger share of recurrent revenues of the Tanzanian government was generated from direct taxation (income taxes) and indirect taxation (import, export and excise taxes), which, together, accounted for between 82 and 88 per cent of the total revenues during 1961–80. Import and excise duties represented the largest single item, although it dropped from roughly 50 per cent of the total revenues during the 1960s to an average of 36 per cent during the 1970s.[21] Development expenditures were partly financed by foreign assistance, of which the relative proportion declined from approximately 90 to 25 per cent during the 1960s, followed by a continuous increase to approximately 65 per cent of the total in 1978. The loan share alone peaked in 1971 close to 100 per cent of the total foreign component, dropping to around 50 per cent in 1978.[22]

Until the early 1970s, the central government's budgetary policy was prudent, leaving a surplus of up to 10 per cent on the recurrent budget. By the 1980s, this surplus had turned into a deficit of approximately the same size (being actually 20 per cent in 1980). Including development expenditures, there was an overall budgetary deficit from the early 1970s, which had doubled by the 1980s.[23] Public expenditures were primarily invested in economic, social and public services. Of the social services, education always constituted the major item due to the manpower needs and the changed priority of the sector.

During 1962–66, economic activities were laid out in two development plans designed and influenced by expatriates, in particular the World Bank. Their objective was to develop a self-sustained national economy through increased economic growth. The means selected was the continued modernisation of primary agricultural production through the application of two different approaches: the improvement approach which aimed at promoting better practices among individual peasant households by way of agricultural extension and community development; and the transformation approach which proposed to create new large-scale villages which practised modern techniques and organisation by way of settlement schemes.[24]

The implementation of the two approaches caused disruption among the peasantry and was largely unsuccessful. Tobacco schemes did, however, lead to higher returns and, in a context of historically high prices, the common peasantry was relieved from the force or persuasion applied by the British administration before independence in the implementation of new agricultural practices. In general, however, the approaches reinforced a social differentiation or class stratification process within the African population, rather than between the African and non-African populations as at independence. This was primarily due to the importance of public institutions in economic life and the consequent dominant role of state officials relying on public or foreign funding. The socio-economic differences increased both within the rural sector and between the rural and urban sectors. Within the agricultural sector, the number of African 'progressive' farmers, who applied machinery and hired labour in large-scale farming, expanded particularly in the export crop-producing areas of the northern highlands (Kilimanjaro and Arusha), and the north-western highlands (Lake Victoria region) and among maize-producing farmers in Ismani (Iringa region). In 1967, some 1,000 African estate farmers alone accounted for approximately 124,000 of the total number of employees.[25]

In the urban sector, Africans were rapidly replacing Europeans in the middle and senior ranks of the civil service. By 1966, they constituted approximately three quarters of the total, compared with roughly one quarter at independence. Both government and TANU officials pressed successfully for salaries equivalent to those of the former British administrative officers, which compared favourably with the incomes of the more successful farmers. There were also substantial increases in the salaries of subordinate staff. In the industry and service sectors, the TANU-controlled trade union, NUTA (National Union of Tanganyika Workers), exerted pressure for nationalisation, Africanisation and higher pay. The wage levels of urban wage earners, who constituted about one tenth of the total labour force, continued to rise, by 1966 being 80 per cent higher than at independence and leaving the wage earner better off than the average farmer.[26]

Trade during the period reflected the pre-independence pattern, the larger share of both exports and imports being undertaken with the Western industrialised nations and the United Kingdom in particular. The pattern of external assistance, however, altered in several different ways: the capital budget was constituted of internal rather than external sources of funds; external capital funds changed from grants to loans; and, finally, there was a more widespread diversification in the sources of overseas development funds. This was mainly due to foreign policy disputes with previous major donors[27] and took place despite the fact that the Tanzanian government was continuing a Western-designed economic development process. The British contribution alone dropped from 96 per cent at independence to 6 per cent in 1966/67. The largest individual donor in 1966/67 was instead China, which contributed 40 per cent of total development funds. In all, only about 40 per cent of expected overseas finance was realised during the two planning periods.[28]

The formulation of the strategy of Socialism and Self-Reliance in 1967 and its implementation during 1969–76 shifted the focus to the extension of the principle of ujamaa in order to meet with the short-term goal of spreading development to the mass of the people. Long-term economic transformation was, on the other hand, to be ensured by public investment in and management of industry and large-scale agri-culture.[29] In the Third Five Year Development Plan of 1976, however, industry rather than agriculture was appointed the key economic sector. Emphasis was put on the production of food and goods essential to people's needs and framed within a long-term basic industry strategy for 1975–95. The planned self-reliant aspect of development efforts was also downplayed as the Tanzania leadership, perhaps learning from experience, set a target of approximately 60 per cent of total investment by foreign investors compared with 40 per cent in the earlier plan.[30]

The emphasis on people's needs reflected the change in international thinking on development which occurred in the early 1970s. At that time development with maximum GDP growth and modernisation through maximum investment were considered, by the international multilateral and bilateral organisations, as having largely failed to bring about broad-scale development in developing countries. Instead, the so-called Basic Human Needs strategy was advocated in 1976, which, in addition to proclaiming the need for economic growth, made a direct attack on world poverty by setting minimum consumption levels in relation to five broad targets: basic consumer goods (i.e. food, clothing, housing); basic services (i.e. education, water, health); productive employment (including self-employment); infrastructure; and mass participation in decision-making and implementation of projects.[31]

The implementation of ujamaa involved the concentration of the major part of the population from scattered homesteads into villages. Due to lack of peasant response to the idea during 1967–69, when implemen-tation relied on voluntary participation, the movement in 1970–71 was undertaken as government 'operations' and, during 1973–76, by the use of coercive measures. The emphasis on communal farming, and there-fore a profound transformation of the mode of production, also had to be abandoned due to lack of peasant response. It was replaced in 1973 by block-farming, i.e. individual 'shoulder-to-shoulder' farming, of a limited number of cash crops on the communal farm.[32]

In all, around 8,000 so-called ujamaa villages with approximately 13,140,229 members, which represented approximately 85 per cent of the population, were registered in 1976. The villages were concentrated in the poorer central and southern regions (e.g. Lindi, Mtwara, Dodoma and Singida) with empty cultivable land suitable for village resettlement, but were much fewer in the richer northern and north-western regions (e.g. Kilimanjaro, West Lake) with population density, land pressure, a stronger peasant differentiation and a peasant population already living among their permanent crops. The villages fulfilled a wide variety of overall purposes which corresponded only partially with the ujamaa philosophy. Many of them were the arbitrary creation of state officials rather than the spontaneous response by the peasants to the ujamaa philosophy. The delegation of authority concerning development activities at the regional, ward and district levels during 1968–72 and the decentralisation reform of 1972 both enhanced socialist leadership through TANU which, in effect, eliminated participation in formulation and decision-making by the peasantry at the village level.[33]

The implementation of ujamaa was generally patchy, except for the nationalisation and regionalisation of more than half of the sisal plantations and many of the large-scale grain farms, some of which were given to ujamaa farmers. Coffee estates in Kilimanjaro were also handed over to local cooperative societies. There was an outflux of the non-African communities in reaction against the policy, which included expropriations. Locally, 'progressive' farmers survived or leading citizens turned themselves from 'progressive' farmers into village leaders, acting as a link between state officials and the villagers. While state funds were much too limited to support all villages, 'progressive' farmers also often abused their position as village leaders to apply government-provided resources, such as fertilisers, insecticides and machinery, on their private farms instead of the communal farm, and often had a vested interest in not starting communal ujamaa villages or specific communal projects, such as cash crop schemes, cooperative bars or shops, which might compete with their private economic enterprises. The lack of peasant response to communal farming was rooted in the fact that increased demands were made on their labour power and time without securing their influence on decision-making concerning production targets and redistribution of economic outcomes.[34]

The trends for most export cash crops and marketed food crops were declining during the implementation of ujamaa and its redirection into the basic industry strategy. This was partly caused by deteriorating world market prices (affecting sisal, pyrethrum, coffee and cotton), the drought in 1973–74 (affecting wheat, rice and maize), and the general dislocation and disruption in production related to the nationalisation policy (affecting cashew nut production), which led to an escalation of food imports in order to support the non-agricultural population. This situation was followed by an overall imbalance in foreign and local investment in favour of industry and infrastructure and away from agriculture.[35] During 1976–81, of the export cash crops only tea, tobacco and coffee expanded. The output of marketed maize, wheat and rice, on the other hand, increased slightly seen in relation to the 1967 output figures and to the average 1969–71 production figures.[36] Total marketed food production far from met the local needs, particularly during 1979–80, when serious weather conditions (both drought and flooding) disrupted production. Tripling food imports and a significant increase in the imports of machinery to support the long-term industrialisation programme contributed to a tripling of the balance of trade deficit. Furthermore, continuously falling prices of the major export crops, another jump in the world prices of oil in 1979–80 and the war against Amin in 1978–79 worsened the foreign exchange deficit and placed the country in a state of bankruptcy, external public debt having increased fivefold during 1970–81.[37]

All of the official social indicators of development did, however, improve in numerical terms and socio-economic and rural–urban divisions also diminished. By 1981, life expectancy had reached 52 years; water supplies were provided for 90 per cent of the urban and 42 per cent of the rural population; the literacy rate had increased to 79 per cent; and the enrolment rate in primary schools covered 70 per cent of the age group.[38] In the public sector, the salaries for civil servants were cut drastically. During 1967–81, the differentials between the highest- and lowest-paid government employees were reduced from 30:1 to 6:1, whereas middle-grade civil servants experienced a 54 per cent drop in real wages during 1970–80. Similarly, real non-agricultural wages are estimated to have fallen by almost 50 per cent. Smallholder incomes are estimated to have increased by 8 per cent during 1970–80 and peasant income from cotton and subsistence production has been estimated as higher than the minimum wage during 1976–82. Commercial farmers, on the other hand, are estimated to have experienced a 46 per cent decline in income during 1970–80.[39]

The total amount of foreign aid increased drastically from US\$ 44.6 million in 1969, US\$ 288.7 million in 1976, to US\$ 648.8 million in 1981, net figures in 1981 equalling exports as a source of revenue and foreign exchange. In 1980/81, total assistance represented approximately 60 per cent of the development budget, grants having increased at the expense of loans. The major proportion of foreign aid came from 'liberal' or social-democratic Western democracies (e.g. the Scandinavian countries, the Netherlands and Canada). Despite a continued diversification of the import/export trade, Western industrialised countries remained, with some fluctuation in individual years, the main partners for both exports and imports. The relative importance of the United Kingdom declined, whereas (then) West Germany gained in significance as an exporter to Tanzania and together with other EEC countries, as an importer from Tanzania.[40]

The Tanzanian society of the early 1980s, therefore, was far from representing the rhetoric or achieving the goals of the official statements and plans on Socialism and Self-Reliance. While state, market and global forces all had an impact on the development process, the implementation of the policy by far exceeded public means and partly caused the failure of agricultural schemes. The adopted top-down approach explains some of its misdirection, although it also appears that the underlying belief in the creation of social commitment and cooperative behaviour was unfulfilled. This could be due, to some extent, to a simplistic misrepresentation of the nature of human interaction in the pre-colonial societies, which was taken as a model for the new Tanzanian society. However, it may also have related to a lack of transformation of social attitudes through a successful use of the educational system as a tool. While this question will be explored in more detail in Chapters 7 and 8, it is first important to analyse how the national educational system was reformed in order to fulfil the goals of mass participation in local and national development, and to secure an equalisation of regional, rural–urban and socio–economic, including gender, discrepancies.

The Priority of the Educational Sector

The reforms of education by the independent government were based on an increased overall priority of the educational sector during 1962–81, compared with the time before independence. This priority was affected, however, by the severe economic conditions in the early 1980s. In addition to the expenditure provided by the central government, funding for education was raised locally by the local authorities and the regional administrations. Parents, churches and various non-government organisations, moreover, contributed on a voluntary basis to private education. The central government funds were channelled through the Ministry of Education and the Prime Minister's Office, the latter being responsible for the subvention of the regional administration (including the districts and towns). Other ministries, such as the Ministry of Agriculture, the Ministry of Health and the Ministry of Labour, were responsible for vocational training and educational programmes within their specific fields.

Like government expenditures overall, total expenditure on education was increasing during the period when education was considered to be a leading force in the social change process.[41] Its share of the monetary GDP was increasing during 1962/63–1975/76 (from 2.7 to 5.7 per cent) and largely retained in 1980/81 (5.3 per cent), although it was declining as a proportion of total government expenditures (see Table 6.1). By far the larger part of educational expenditures derived from the recurrent

Table 6.1 Expenditures on Education in Relation to Total Recurrent and Development Expenditures in Tanzania 1962/63–1980/81 by Source. Current Prices

Source	1962/63 Msh.[a]	1966/67 Msh.	1975/76 Msh.	1980/81 Msh.
Recurrent				
1. Total govt expenditure	479	740	3,716	9,986[b]
2. Total expenditure on education	101[c]	173	776	1,811
Min. of Education	101	173	357	1,811
Regional expenditure	-	-	324	n/a
Other ministries	n/a	n/a	95	n/a
Item 2 as % of 1	21.0	23.3	20.9	18.1
Development				
3. Total govt expenditure	113	259	2,253	5,184[b]
4. Total expenditure on education	15	27	201	337
Min. of Education	15	20	93	245
Regional expenditure	-	-	54	92
Other ministries	n/a	7	53	n/a
Foreign composition of 4	n/a	16	n/a	175
Local composition of 4	n/a	11	n/a	71
Item 4 as % of 3	13.3	10.4	8.9	6.5
5. Total govt expenditure (1+3)	592	999	5,969	15,170
6. Total expenditure on education (2+4)	116	200	977	2,148
Item 6 as % of 5	19.6	20	16.4	14.1
7. GDP (factor cost)	4,227.5	6,514	16,988	39,822
Item 6 as % of 7	2.7	3.0	5.7	5.3

n/a Not available.

Notes: a The figures have been converted from £ (£1 = sh. 20).
b Estimate.
c Approved estimate. Including £455 for information services.

Sources: *Estimates of the Revenue and Expenditure of Tanganyika 1st July-30th June 1964*: xiii; *Appropriation Accounts, Revenue Statements, Accounts of the Funds and Other Public Accounts of Tanzania for the Year 1975/76*: 159–165; *Background to the Budget. An Economic Survey 1966/67*: 70–72, *1968/69*: 79–92; *Economic Survey 1977–78*: 9, 34–36; *Annual Plan for 1977–78*: 5; *National Accounts of Tanzania 1960–62*: 9, *1964–72*: 11, *1970–82*: Table I; Goranson 1981: 6; *Speech by the Minister of State for Planning and Economic Affairs in the Vice-President's Office*: 9; Ministry of Education, *Recent Educational Developments in the United Republic of Tanzania (1981–83)*: 9.

rather than the development budget. As a percentage of total expenditures, recurrent expenditures on education peaked in 1966/67 (23 per cent), followed by a falling trend to an estimated 18 per cent in 1980/81. Of the development budget, education was allocated its largest proportion in 1962/63 (13 per cent) and its lowest in 1980/81 (6.5 per cent).

The foreign component of the educational development budget has been estimated to average approximately 42 per cent during the 1960s and 67 per cent during the 1970s.[42] As the total development expenditures averaged only about 19 per cent of the total recurrent expenditures on education in the selected years, education seems to have been primarily financed by the Tanzanian government during the period. The relative unreliability and unavailability of data on the total foreign assistance to the development budget and the increased contributions to the recurrent budget in the 1980s (and 1990s), however, hamper any firm conclusions on the relative foreign impact. That it was significant, and perhaps did not always fulfil stipulated national goals, appears from the fact that it was often concentrated in sub-sectors and projects of the donor agency's preference and choice rather than those of the Tanzanian government's. This was increasingly so with the general redirection of economic and educational policies in the 1980s in the context of structural adjustment.

The changed emphases from manpower development to Education for Self-Reliance were reflected in the support to the sub-sectors of education (see Table 6.2). Thus, while secondary education expanded on the recurrent budget (from an estimated 24 to an estimated 31 per cent) during 1962/63–1966/67 and together with higher education consumed the total development budget in 1966/67, primary education dropped from an estimated 47 to an estimated 41 per cent of the total during the same period. Between 1966/67 and 1980/81, on the other hand, the relative proportion of primary (and adult) education was substantially increased, by an estimated 13 per cent on the recurrent budget and by an estimated 37 per cent on the development budget, whereas secondary education dropped by an estimated 20 per cent on the recurrent budget and by an estimated 19 per cent on the development budget. Teacher training and higher education had fairly constant proportions of the recurrent budget during the whole period (an estimated 6 and 13 per cent respectively), their relative proportions of the development budget fluctuating at a higher level, an estimated 8 and 35 per cent respectively.

The Provision of Education

The relatively high priority of the educational sector and of mass education as a sub-sector was established in a context where the achievement

Table 6.2 Recurrent and Development Expenditures on Education in Tanzania 1962/63–1980/81 by Level. Current Prices

Level	1962/63 Msh.[a]	%	1966/67 Msh.	%	1975/76 Msh.	%	1980/81 Msh.	%
Recurrent								
Primary	44.5[b]	47	61[c]	41	309	45	872[c]	48
Adult	-		-		41	6	106[c]	6
Secondary and technical[j]	22.4[b]	24	45[c]	31	142	21	194[c]	11
Teacher train.	6.6[b]	7	12[c]	8	43	6	65[c]	3
Higher	18.0[bd]	19	17[c]	12	107	16	219[c]	12
Other	2.7[be]	3	12[ck]	8	39[d]	6	373[cf]	20
Total	94.2[h]	100	147[h]	100	681[g]	100	1,829[hi]	100
Development								
Primary	1.4[c]	10	-		56	38	73[c]	23
Adult	-		-		23	16	44[c]	14
Secondary and technical[j]	7.4[c]	53	11[c]	39	43	29	64[c]	20
Teacher train.	0.1[c]	1	-		11	8	42[c]	13
Higher	4.0[c]	28	17[c]	61	12	8	60[c]	19
Other	1.1[c]	8	-		-		35[c]	11
Total	14.0	100	28[h]	100	145[g]	99	318[hi]	100

Notes:
a The figures have been converted from £ (£1 = sh. 20).
b Approved estimate.
c Estimate.
d Including administration and general services.
e Information services.
f General education.
g Excluding spending from other ministries.
h Note that actual spending differed somewhat (see Table 6.1).
i Note that the actual distribution of the total recurrent and development budget was: primary 44%, secondary 12%, teacher training 5.5%, adult education 6.6%, higher and technical 1.6%, university 11.4%, general education 6.8% (Ministry of Education 1984b: Table III).
j Exclusive of spending on vocational training from other ministries.
k General services.
l All remaining subvotes of the Ministry of Education.

Sources: Estimates of the Revenue and Expenditure of Tanganyika 1st July–30th June 1963: 230–231, *1st July–30th June 1964*: 45–47; *1st July–30th June 1967*: 48–50, D.3; *Appropriation Accounts, Revenue Statements, Accounts of the Funds and Other Public Accounts of Tanzania for the Year 1975/76*: 159–165; Goranson 1981: Table 5; Ministry of Education, *Recent Educational Developments in the United Republic of Tanzania (1981–1983)*: Table III.

of independence had released widespread popular expectation of social equality and improved welfare. As long as the interrelationship between formal educational qualifications and access to restricted modern sector occupations with high income opportunities was maintained, education could be rightly considered by the wide population to be the most important means of social mobility and an access card to wider social opportunities. The maintenance of political stability, therefore, partly depended on the government's will to provide educational opportunities which satisfied this expressed popular demand.[43]

The government initiated reforms of the educational system which affected its structure, organisation, access criteria and contents. The racially segregated educational systems were unified in 1961. The new system was to operate according to one national curriculum, and access to education was permitted in all educational institutions, irrespective of race and religion. The government also extended its influence on voluntary agency schools by exerting supervision over primary schools, control of the selection of students and maintenance of discipline in secondary schools and teachers' colleges, and control of the salaries, working conditions, recruitment and posting of teachers to all voluntary agency institutions. The ownership and management of all publicly-supported voluntary agency schools were transferred to the central government. Private schools could still be registered provided they fulfilled government conditions for the provision of education, which was always centrally planned. The shared responsibility for primary (and adult) education by the local authorities and post-primary education by the central government was maintained after independence.[44]

After 1968, formal education comprised seven years of primary, four years of 'ordinary' secondary and two years of 'advanced' secondary education (see Figure 6.1). The examination and certification points introduced by the British administration were maintained after standard VII (the Primary School Leaving Certificate), form IV (the Certificate of Secondary Education) and form VI (the Advanced Certificate of Secondary Education), with additional examination points for quality control at standard II and form II. One year of national service and, during 1974-84, two years of work experience were introduced by the new government as conditions to enter higher education. During the period, vastly expanded options were developed for training and professional education at different levels after standard VII, form IV and form VI and after various undergraduate degrees. Some of these options for training and education did not, however, function in reality. Adult education (for persons over the age of 13) was formalised as a channel for both literacy and vocational training and was planned in 1982 for use even at the university level.

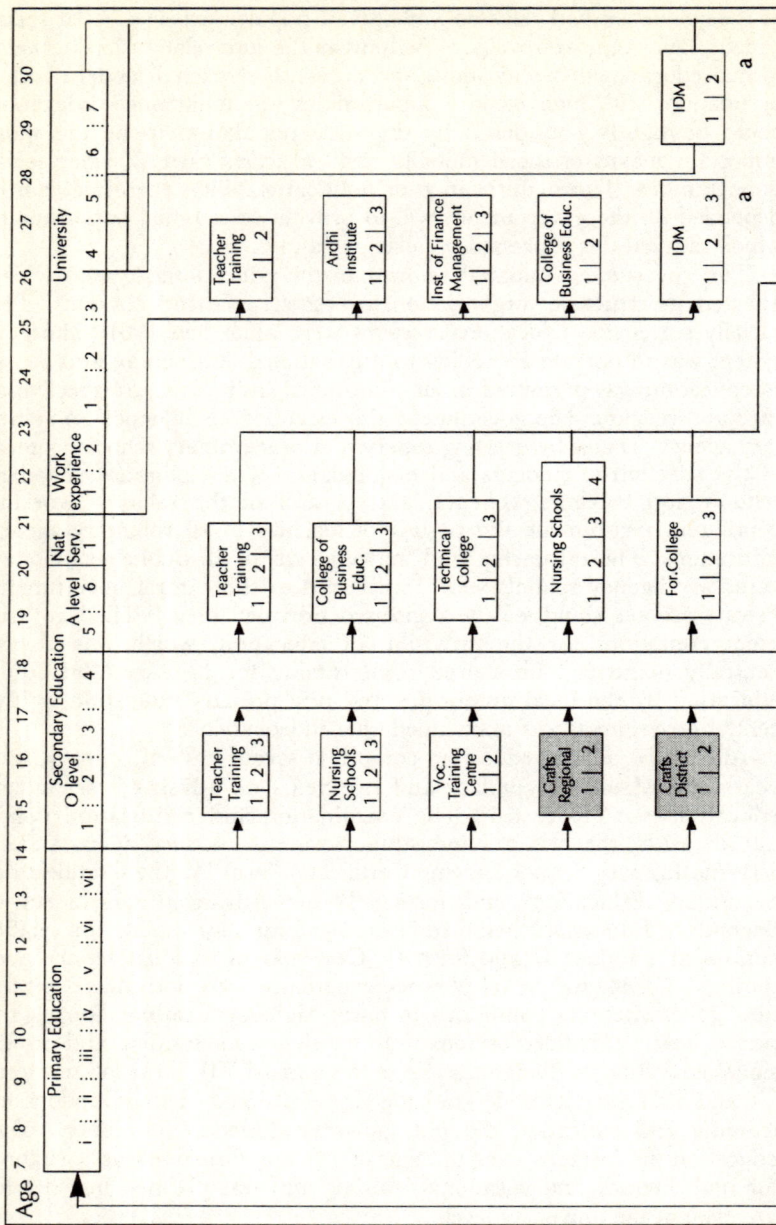

Figure 6.1 The Structure of Formal and Adult Education in Tanzania towards the Year 2000

Note: The hatched boxes refer to recommendations by the 1982 Presidential Commission to establish additional vocational and crafts training centres at the district and regional level as well as an institute for Higher Studies by Distance Learning in one of the Universities.

a = Institute of Development Management

b = East African Statistics Training Centre

Sources: Ministry of Education, *Educational System in Tanzania: Towards the Year 2000*, Dar es Salaam, 1984: 18; Ministry of Education, *Recent Educational Developments in the United Republic of Tanzania (1981–83)*, Dar es Salaam, 1984: Appendix 1.

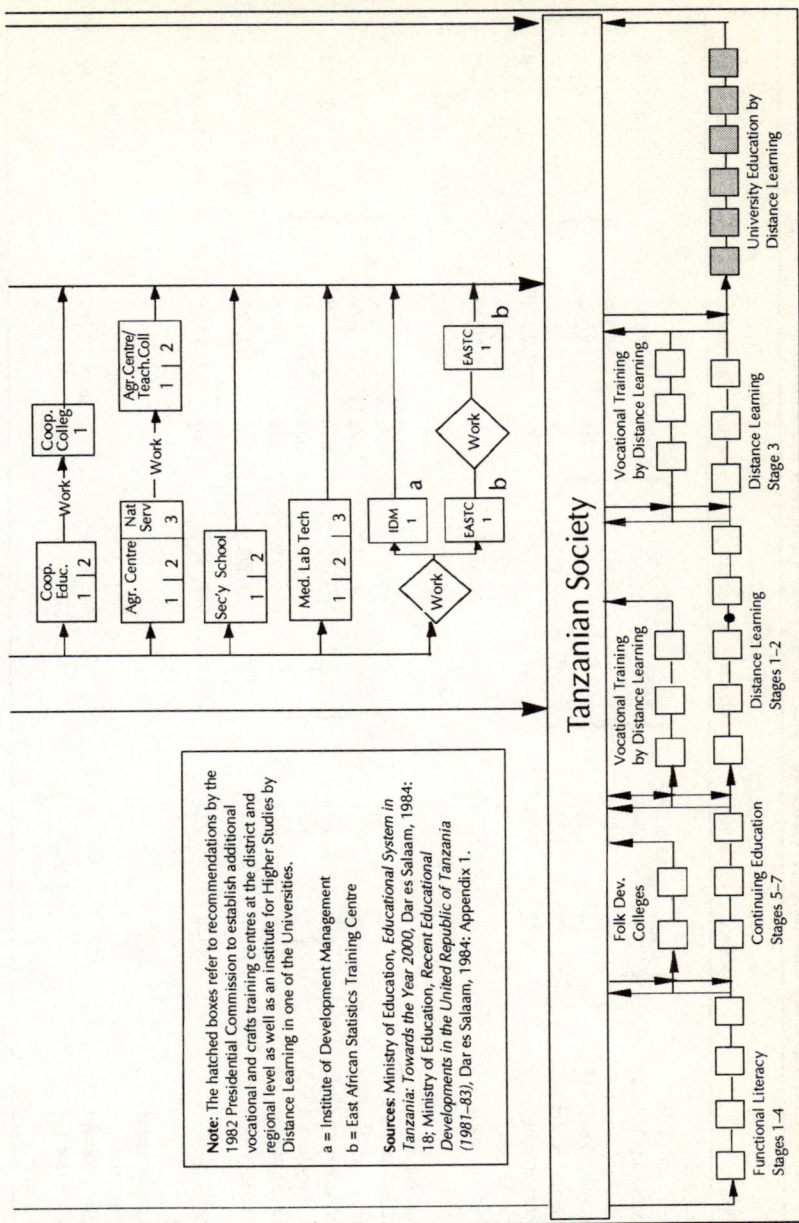

Table 6.3 Formal and Adult Education in Tanzania 1962–81 by Category: Schools and Enrolment

Category	1962 Schools	1962 Enrolment	1966 Schools	1966 Enrolment	1976 Schools	1976 Enrolment	1981 Schools	1981 Enrolment
Formal (govt)								
Primary (stds I–IV)	3,342 {	443,799	3,853 {	561,755	5,804[b] {	1,954,442	9,947 {	3,530,622
Primary (stds V–VIII)[a]		74,864		179,236		36,218		34,748
Secondary (forms I–IV)	51	13,690	70	22,241	n/a	3,729	83 {	3,544
Secondary (forms V–VI)	10	485		1,595		n/a		1,360[d]
Vocational & technical	3[c]	1,516	3[c]	1,444[c]	n/a	n/a	2[d]	
Teacher training	21	1,851[e]	17[f]	5,011[f]	n/a	9,471[b]	37	13,138[g]
Higher (E. Afr.)[h]	–	193[i]	–	997[i]	–	2,828	1[j]	2,952
Higher (overseas)	–	1,327[k]	–	2,325[k]	–	1,070	–	1,497
Sub-total	3,427	537,725	3,943	774,604	5,804	2,007,758	10,070	3,587,861
Formal (private)								
Primary (stds I–IV)	n/a	n/a	631 {	49,025	n/a	n/a	33 {	7,561
Primary (stds V–VIII)[a]	n/a	n/a		4,703	n/a	n/a		n/a
Secondary (forms I–IV)	1 {	n/a	26 {	3,786	n/a	17,039	75 {	29,078
Secondary (forms V–VI)	1	n/a	2	6	n/a	157		232
Teacher training	1	n/a	2	72	n/a	n/a	n/a	n/a
Sub-total	2		659	57,592	n/a	17,196	108	36,871
Grand total	3,429	537,725	4,602	832,196	5,804	2,084,954	10,178	3,624,732
Adult								
Functional literacy		–		–		n/a		3,526,565
Post-literacy		–		–		n/a		1,386,069
Folk dev. colleges		–		–		n/a		13,654
Illiteracy rate (%)		90.5		71.9		27[l]		20
Sub-total								4,926,308

Footnotes to Table 6.3

n/a   Not available.

Notes: Excluding figures on vocational training under the Ministry of Labour and Social Welfare (now the Ministry of Labour and Manpower Development). Formal education includes registered private institutions which received government grants-in-aid. The number of students represented gross enrolment.

a   Standard VII was abolished in 1968.

b   1975 figure.

c   Including Dar es Salaam Technical College, secondary technical schools (Ifunda and Moshi), craft courses (at Moshi) secondary schools only. These courses were phased out by the four-year secondary technical course). There were also 1,580 part-time students at Dar es Salaam Technical College in 1966.

d   Dar es Salaam and Arusha Technical Colleges. Excluding students in vocational training centres and post-primary vocational centres under the Ministry of Labour and Social Welfare/Manpower Development.

e   Including grade A, B and C in both government (in all 439 students) and voluntary agency colleges as at November 1962.

f   Including 1st year intake and 2nd year output (2 year courses only) in teachers' colleges, education officers grade III, grade A, B and C.

g   Note that the output from the distance training programme is not included in the figure. During 1979–84, output was 37,988 people of whom 35,028 had passed their examinations by 1981 (Mälck and Temu 1989: 27).

h   The University of East Africa was split into three autonomous universities in 1970. In Tanzania the University College became the University of Dar es Salaam.

i   Including enrolment in all courses 1966/67.

j   University of Dar es Salaam.

k   Including universities overseas, other post-secondary institutions and other courses.

l   1977 figure.

Sources: *Annual Report of the Ministry of Education 1962:* 10–16, *1966:* 54–86; *Statistical Abstract 1964:* 154–158; *Annual Report of the Ministry of Education 1966:* 54–86; *Economic Survey 1977–78:* 111–112; Ministry of Education, *Basic Education Statistics in Tanzania (BEST) 1981–85:* 1, 5, 8–10, 12–13, 15–20, 22; UNESCO 1977: 1.3.

The Access Dimension of the Educational Reform

While the racial and religious dimensions of social inequality were the particular concern of the post-independent government at independence, regional (rural–rural and rural–urban) as well as socio-economic inequality came into focus with the Arusha Declaration in 1967. In education, this concern was reflected in policies which aimed at incorporating deprived social groups, including women, and deprived geographical areas into the educational system and at securing access for some of them to post-primary education. The year 1975 was targeted for the eliminatation of adult illiteracy and the year 1977 for the achievement of universal primary education. The emphasis on mass participation in education, which was seen in relation to the development of the rural sector through Education for Self-Reliance, restricted the expansion of post-primary education. While the student population at the University of Dar es Salaam reacted against the decline in privileges and trained personnel showed reluctance for posting to rural areas, the more long term effect of the policy was the creation of severe tensions with parents and social groups, who were still hoping for higher education for their children in order to secure access to economic and political opportunities.

The impressive quantitative effect of the government priority is displayed in Table 6.3. As far as mass education was concerned, there was a sixfold increase in the primary school population, which tripled between 1966 and 1976 and again between 1976 and 1981 in accordance with the goal of universal primary education by 1977. The 1981 enrolment figure corresponded to roughly 97 per cent gross enrolment, but represented only 70 per cent net enrolment of the child population between 7 and 13 years.[45] The provision of adult education reduced the number of illiterates from 90 to 20 per cent of the population during 1962–81.

At the post-primary level, provision was sharply reduced. Gross enrolment expanded in secondary schools in support of the manpower planning policy until the mid-1970s (roughly tripling between 1962 and 1976) but declined during 1976–81. The private secondary sector, on the other hand, expanded significantly from 1966, approaching the intake in the public system by 1981. While enrolment in technical and vocational training was fairly constant (around 1,400 students),[46] the number of students in teacher training and higher education increased. The number of students in the local universities rose at the expense of those studying abroad. The total, however, represented a declining percentage of the secondary school leavers.

The adopted policies of eradication of adult illiteracy, universal primary education and direct access to higher education for women promoted female participation. Certain patterns of inequality, never-theless, remained. Female illiteracy was always higher than male illiteracy, though decreasing from 95 per cent in 1962 to approximately 69 per cent in 1978.[47] In formal education, female participation was highest at the bottom of the system (primary education). At the post-primary levels, particularly beyond form IV, females were never represented in equal proportion to males. While in 1961 constituting 40 per cent of standard I and 23 per cent of standard VII, in 1981 females accounted for 47.7 per cent of the total enrolment in standards I–VII (49.8 per cent of standard I and 43.3 per cent of standard VII). At the secondary level, female enrolment in 1961 equalled 29 per cent of form I but only 9 per cent of form VI. By 1981, it had increased to 34 per cent of total public and private enrolment in forms I–VI, constituting 33.6 per cent of form I in public schools (38.3 per cent in private) and 22.9 per cent of form VI in public schools (14.3 per cent in private). The female student population was concentrated in traditional 'female' subject areas. In the diversified secondary schools which were created in the early 1980s, well over half of the girls attended domestic science and commerce but only very few the technical stream. The number of female undergraduates doubled from 8 per cent of the total in 1961 to 24 per cent in 1981.[48]

Regional and socio-economic disparities in education were, like gender inequality, positively affected by the comprehensive mass educa-tional efforts. At the secondary level, 'free' secondary education and the introduction of a quota system which allocated form I places in relation to the total number of primary school leavers in each region and district, in addition to promoting relative female participation, evened out the regional and socio-economic proportionate enrolment for form I. By 1976, it was close to the national average of 6.2 per cent in all regions except for Dar es Salaam (where the figure was as high as 17 per cent).[49] In 1982, more than half of form IV and form V students in a repre-sentative sample of public secondary schools came from families where the father's occupation was 'farming' and where the father had received at most four years of education and the mother no schooling at all. Between one third and two-fifths of the students came from a small-holder peasant background.[50]

The expansion of the private secondary sector, however, had an important neutralising effect on the tendency towards equalisation. While it widened the supply of students for needed manpower develop-ment, it also reinforced existing social and regional differentiation. The private schools were concentrated in the cash crop-producing areas, particularly Kilimanjaro and the West Lake region, and in the urban locations of the political-administrative and intellectual elite. The loca-tion of the schools, in combination with the fact that they concentrated

concentrated on academic education, charged fees and directed their students back into the public system at A level, influenced the composition of the total student population in secondary education with regard to both geographical and socio-economic origin. In 1982, Kilimanjaro region alone accounted for over one-quarter of form V students enrolled in government schools, while five regions alone (Kilimanjaro, Iringa, Kagera, Mara and Mbeya) accounted for nearly 60 per cent of all form V students, but for less than 30 per cent of the relevant national cohort.[51] In 1982, a representative sample of form I students in private schools in four regions showed that children of parents with no educational background constituted less than half of their population representation in public secondary schools, whereas children of parents with an upper secondary school background constituted more than double their population representation in public secondary schools.[52]

The identified strong interest in private education, in effect, represented a continuation of the relative influence of the social groups who became incorporated in the modernisation efforts during the pre-independence period and who were already relatively well provisioned with educational facilities at independence. For the Chagga in Kilimanjaro and the Haya in the West Lake region, education represented the most important channel for investment in their children's future in a situation of land pressure and restricted alternative opportunities for private economic investment after the Arusha Declaration.[53] Despite significantly reduced salaries at the higher income levels, public sector jobs continued to provide comparatively more political influence as well as access to scarce resources (e.g. food) and fringe benefits for the bureaucratic and intellectual elite.[54] The expanding private sector, thus, represented a force opposing the Education for Self-Reliance policy with its reorientation of educational 'relevance' towards the rural sector of the economy.

The Content Dimension of the Educational Reform

The content of the primary school curriculum was gradually adapted to Tanzania's status as an independent state and to its expressed political ideology. During 1961–66, the curriculum was 'Africanised', 'politicised' and directed to developing needed manpower skills in accordance with the manpower development strategy. The teaching of vocational (agricultural) education was abandoned, turning the curriculum into a purely academic one in order to consolidate the needed middle- and high-level manpower skills. The outlook of students, and the population in general, was to be directed towards a nation-state promoting national integration and nationhood instead of ethnic or tribal affiliation. Subjects such as history, geography and general science were to become relevant to Tanzanian society, i.e. to reflect a proper African and Tanzanian perspective and to include material on local conditions and problems. Kiswahili was designated in 1964 as the national language. It was introduced in 1967 as the medium of instruction in all primary schools, thereby eliminating the immediate barrier to integrated education. Specific subjects, such as civics, current affairs and political education, as well as extra-curricular activities, such as the participation in local development projects and in TANU Youth League branches, which were to be established in all schools, were used to promote understanding and support for the national political process, the national party and its ideology.[55]

After the Arusha Declaration in 1967, vocational activities were reintroduced in the form of Education for Self-Reliance. They mostly materialised as very basic agricultural work on the school farm (shamba) in the afternoon, as was the case before independence. The underlying rationale was both economic and political. Income-producing self-reliance activities were to alleviate public expenditure on education by meeting 25 per cent of the recurrent costs of each school.[56] They were also to sustain positive attitudes and skills needed for work in the rural sector and the village economy. In reality, however, school income hardly met 10 per cent of the running costs, with primary schools generally performing worse than post-primary institutions (secondary schools and teacher training colleges). While some research evidence suggested that the attitudes of primary school students and parents towards wage employment were altered, i.e. expectations were lowered and the teaching of vocational skills was seen as more desirable,[57] the skills taught were generally at too low a technological level to promote the village economy and improve the living conditions. Many primary school leavers, therefore, left their home areas and added significantly to the influx into urban areas and to the unemployment problems.[58] The rapidly expanding private secondary sector was, similarly, an alternative road for students who did not gain access to the public system and who, supported by their parents, reacted against the idea of being restricted to the village economy.

Except during the years from the Arusha Declaration in 1967 to the Musoma Resolution in 1974, the introduction of self-reliance activities and political education did not affect the stipulated relative balance in the school curriculum of individual subjects. Core academic subjects, such as Kiswahili, arithmetic and English, always retained their relative proportion, although English was deferred to standard III in 1980. The addition of the new subjects, however, led to an overcrowding of the curriculum, low competency in the academic subjects and a deteriorating educational quality, due also to insufficient inputs into the teaching process, such as school materials and adequately trained teachers.[59] Even though 'attitudes toward work' formed part of the continuous assessment of performance in standards V, VI and VII, they did not replace traditional rote-learning methods and seemed to have played virtually no part in the selection for secondary schools, i.e. very few students failed due to a low 'character' assessment.[60] Research evidence during the 1970s indicated a somewhat more egalitarian outlook among the primary school population and a greater orientation toward what were considered to be African and Tanzanian cultural norms and attitudes as expressed in the official ideology.[61] It is, however, doubtful not only how widespread such attitudes were and whether they were sustained in the medium and long run, but whether they were simply indications of the expected correct answers to questions set in the context of a still authoritarian school system.

At the post-primary level, the curriculum was equally 'Africanised' and somewhat changed to break the barrier between mental and manual work. Kiswahili became a compulsory subject for all secondary schools in 1964. However, it never replaced English as the medium of instruction for secondary and higher education, despite the stated intentions in the development plans, because of the continuing struggle over the orientation of the educational system and the interpretation of national needs. Political education and/or development studies were introduced as subjects at the different post-primary levels to familiarise students with the history and principles of socialism and the Tanzanian interpretation of Socialism and Self-Reliance. While not occupying as predominant a part of the educational activities as at the primary level, the subjects probably developed among the students the specific understanding of one particular ideological framework rather than the selection from different alternatives which would seem to have been desirable in order to develop the capability for critical thinking and strategic choice-making which was central to the philosophy of Education for Self-Reliance.

At the secondary level, one third of the curriculum of forms I–IV was, in the early 1980s, under strong World Bank support, taken up by different vocational biases, either agricultural (in 33 public secondary schools), commercial (29), technical (16) or domestic science (7), in order to stream students towards their future occupations, provide them with better skills, and fulfil the notion of integration of mental and manual labour. Generally speaking, the value of the income-producing activities in secondary schools (and teacher training colleges) was considerably higher than at the primary level and even expanding during the period.[62] As at the primary level, 'attitudes toward work' formed part of the internal assessment of secondary school students. Their relative weight in the final grading for the 0 and A level examinations, however, rarely influenced the result of the academic tests, exercises and examinations which secured entry into higher education. In 1976, a mere 0.1 per cent of all form IV candidates failed due to low 'character' assessment and low 'character' assessment generally correlated with poor academic performance.[63] While studies in the 1980s of samples of agricultural secondary school students indicated positive attitudes and aspirations toward farming and rural life, a World Bank evaluation study of the diversified secondary schools questioned whether the measurable financial benefits to society of diversification were greater than those of conventional education. Seen in relation to the higher costs for diversified than conventional education, and the fact that there was an important time lag between the possible changes of occupational aspirations and the expectations of students, on the one hand, and their future effect on the productivity level of society, on the other, diversification was recommended to be discontinued.[64]

Work attitudes and social commitment were also promoted at the higher educational level by the introduction of one year's national service at the end of form VI, which included para-military training and community development work (see Figure 6.1). Between 1974 and 1984, 'attitudes toward work', based on two years of work experience, formed part of the admission criteria to university, except for women and with respect to courses preparing for professions in short supply, such as engineering.[65] University candidates were also obliged to work for five years in the country stationed by the government, as a recompense for their education. The effect on students' attitudes has, however, been hard to isolate and evaluate. Visible differences in life style and behaviour between the few well-educated students who were influenced by and adopted a Western orientation and the many who were not still persisted.[66] Furthermore, the changing admission criteria to higher education and the quota system at the secondary level were seen as partial reasons for the lowering of the academic quality of candidates in the 1980s and 1990s.[67]

Thus, in summary, the educational reforms during 1962–81 led to widespread expansion of the system compared with the pre-independence situation. In contrast to the pre-independence curriculum, work-related activities were introduced as part of the student's experience even beyond the primary level and 'attitudes toward work', as an expression of social commitment, were made a limited part of the assessment procedure. The work-related primary school activities were, however, so basic that they could not fulfil stipulated economic and political purposes and were seen by students and parents as conflicting with academic learning which could bring better opportunities. While providing higher economic benefits at the post-primary level, work-related activities were also questioned with respect to their relevance for the future occupations of students. Similarly, 'attitudes toward work' never strongly influenced choices concerning access for students to the ensuing educational level and did not create uniform social commitment toward the overall economic and educational goals. The rapid expansion of the system also led to an even stronger quantitative division between mass and elite education. In practice, equity in education implied access for all to basic education, not increased opportunities beyond the primary level, the transition rate from standard VII(I) to form I (public schools) having dropped from 35 per cent in 1962, 15.5 per cent in 1966, to 2.6 per cent in 1981.[68] While there were positive indications of reduced regional, socio-economic and gender divisions in education, these developments were counterbalanced by the private educational efforts. Private education was an expression of disagreements over the defined Education for Self-Reliance policy and reflected the limitations of schemes for which popular participation was expected but not fully accepted by all concerned.

Education for Economic Development and Social Participation: Concluding Remarks

Education was intended to play a primary integrating role in the development of independent Tanzania. On the assumption that an educated population was crucial to the promotion of political stability and economic development, the Tanzanian government initiated educational reforms to readdress the situation inherited at independence. In conformity with the thinking behind the general development strategies and their transformation during the implementation process, the prevailing educational concepts underwent an identical transmutation. The crucial distinction was the change of emphasis away from skills development at the post-primary level during 1961–66 in order to support a market-oriented modernisation process, to an expressed concern with the formation of social attitudes and skills relevant to a socialist and self-reliant state during 1967–81. While curricular changes were introduced in the years immediately after independence to strengthen nation-building efforts, it was not until 1967 that these efforts were directed at the mass of the people. Mass provision of education relied on the participation of the local communities and was seen as a channel to further national cohesion by creating mass support for the national politico-economic goals and a common socio-cultural outlook. Similar efforts were undertaken at the post-primary level in an attempt to direct the education of the few to service for the many.

The specific activities intended to implement the Education for Self-

Reliance idea, however, never replaced the traditional academic subjects as the primary focus of formal education. The maintenance of the British 7–4–2 educational structure with examination points to select the few who could proceed to further education, largely assessed on their academic achievement, reinforced a concern and interest for the ensuing level of education, rather than a primary orientation towards the quality and outcome of the educational process at each terminal stage. The very structure, in effect, mitigated against the basic notion of mass education. The incorporation of work-related activities in the curriculum seemed not to have directed the choice of future occupations among the students or to have improved the quality of the basic skills. Instead, rural–urban migration of primary school leavers increased and job opportunities for secondary school leavers were determined by the job market, not created by the school system. While both may indicate an underlying disagreement concerning the area of work which was defined beforehand by the government, there was also an obvious connection to declining investments in the agricultural sector and infrastructure from the mid-1970s to 1981, which prevented the expansion of opportunities and incentives to become employed or self-employed in the village economy. This lack of an integrated approach in the implementation of economic and educational policies underlined the underlying moralistic aspect of the policy, i.e. the obligation of the people to participate in national development as defined for them by the leadership.

The incorporation of the mass of the population in educational efforts at the primary and adult levels was largely successful when measured in a quantitative sense. The establishment of ujamaa villages undoubtedly furthered this purpose by removing any physical barrier to access to education. The decentralisation reform, however, never incorporated the villages, or other local levels of administration, in decision-making concerning curricula. This could conceivably have affected the relative success of Education for Self-Reliance, particularly if the design of relevant curricula was also supported by resources to implement them adequately and by opportunities for the graduates to use the skills after completing school. Instead, Education for Self-Reliance activities were implemented uniformly across the country and were in most cases as rudimentary as before independence, leaving little realistic prospect of furthering local development potential. In a situation of rapid expansion, the quality of primary education was badly affected because of the sheer lack of infrastructure and the unavailability of sufficient and satisfactory inputs into the educational process, for instance trained teachers, book supplies and other equipment.

The mushrooming of private secondary education indicated a reaction to the stipulated policy of Education for Self-Reliance by those ethnic groups that were surplus-producing during the pre-colonial period

They also refused to establish ujamaa villages and displayed a stronger Western orientation than the mass of the population. The effect of the expressed orientation towards Western education as an additional and alternative road to status and power was to neutralise the official public measures, which aimed at ensuring a more widespread access to education for formerly deprived social groups and geographical areas.

This expressed conflict of interest questions one of the core assumptions of the self-reliant socialist strategy, namely whether the Tanzanian population was traditionally collectivist and whether common goals could be successfully enacted by way of the educational system. While measures of a national civic psychology are hard to define and substantiate, and while it only seems possible to establish the apparent will on behalf of the government to use the educational system as a tool to strengthen national cohesion, the government did initiate specific experiments to bring more life to the Education for Self-Reliance idea at the primary level through the so-called community schools. The prototype for this experiment, Kwamsisi, was replicated as a model in a number of other primary schools across the country in the mid-1970s. As will be discussed in the following chapter, there were, however, significant barriers to the implementation of the Education for Self-Reliance idea in the community schools, as there were in the educational system in general. More successful, although during a rather restricted time period in the late 1960s and early 1970s, were the widespread adult functional literacy campaigns. The arrested development of these campaigns was, on the other hand, probably one of the clearest expressions of the negative impact of changing national policies related to the structural adjustment programmes in the 1980s, the topic for Chapter 8.

Notes

1. Nyerere 1962: 162–163.
2. Nyerere 1967b: 231–250.
3. Nyerere 1967c: 272–290.
4. Nyerere 1962: 161–171, 1967d: 337–366.
5. Nyerere 1967f: 385–409.
6. Nyerere 1962: 162–171, 1965: 104–106, 1967d: 337–366.
7. See von Freyhold 1979: 22–31.
8. UNESCO n.d.; 1963.
9. Schultz 1961; Skorov 1966; Thomas 1968.
10. Nyerere 1967e, 1968c.
11. Nyerere 1966a, 1966b, 1968b.

12. Nyerere 1967c: 272.
13 Nyerere 1967c: 267.
14. Nyerere 1967c: 267–275, 1967g.
15. See, for example, Fanon 1963; Memmi 1974; Freire 1977 (1970), 1982 (1972).
16. Nyerere 1969, 1970b, 1974a.
17. Nyerere 1974b: 48.
18. Pratt 1972; Hartmann 1983: 75–88, *passim*, 1988.
19. Pratt 1976: 194–201.
20. Nyerere 1961, 1970a.
21. *Budget Survey 1964–65*: 88; *Economic Survey*, various years; Kahama *et al*. 1986: Table 11.2.
22. Goranson 1981: Diagrams 4 and 5.
23. Svendsen 1986: 64–65.
24. *Development Plan for Tanganyika* 1962; *Five Year Plan for Economic and Social Development* 1967. See also IBRD 1961; Little 1966.
25. Gottlieb 1973: 246; Boesen and Mohele 1979; Coulson 1982: 162–167.
26. Rweyemamu 1973: 52–53; Pratt 1976: 215–226; ILO 1978: 4.
27. International aid was either withdrawn, frozen or restricted because of the 1964 dispute with West Germany over East German relations with Zanzibar; during the 1964/65 clash with the United States over two alleged plots to overthrow the Tanzanian government; and in the 1965 severance of diplomatic relations with Britain over the British stance concerning Rhodesia (Pratt 1976: 134–152).
28. Pratt 1976: Tables 8, 9 and 10; Resnick 1981: 54; Crouch 1987: 28.
29. *Second Five Year Plan for Economic and Social Development* 1969.
30. *Third Five Year Plan for Economic and Social Development* 1976: i–iv, 5–13.
31. Green 1978; ILO 1978, 1982.
32. Boesen *et al*. 1977: 164–166, 170–172; Hyden 1980: 100–105.
33. Nyerere 1972; Boesen *et al*. 1977: 167–169; von Freyhold 1979: 38–43; Hyden 1980: 100–123; Ministry of Agriculture 1983: 16; Okumu with Holmquist 1984: 54–59; Kahama *et al*. 1986: 53.
34. von Freyhold 1979: 42–43, 62–63, 78–79, 151–155; Hyden 1980: 104, 113–121.
35. Aid to agriculture decreased from 40 to 10 per cent, whereas aid to industry increased from 9 to 20 per cent of total assistance. The Tanzania government's recurrent and development expenditure on agriculture decreased from 40 to 10 per cent compared with an increase of industry from 1.9 to 8.3 per cent (Bryceson 1986: note 11; Svendsen 1986: 67).
36. Buchert 1991: Figures 5.1 and 5.2; ILO 1982: Table 16.1.
37. IBRD 1983: Table 16; Barkan 1984b: 19; Bryceson 1986: Table II, Figures I and II.
38. Barkan 1984b: Table 1.3.
39. ILO 1982: 270; Leonard 1984: Tables 6.1 and 6.4; Bryceson 1986: Figure IV; Svendsen 1986: 69.
40. Buchert 1991: Table 5.2; Gordon 1984: 303, 305.
41. As before independence, official figures on expenditure and enrolment are unreliable. Generally speaking, figures on recurrent expenditures are

unreliable. Generally speaking, figures on recurrent expenditures are considered to be more reliable than those on development expenditures because of the lack of standard accountancy measures for foreign aid, which is part of the development budget. The contributions at the local level and from other ministries are generally not available in a systematic way. Despite the high degree of unreliability, the figures here presented are considered useful to indicate the probable changing allocations to education, which coincided with changes in policy formulation for education and for economic development more broadly.

42. Goranson 1981: Appendix 3.
43. Court and Kinyanjui 1980: 327–333; Court 1984: 265–272.
44. *Ordinance for Education* 1961; *Education Act* 1969; Morrison 1976: 95–96; *National Education Act* 1978.
45. Ministry of National Education 1981. Cf. Carr-Hill 1984: 9.
46. To this figure should be added the number of trainees under the national vocational training programme which during 1973/74–1982/83 was 8,932 apprentices within 25 different trades and 23,625 trainees in evening skill-upgrading courses (Ministry of Labour and Social Welfare 1983: 1).
47. UNESCO 1977: 1.3, 1991: 1.3.
48. Malekela 1983: 211. Cf. Cooksey 1985: 49; Ministry of Education 1986: 21.
49. Court and Kinyanjui 1980: Table 13.
50. Malekela 1983: 3–20. Cf. Cooksey 1985: 19–21.
51. Malekela 1983: 154. Cf. Cooksey 1985: 16–17.
52. Carr-Hill 1984: Table 28B.
53. See, for example, Samoff 1974: 35–58, 1979, 1987.
54. See, for example, Shivji 1982; Court 1984; Bryceson 1990.
55. Morrison 1976: 215–30.
56. ILO 1982: 112.
57. Carr-Hill 1984: 92.
58. Mbilinyi 1977; Ishumi 1984: 46–51.
59. See, for example, Mbilinyi 1979; Carr-Hill 1984: 41–45; King 1984; Ishumi 1988.
60. Court and Kinyanjui 1980: 386.
61. Prewitt 1971; Court 1973.
62. Ministry of Education 1986: 11, 14; Komba and Temu 1987: 46; Temu and Komba 1987: 47–54.
63. Court and Kinyanjui 1980: 386–387; Komba and Temu 1987: 109.
64. Psacharopoulos and Loxley 1984: 226–227. See also King 1988.
65. See, for example, Mmari 1976.
66. Court 1984: 278–279. See also Foster 1969.
67. Omari 1991.
68. Ministry of Education 1986: 7.

Seven

Societal Innovation
through Education
The Community School Movement
1971–82[1]

The particular purposes of the community school as defined in the Education for Self-Reliance document in 1967 were to contribute to village development by breaking down the barrier between the school and the surrounding society and between academic and manual skills, in other words to 'integrate' the school with village life and theoretical learning with practical work. Through the cooperation or 'participation' of village members in school life and school members in village life, the community school was seen as an important means of forming the 'relevant' skills and attitudes which were needed to further socialist and self-reliant development.[2] Being regarded as an educational and economic unit in the context of the village society, the school was to be a centre for basic educational activities for the young and for adults, whereas the village economy was to provide subsequent opportunities for young people in order that they would remain in the village after having finished school.

Compared with the innovative agricultural centre of Nyakato before independence, the community school idea was far-reaching. It went beyond the immediate technical and economic aim of Nyakato, i.e. to improve peasant agricultural production through the teaching of specific agricultural skills, to focus on a number of socio-cultural, political and economic purposes. Furthermore, in contrast to the orientation of Nyakato towards individuals, the guiding principle for the community school was the high degree of involvement of the local communities in the management of school affairs and the desire to incorporate students and school leavers in village life. However, as in the case of Nyakato, the implementation of the idea was affected by contextual factors at

123

both the national and local levels, and by the changing priorities of national policy-making in the context of severe economic difficulties. Like Nyakato, the community schools existed in isolation from the dominant educational patterns in the formal system. They owed their rise and fall primarily to the economic and political climate surrounding them instead of to convincing educational evidence concerning their effectiveness, impact and prospects. In reality, therefore, the community school remained more of a political idea than an educational movement working toward societal innovation or broader social change.

The Context of the Community School Idea

The community school idea was implemented in three specific time phases (Table 7.1). During 1970–75, it was concentrated on the setting up of the prototype for the experiment, Kwamsisi community school in Tanga region (see Map 3), in the context of the implementation of the ujamaa policy and significant interest from the international community, in particular UNESCO and UNICEF. During 1976–79, in the context of the Basic Human Needs strategy and continuing foreign interest, Kwamsisi was replicated as a model in 35 other primary schools in 35 different villages across the country. In 1979, it was decided by the Ministry of Education that all primary schools in Singida and Dodoma regions were to be converted into community schools. In 1981, 80 primary schools in the two regions were converted as the beginning of a complete conversion of all primary schools, first in the two regions and then in the rest of the country. The conversion in Singida and Dodoma was to go hand in hand with the implementation of a health programme by the Ministry of Health in cooperation with the United States Agency for International Development (USAID).[3]

Table 7.1 Chronology and Policy Context for the Community School (CS) Movement

Dates	Policy context	Sub-aspect of CS movement
1970–75	Ujamaa	Kwamsisi pilot project
1976–79	Basic Human Needs	Replication in 35 villages nationally
1979–81	Basic Human Needs	Conversion of 80 primary schools in Dodoma and Singida regions to be followed by complete conversion of all primary schools regionally and nationally
1982	Structural adjustment	CS policy abandoned

124

In 1982, however, the community school idea was abandoned as a policy 'for lack of understanding of integrating school and community by the villagers'.[4] This took place concomitantly with wider changes in the national educational policy aims in the context of structural adjustment and with new priorities for international educational assistance to Tanzania. The already established community schools are, however, still so considered by the Ministry of Education.[5]

The concept of community school was never clearly defined. While its most important characteristics remained those of 'integration' of school and society and joint 'participation' of school and village members in common affairs, the mechanism to achieve such purposes and the particular areas of cooperation remained open for interpretation by policy implementors and the specific local communities. Moreover, in the changing political and economic circumstances during the three phases of implementation, the overall purposes of the school were re-directed in accordance with the new priorities of the national economic and educational policies and the transmutation of the concept of Education for Self-Reliance.

Many of the contradictions in the implementation of the wider economic policies and of decentralisation, which was designed to mobilise the mass of the population in national and local development efforts, were, therefore, also apparent in the implementation of the community school idea. This partly related to the interaction between national officials and local communities. As will appear from the following analysis of two selected cases, namely Kwamsisi as the prototype for the experiment and Kwalukonge as a replicated experiment in the same region, the qualitative outcomes of the schemes were highly dependent on the interplay between national and local material and human resources, national and local contextual factors, and the relative importance of both educational and non-educational variables. The analysis is based on a field visit to the two sites during spring 1991. It combines a qualitative methodology with an analysis of official reports concerning the experiment in Kwamsisi and the movement in general.[6]

The Rise and Fall of Kwamsisi
as an Innovative Experiment

The Kwamsisi community school experiment was designed in the context of the implementation of the policy of ujamaa during 1969–76. As the prototype for the community school movement, it was to further the creation of the self-supporting communal villages through the establishment of a formal cooperation between the school and the village, and through a reform of the curriculum to promote the skills and attitudes of relevance to the village economy and the declared political philosophy.

The pilot project in Kwamsisi was a part of the wider Tanzania/ UNICEF/UNESCO Primary Education Reform Project (Mpango wa Tanzania/UNICEF/UNESCO (MTUU)), which was launched in 1970 in order to reform primary education in accordance with the newly stipulated national policies. The reform project was executed by the Tanzania government and combined the expertise of UNESCO with the financial, technical, professional and other assistance of UNICEF. MTUU operated within the teacher education directorate of the Ministry of Education, the Director of Teacher Education also being the Director of MTUU. The Director of Teacher Education formulated the policies concerning MTUU and consulted with the Commissioner for National Education in all matters related to the project. Under the director was a MTUU administrator, who was the chief executive officer of the project. At the local level, MTUU activities were directed from the Colleges of National Education. The college principals were the local heads of MTUU and responsible to the national officials. The principals acted as the link between the Ministry of Education and the villages where community schools were established. The principals implemented the educational reform at the village level, assisted by itinerant teacher educators, who helped organise courses at the college and supervised the implementation in the schools. All curriculum changes had to be approved by the regional and district officials of the party and the government.[7]

Kwamsisi was selected by MTUU officials at a meeting in Bagamoyo in 1970 because the principal of Korogwe teachers' college, as the patron of the primary schools in his area, expressed a keen interest in and willingness to implement the community school idea in one of his schools. He selected Kwamsisi because of its proximity to Korogwe (approximately 15 km), its accessibility all year, and the fact that Kwamsisi was considered to be an already well-functioning village in accordance with the ujamaa philosophy. No reasons or factors were indicated which related specifically to the functioning of Kwamsisi primary school or to the particular capacity of the principal in question. There is, however, some evidence that, in the early 1970s, parents in Kwamsisi expressed concern that the kind of education provided for their children was not relevant for their future occupations. Such attitudes were probably important to MTUU because they were in accordance with one of the most fundamental ideas behind the community school in the Education for Self-Reliance policy.[8]

Kwamsisi is located in one of the key sisal plantation regions on relatively fertile soils with relatively reliable rain. The village was founded in 1925 and was from 1935 the homestead of Mzee Msisi, who migrated from the nearby poorer Handeni district. Msisi was the village chairman when the Kwamsisi community school experiment was started, in 1971, until 1982, when he died. The village chairman at the time of the field visit was the vice-chairman when the scheme was started. Kwamsisi is almost solely inhabited by Zigua farmers, and at the beginning of the experiment constituted approximately 60 families, mostly belonging to Msisi's extended family. Attracted by the relatively fertile soils, an even larger number of outside Zigua families, who were then living in scattered homesteads, settled in the village under the impact of the ujamaa policy during 1975–76. The total population increased from 1,359 in 1976 to 2,352 in 1991. The villagers subsist on mixed farming activities, the main crops being maize, rice and cassava. In 1991, the village had a dispensary and water facilities but no mechanised equipment, except for a privately owned grinding machine. The literacy rate was estimated at 68 per cent in 1991 and was thus considerably below the official (1986) national average literacy rate of 90 per cent.[9]

Kwamsisi had a village council and village committees before the initiation of the Villages and Ujamaa Villages Act in 1975. The villagers, moreover, practised communal farming activities before it was demanded by the ujamaa policy. This administrative structure and established practice of cooperation was considered by MTUU officials likely to facilitate the introduction of the community school idea. In particular, it was believed that the inclusion of village members in the school committees (for instance the self-help and finance committees) and of school members in the village committees (for instance the executive committee) would enhance the joint cooperation between the school and the village.[10]

The Goals and Reality of Kwamsisi Community School 1971–75

According to MTUU, a community school was one in which the form and pattern of life in the community, the main features of the environment, the social practice of work, and politics would figure prominently in the curriculum.[11] A particular Kwamsisi community school curriculum and supportive curricular materials were designed by MTUU and approved by the Ministry of Education. The curriculum covered standards V–VII and attempted to integrate the traditional primary school subjects into four main areas: literacy and numeracy; political education; community studies; and cultural studies and skills related to village life. Literacy and numeracy contained the normal school programme in Kiswahili, English and mathematics, although with a clear vocational bent. It included, for instance, the study of better methods of farming, craftwork, building techniques and commercial methods as well as general science related to the local physical and human environment, health education and hygiene. Political education did not deviate in content from the ordinary primary school curriculum, whereas both community studies and cultural studies aimed at maintaining the integration of the pupils in the local culture and environment, and at heightening their capability to solve local problems and further the ujamaa philosophy. The emphasis on the integration of the school with the community implied both the active participation of the community in school affairs and the active participation of the school in village affairs.[12]

The implementation of the experiment was overseen by the principal of Korogwe teachers' college supported by MTUU officials. It involved the reorientation of the teachers of Kwamsisi through courses arranged at the college, and visits by an itinerant teacher educator to the village to supervise the teaching practice. Exchange visits were also arranged with other schools in other villages, including nearby Kwalukonge. For the teachers, the implementation of the scheme was, however, primarily a learning-by-doing experience, which, although supported by the material and human assistance of MTUU, demanded knowledge, skills and attitudes which had not been part of their formal teacher training programme.[13]

The former MTUU officials who were involved in the project and the village officials and villagers of Kwamsisi agreed that a successful level of cooperation between the school and the village was achieved during 1971–75. The common areas of cooperation identified by villagers, ex-students and ex-teachers included certain economic projects, the use of villagers as teachers in the school and the use of students as teachers in the village. In order to become a community school, Kwamsisi primary school had to be extended from standard IV to standards V–VII. This required new classrooms, which were constructed by the villagers, students and teachers in cooperation. Various economic projects to diversify the crop production pattern, generate additional income and alleviate shortages were successfully established, such as the cultivation of tobacco and cotton, the production of desks for the school and the serving of midday meals for the students based on the output from the newly established school farm. The students taught the villagers 'modern' farming techniques on the communal farm, for instance row-planting and spacing of maize, the use of manure and the selection of proper seeds, which helped to increase the output. Students were also assistants in the adult literacy classes. Villagers, on the other hand, taught some of the subjects in the curriculum in which they had a special expertise, such as basket-weaving, local dancing and local history.[14]

The establishment of Kwamsisi as a community school seems to have furthered the application of new farming skills, which the former students indicated they had continued to practise after they left school. Some of them acquired their own plots after leaving school, while most worked for a number of years with their parents before they were given one. A minority never got their own. Parents and village officials also stressed that the more widespread interaction between the students and the villagers at the time led to a generally more cooperative and respectful attitude among the students than is the case today. The former students confirmed that during the time of the community school experiment, most of the children stayed behind in the village after they had finished school. Later on, and particularly since the mid-1980s, a high percentage of the school leavers have joined relatives in the urban areas who, themselves, had left the village. There was a general preference for the academic subjects in the curriculum, among both the former and the present students. Only the latter, however, expressed a dislike for agricultural activities because they were not taught regularly and for lack of proper tools. In contrast to the former students, they would like to leave the village once they have finished primary school, whether or not they can fulfil their hope for further education.[15]

The designed curriculum was, however, not successfully implemented as an integrated curriculum to promote the understanding and development of the village society, or to establish the students as agents of change with a heightened problem-solving capacity. Not only were the teachers inadequately trained for such a sophisticated approach, but their primary responsibility for the teaching outcome remained, in the final instance, with the Ministry of Education, not with the village. In addition, even though standards V–VII were established for the community school experiment, the students of Kwamsisi in these standards were tested along with other primary school students in the ordinary subject areas. Their progress to secondary school, which was then the measure for successful achievement, was based on good grades in the academic subjects, not on an evaluation of the particular skills and attitudes which the experiment was trying to promote. Finally, according to the villagers, MTUU never kept a promise to reserve a number of places in a secondary school for bright Kwamsisi students, who might also have been disadvantaged by the experiment in their attempts to obtain further education. A former top MTUU official maintained that no Kwamsisi students were that able – which is perhaps rather an indication of the lack of long term interest in and commitment to the scheme by MTUU.[16]

It is, therefore, doubtful whether, even at its height during 1971–75, Kwamsisi ever became the kind of community school defined by MTUU and whether it succeeded in achieving the far-reaching goals of the specifically designed curriculum. The 'integration' of school and community and the 'participation' in common affairs were restricted to particular *ad hoc* activities which, like the curriculum itself, were designed by MTUU officials in consultation with the village, rather than by representatives of the school and the village. Although the Kwamsisi villagers expressed a clear 'ownership' of their school as a community school – 'the school belongs to us' – they appeared not to have been widely involved in the decision-making and planning process concerning the direction of the school. Former students (in contrast to the present students) did, however, state that, in the early days, each standard had a student representative on the joint village and school committee, which decided when and how to undertake common projects. To the Kwamsisi village officials, villagers and students, the community school concept, in effect, covered only the more practical aspects of both the MTUU concept and curriculum, namely that the school and the village cooperated in certain common areas which could help the village in its development and which could help to keep the children in the village after they had finished school. None of the groups referred to the particular innovative role which MTUU envisaged the students were to play in village development, or to the importance of the community school for politicisation purposes.[17]

The Interaction of National and Local Factors

None the less, in 1975, Kwamsisi was considered by MTUU to be successful enough to act as a model for replication in other schools. For Kwamsisi, however, this decision led to the transfer of some of its most valuable resources, particularly the headteacher and other teachers, to nearby Kwalukonge. Other material resources promised by MTUU in support of village development were withdrawn and, according to the village officials, distributed probably to some of the new selected schools and villages. The Kwamsisi village officials also maintained that their new teachers were unfamiliar with the community school concept and neither trained in nor supportive of its implementation. Whereas the former MTUU officials disagreed with this point of view, the fact remains that Kwamsisi experienced a continuous and rapid transfer of its teachers to other schools and has had, in all, seven different headteachers from the beginning of the experiment in 1971 until 1991. None of the headteachers was appointed from within the Kwamsisi community school, which, consequently, experienced continuous breaks of continuity in the implementation of the scheme.[18]

Furthermore, Kwamsisi lost its strong village cohesion when the outside families settled there during 1975–76. According to the village officials, these families were unsupportive of any level of cooperative activities, whether farming or educational, as they preferred to see the immediate personal benefits of their own labour. Coinciding with the settlement of the new families, tools provided by MTUU in support of the experimental scheme began to disappear. This fact was, in turn, used by MTUU as an argument not to provide any further support.[19]

After 1975, the Kwamsisi community school experiment went gradually downhill and finally died out. The former MTUU officials pointed to the lack of a cooperative spirit in the village as the main reason for the decline. They associated the lack of cooperation with poor village leadership, inadequate support of the community school idea by the village chairman and the fact that 'Zigua people are reluctant to change'. It was, furthermore, indicated that it was always expected by MTUU that the experiment had to stand on its own after a period of initial comprehensive support.[20]

The stated reasons stand in contrast to the original argument to select Kwamsisi in part because of its successful cooperation in village management and activities. They do reflect, however, the changed situation in the village with the influx of outsiders during 1975–76 when the scheme was essentially given up by the officials. These changed circumstances and conflicts of interest were, however, not mentioned specifically by the former MTUU officials during the interviews. The role of Msisi as village and party chairman was undoubtedly crucial. According to the Kwamsisi villagers, Msisi alone discussed the introduction of the community school idea with the MTUU officials. While the villagers liked and supported the idea once they had been informed, they were apparently not included in a process which would have made the idea become theirs and which might have secured their stronger influence on the medium-term development of the school. According to a former itinerant teacher educator, Msisi did not cooperate in the implementation of the project after 1975, except by nominal participation in the presence of outside officials. The Kwamsisi village officials indicated that Msisi was probably hesitant to extend cooperative activities to and share proceeds with the new families who did not belong to his extended family.[21]

The nature of Zigua people can, however, hardly have changed in the brief implementation period of the scheme. Claims of their resistance to change as an explanation for the failure of the scheme probably bears more witness to unfortunate attitudes among the MTUU officials than to sound criteria of evaluation. If Zigua people were resistant to change, it seems that more effective and qualitative criteria ought to have guided the selection of the prototype for the experiment in the first place. Moreover, it is questionable whether an adequate and substantial evaluation of the medium- and longer-term need for support of the experiment was undertaken by MTUU, including the actual effect of the transfer of Kwamsisi teachers, which was decided at the regional level.

As an innovative educational scheme, Kwamsisi probably rose and fell primarily with the tide of wider policy-making. It was implemented at a time when Tanzanian society was to be restructured and was, thus, but one part of more extensive 'packages' of societal innovation. The political pressure to innovate undoubtedly disregarded crucial ingredients of the innovation process, such as the time and effort needed to sustain the experiment and the proper mix of nationally and locally provided resources. Once it was decided to replicate the experiment in other schools, it was apparently also implicitly decided to limit or eliminate resources spent on Kwamsisi, irrespective of the actual needs there.

The Local Defence of a Nationally Abandoned Idea

The brief experiment does, however, seem to have made its mark on Kwamsisi. The villagers confirmed that they still applied some of the modern farming methods (such as the use of manure and row-planting and spacing of maize) which they were taught by the community school students and which the ex-students also indicated that they had continued to apply. No extensive corroborative evidence was, however, gathered during the field visit in support of such statements, or as a basis to evaluate whether the part of the community that was uncooperative with the community school idea also adopted the new agricultural skills, or whether the villagers followed a practice which was common for the area in general. While parents and village officials pointed to an apparent difference in attitudes to cooperative endeavour between the former students of the community school and the present students, and while the discussions with the ex-students and the present students revealed a difference in attitude to the teaching of agriculture, to involvement in agricultural activities and to a future life in the village, much more detailed observation and enquiry over a longer period would be needed to make affirmative conclusions concerning the possible isolated effect of the community school on expressed attitudes of cooperative behaviour, which was a crucial ingredient of the self-reliance policy.

The village officials, parents and ex-students were, at the time of the field visit, still supportive of the community school idea, even though community schools are no longer emphasised as a vehicle for societal innovation by policy-makers. The villagers considered the teaching of vocational, in particular agricultural, skills as essential because these were the skills most children would need in their future lives. They also wanted to reestablish integrated school and village activities and were hopeful that further discussions with village members, who may still object to the idea, would lead to their support of such efforts. The villagers saw new prospects for village development through the village cooperative society which had been established after the reintroduction of primary cooperative societies in the country in 1982 and through which cooperative members could now take loans on a voluntary basis under certain financial conditions without the consensus of the whole village. They were, however, also aware that only renewed outside support from the Ministry of Education and/or international agencies, such as UNICEF, could change the present status of their school.

The expressed attitudes stand in stark contrast to the general dominance of the 'vocational school fallacy' in the debate on education in Tanzania and to some of the strong reactions against Education for Self-Reliance as an overall policy for the formal educational system. In the situation of general deprivation which existed at the time of the field visit, it seemed obvious, however, that those Kwamsisi villagers who had supported the community school experiment of 1971–75 also looked back to a time when constant visits by international and national officials brought contact with the outside world and material resources to the village. Now, in contrast, they 'felt forgotten'. Their defence of the community school idea can, therefore, be seen, in part at least, as a hope for outside help in order to reach higher levels of development under the present constrained conditions.

The Replication of Kwamsisi as a Model: The Case of Kwalukonge

The replication in 1976 of Kwamsisi community school as a model for other primary schools coincided with an official recognition that the establishment of ujamaa villages in the country was complete. Instead, the wider economic policies, in conformity with the internationally designed Basic Human Needs strategy, supported the basic industry strategy and a distribution of basic services, such as water, health and education, in the established villages. The purpose of the replicated community schools was directed, in part, to the introduction of these basic services into the villages.

In contrast to the Kwamsisi scheme, which only involved the Ministry of Education, the replicated experiments, including the community schools established in 1981 in Dodoma and Singida, involved the other ministries concerned with the introduction of basic services into the villages, for instance the Ministry of Health. The community schools were to cooperate in the introduction of new basic services, for instance, widening the understanding among the village populations of the use and importance of water and health facilities, and supporting general village development through economic projects. In contrast to the Kwamsisi scheme, there was no emphasis in the new community schools on the formation of cooperative attitudes and problem-solving skills. As in the case of Kwamsisi, ideas for implementation of the basic services approach to community schools were discussed with national and international organisations, such as UNICEF and the Community Development Trust Fund, rather than with the local communities.[22]

The Kwamsisi community school curriculum was replaced by a new curriculum planned by the Institute of Education of the (now) University of Dar es Salaam. Instead of the four integrated curriculum areas designed for Kwamsisi, the new curriculum had ten individual subjects, which overlapped greatly with the traditional primary school subjects. The area of literacy and numeracy was dissolved into individual subjects (Kiswahili, English and mathematics). Community studies were replaced by environmental studies, which, however, had no clear specification of subject matter. Political education and cultural studies were maintained, and a number of new subjects added, including adult education and productive activities. It was generally unclear from the curriculum how the community school was to further the introduction of the new basic services. From 1982, all so-called community schools have taught according to the primary school syllabus of 1982, which comprises thirteen different subjects and has no direct emphasis on integrated activities between the school and the village.[23]

The Local Context of Kwalukonge

Kwalukonge is located in the Usambara mountains (approximately 60 km from Korogwe), on soils which are less fertile than those of Kwamsisi and exposed to less reliable rain. Like Kwamsisi, it is surrounded by sisal plantations. Kwalukonge was a relatively small village until 1970, when it registered as an ujamaa village. During 1970–80, it experienced a large increase in its population because plantation workers from the surrounding sisal estate decided to settle in the village and reestablish themselves as peasant farmers. Many of the workers had migrated from different areas of Tanzania and the population of Kwalukonge in 1991 incorporated in all fourteen different ethnic groups. Of these, the Bena who migrated from the southern Iringa and Njombe areas, the Sambaa, from the hills, and the Zigua from the plains and the coastal strip, together constituted 95 per cent of the total population, which amounted to 2,663 people in 1991. According to the village officials, the mixed ethnic groups form a pool of varied knowledge and skills that compete in a healthy manner, stimulated by the economic accomplishments of the more advanced elements and members.[24]

The total acreage under cultivation in Kwalukonge is higher than in Kwamsisi (5,183 acres compared with 1,672), the average acreage per person being as high as 8 acres compared with 3 acres in Kwamsisi. Agricultural production encompasses both food and cash crops, including maize, millet, peas, beans, cotton, groundnuts and sunflower, and there is a sizeable number of livestock (although less than in Kwamsisi). The production methods within the village appeared to be continuously transformed with outside technical assistance and in cooperation between village officials and government experts.[25]

Unlike Kwamsisi, the village is highly modernised. Agricultural production activities are partially mechanised, the village owning tractors, ploughs, planters and grinding machines. It has its own transport facilities, in the form of a pick-up truck and a lorry, and it runs a daily bus service to Tanga. There is hydro-electric power, tapped water, a dispensary with a medical assistant and two nurses, cooperative shops, a bar and a hotel, and an increasing number of permanent houses. In 1991, the literacy rate was estimated at 81 per cent, i.e. considerably above that of Kwamsisi but still somewhat below the official national literacy rate.[26]

According to the Kwalukonge village officials, any private wealth that existed originally among individuals in the village was voluntarily transferred to communal ownership when Kwalukonge was established as an ujamaa village in 1970. Since then, expanded economic activities and loan-taking have enabled the village to invest in communal equipment for the village, such as tractors. More comprehensive village projects were financed through loans from national or international bodies, for instance the Tanzania Rural Development Bank. All village facilities are communally owned by the registered village members (approximately 5 per cent of the population are not officially registered). The village leadership and the villagers of Kwalukonge were expecting that the village could continue to develop by applying still more advanced production methods and by creating industrial activities.[27]

For more than ten years, Kwalukonge won the first prize as the most successful ujamaa village in Tanzania (it was number two in 1990). It is one of only five ujamaa villages which have reached high enough standards of development to have a 'village institutional secretary' (katibu wa chama (CCM) wa taasis ya kijiji) to head the village administrative structure. The 'village institutional secretary' had been appointed at the highest political level by the central committee at the CCM headquarters in Dodoma.[28] He acted as a link between the village, the region and the party headquarters. Besides his political obligation to ensure that party policies were duly implemented and adhered to in the village, he was the crucial resource person with respect to the implementation of village targets for development and the maintenance of communal property. This took the form of continuous evaluations of the ongoing economic activities in the village and the design of strategies for amelioration and development of the village as a whole, including further education of the heads of specific village activities. His work was undertaken in active cooperation within the village with the village chairman, the village secretary, the village council and the village committees and outside the village with government experts. This direct and workable link between the village and the highest political level of the party presumably also paved the way for government attention to important village matters and smoothed the operation of bureaucratic procedures. The top leadership of the village has, moreover, secured a strong continuity of efforts within the village, as both the village chairman and the village secretary have been in office since 1971.[29]

The Functioning of Kwalukonge Community School

In contrast to Kwamsisi, Kwalukonge community school was, therefore, established and functioned in a context of higher level economic activities, continuous village cohesion and voluntary cooperation, and a strong village leadership. As in Kwamsisi, the initial establishment of Kwalukonge community school was supported by MTUU and other bodies, such as relief services, in the form of human and material resources and, during 1977–79, by TIRDEP (the Tanzania Integrated Rural Development Programme). It was stressed, however, by both the former MTUU officials and the village officials and headteacher of Kwalukonge that, similar to Kwamsisi, outside support was concentrated in the early years of the community school, after which the achievements of the school have rested primarily on self-help efforts and resources from within the village. Like the village in general, the school has had strong continuity of leadership, with only four headteachers since it was established as a community school. The first one, who was transferred from Kwamsisi, where he taught for seven years in all, functioned for as long as ten years and still teaches in the school. He, by far, preferred Kwalukonge to Kwamsisi because of the well-organised village community, the interaction between the different groups in the village and the general living standards in the village. The following two headteachers taught in Kwalukonge before they were appointed headteacher, whereas the present one was appointed from outside the village and had functioned for only approximately one year in 1991.[30]

The concept of community school was understood in a similar way to that in Kwamsisi. For village officials, teachers and parents, the concept implied that the school belonged to them and that there was co-operation between the school and the village in common areas. The headteacher indicated that, despite the lack of emphasis in the present syllabus, it was still possible to undertake integrated school and village activities by using the time-table flexibly. To do this, neither the head-teacher nor the village officials felt a need to participate in curriculum planning or to design the teaching, for instance of agriculture, in relation to their peculiar local conditions.[31]

The students were, however, unfamiliar with the community school concept and both the present and former students had difficulty exemplifying how integrated school and village activities had been undertaken. The concrete examples that were given corresponded with those in Kwamsisi, i.e. students taught villagers literacy and improved farming methods, such as row-planting and spacing of maize, the selection of good seeds and the use of fertilisers; and villagers taught students local crafts. The former students mentioned that they probably did not think of such activities when they were asked, because the activities were not important in the context of their examinations. This statement supports the view that non-academic activities commanded less interest among students, and therefore probably among teachers, because only academic subjects were tested and because of the high interest in further education in the village in general. As in Kwamsisi, the present students were not members of any of the committees which dealt with the affairs of the school and the village. While this could seem somewhat surprising for a village which otherwise attempted to fulfil the philosophy of ujamaa, it also appeared that, except for some group work, the dominant teaching method was still authoritarian and the teaching–learning process relied on a punishment–reward system.[32]

There were continuing efforts in Kwalukonge to solve problems related to the school. In contrast to Kwamsisi, Kwalukonge community school did not suffer from the lack of basic inputs into the teaching process, for instance exercise books and pencils. The area of attention was rather the improvement of opportunities for further academic education. Despite the fact that teachers and village officials agreed that the school was functioning well and that the standard among their students was high, only very few students managed to proceed to secondary education as a result of the quota-directed access to secondary schools. The village had, therefore, applied for permission to establish its own day secondary school with an agricultural bias. The village was also in the process of producing 70 school desks to cover a present shortage. To solve the problem of accessibility to textbooks which is rooted in national distribution problems, the village authorities were considering establishing their own printing services.[33]

As in Kwamsisi, the village officials and the parents spoke in favour of the teaching of agriculture in school, which, they believed, was a way for further development. This attitude was reflected in their choice of an agricultural bias for the planned secondary school. The former students confirmed that they still applied the modern methods they were taught in school, and the present students, while favouring academic subjects, expressed no dislike for agricultural science and agricultural activities. The teachers, parents and village officials did, however, see a need for improved training of the agricultural science teacher (who had been offered a three months' course) and for technical support of the subject in the form of textbooks and tools.[34]

Despite these perceived shortcomings, the school is capable of running a highly successful school farm, half the income from which covered the total school expenditures in 1990. This achievement, which stands in stark contrast to the average performance of the national educational system, where primary schools contribute on average approximately 10 per cent of the recurrent costs of the school, is probably a reflection of the successful agricultural activities in the village in general. These are partly promoted on the experimental farms in the village, which are cultivated under advice from the Mlingano agricultural research centre in Tanga. The continuously improved knowledge is disseminated to the school and is applied on the school farm. The village officials and the parents also indicated that, in contrast to students from other places who came to visit Kwalukonge, the students of Kwalukonge express a general willingness to cooperate in communal activities and demonstrate a pronounced respect for public property, despite the fact that neither the curriculum nor the organisation of the teaching–learning process is set up to enhance such attitudes.[35]

In contrast to Kwamsisi, Kwalukonge community school, thus, existed within a village organisation which apparently managed to implement some of the aspects of the ujamaa philosophy in a highly successful manner and which maintained a workable and beneficial link with outside authorities. The village seems to have relied on an exceptional combination of human and material resources, which were critical to its long term self-sustained development efforts. The settled and enterprising atmosphere of the village undoubtedly furthered the performance of the community school. Like the village in general, the school experienced a strong continuity in the educational process in terms of stability of staff. Although the objectives of the curriculum were considerably narrowed compared with the originally designed purposes for Kwamsisi community school, and although there is a strong orientation towards traditional academic achievement among the teachers, the village officials and the students, the school seemed to be able to contribute to the development of agricultural skills in the same way as and perhaps more successfully than Kwamsisi probably did in its early phase. While the school has probably influenced the attitude to agricultural activities and the transfer of agricultural skills, the expressed social attitudes may, however, be a reproduction of the apparently strongly held social values and behaviour of the community in general rather than being an independent impact of the school.

The Use of Education to Promote Societal Innovation: Concluding Remarks

The underlying purpose of the community school movement was to fulfil the central idea of the Education for Self-Reliance policy, namely that educational institutions could be used as tools to transfer specific skills and attitudes in order to create a defined society. While the analysis undertaken would have benefited from the inclusion of additional corroborative evidence and a more substantial time-frame for in-depth analysis of the expressed social attitudes and the nature of skills, it has, nevertheless, pointed to factors and conditions which seemed to either stimulate or hinder the use of education for such purposes.

As displayed in Table 7.2, there was a different constellation of a number of important internal and external factors which interacted and seemed to determine the relative success or failure of the schemes in Kwamsisi and Kwalukonge. While the particular constellation in Kwalukonge generally had a positive effect, such was the case only in the early period (1971-75) of the Kwamsisi experiment and then probably with less effect than in Kwalukonge. Even though Kwamsisi apparently has a more favourable geographical environment than Kwalukonge, it did not manage to initiate the kind of self-sustained development process which Kwalukonge apparently did. The relative need for medium- and long-term external assistance, therefore, varied in the two sites. In Kwamsisi, the combined effect of national and regional policy-making, lack of external assistance and of internal strong leadership, and changing internal circumstances was severe and all contributed to the downfall of the experiment. The opposite was the case in Kwalukonge, although the school was less experimental than Kwamsisi when it was originally started.

Both Kwamsisi and Kwalukonge probably succeeded in the transfer of some new agricultural skills to the local communities. The formation of positive attitudes to cooperative endeavour through the schools was, on the other hand, more questionable, both with respect to their medium- and long-term effect and with respect to the relative impact of the school compared with the prevailing value patterns in the village. These results seem to indicate that education can possibly be used as a tool of transformation, but only if sustained in the medium and long run, and only when positive educational factors combine with positive non-educational factors in the surrounding society at both the national and sub-national levels.

While underlining this important interaction between educational and non-educational variables in the use of education for societal innovation, the case analyses also identified factors in the national policy-making process which restricted the effect of the implemented schemes. The variation in the interdependent set of influencing factors was partly determined by the diversity of the local conditions. Instead of merely replicating experiments, governments must, therefore, apply resources differentially in order for innovations to achieve maximum impact in response to the needs and boundaries of the particular effort and setting. A precondition for success is, as was the lesson for the British authorities before independence, the positive acceptance in advance by the local communities of the underlying objectives of the particular innovative idea, and their full integration in the planning and implementation of the scheme in order to maximise its largely undistorted implementation. Furthermore, effective qualitative criteria must be applied in the

Table 7.2 Factors Determined as Explanatory of Relative Success of Community Schools and their Relative Influence in Kwamsisi and Kwalukonge

Factors	Relative presence[a]	
	Kwamsisi	Kwalukonge
Internal		
Strong village organisation and management	++/+	+++
Continuity of school and village leadership	+/−	+++
Cohesion of village community	++/+	+++
Strength of human and material resources	++/+	+++
External		
National policy–making	++/− −	+/0
Regional policy–making	++/− −	++
Nature of human and material resources	+++/− − −	++/+
Adequacy of teacher training	+/−	+/0
Nature of student assessment	−/0	0
Adequacy of evaluation	− −/0	0

Note: a Scale:

(+++)	strong positive effect	(− − −)	strong negative effect
(++)	medium positive effect	(− −)	medium negative effect
(+)	slight positive effect	(−)	slight negative effect
(0)	no effect or not relevant	/	early period/late period

selection of the site, there must be careful training of the key personnel, including teachers, in the innovative idea and its proper implementation through altered teaching methods, and proper evaluation of medium- and long-term sustainability must be undertaken. A stronger impact of the taught attitudes and skills on the village economy would, as in the case of Nyakato, have depended on an integration of the educational innovation with reforms of the wider society in order to stimulate further prospects and opportunities.

Thus, while education cannot stand alone as an agent, it seems that it can contribute to societal change when adequately supported in the short, medium and longer term. However, the relative priority given to the educational sector as a driving force in development remains a political question. In Tanzania, under the severe economic constraints and with increasing international impact on policy-making during the 1980s, new goals for education were formulated. The community school movement was abandoned as a failed experiment because 'the villagers did not understand the concept', despite the existence of communities that still defend the idea because they consider it relevant for their needs.

Underlying the abandonment of the community school movement were cost considerations and the 'vocational school fallacy'. It is probably correct that students and parents generally prefer academic education for modern sector opportunities to vocational training (understood as basic rural skills). Part of their reason for doing so may, however, be that, in the context of Tanzania, the educational innovation represented by the community school was an isolated phenomenon which never took over as the dominant pattern of the formal educational system. This was similar to the competition in ordinary primary schools between Education for Self-Reliance activities and the academic subjects on which students were tested for possible access to further education. Both the community school and the Education for Self-Reliance activities could, therefore, easily be associated with an 'education for the poor' as long as they did not transfer advanced skills which could be the basis of future improved living, and as long as the policy-makers who invented the innovation secured further education for their own children in the alternative private system. A true comprehensive reform of the formal educational system through the community school, supported by a consistent high priority, clear goals and adequate support, thus never materialised. It was probably abandoned because of fatigue on the part of policy-makers rather than convincing proof of failure or resistance among local communities.

Many of the outlined limiting factors and general issues also impeded the adult education programmes which were implemented in Tanzania during the same general period as an alternative mode for the creation of the skills and attitudes for the new socialist and self-reliant state. While relatively successful in the early period, 1968–73, their importance in national policy deteriorated simultaneously with declining interest from the international community in the context of structural adjustment during the 1980s. This will be discussed in detail in the context of adult literacy in Dodoma in the following chapter.

Notes

1. An earlier and less extensive version of this chapter was published in Buchert 1992b.
2. Nyerere 1967c.
3. Katunzi 1988: 37.
4. Quote by the Presidential Commission in Katunzi 1988: 39.
5. Wizara ya Elimu 1984; Komba and Temu 1987: 68.
6. During the field visit to the two sites during spring 1991, extensive oral and statistical evidence was collected. The oral data were gathered during semi-structured interviews with the following groups of people in the two villages: village officials; teachers; parents; standard VII students; and ex-students who were pupils when the schools were started as innovative institutions. The groups of teachers, parents, standard VII students and ex-students all contained men and women, whereas all village officials were male. In the case of Kwamsisi, interviews were, moreover, undertaken with former teachers involved in the initiation of the experiment and with UNICEF and Ministry of Education officials in Dar es Salaam responsible for the formulation, execution and evaluation of the project. Most of them had also been involved in or were familiar with Kwalukonge community school.
7. Ministry of National Education 1978: v, 5–11; Mwajombe 1978: 81–83; Kayuza 1979: 100–101; Meena 1983: 127.
8. Interviews with former MTUU officials and Kwamsisi village officials; Ministry of National Education 1978: v; UNESCO 1978: 83; Meena 1983: 124.
9. Kwamsisi village statistics; interviews with Kwamsisi village officials.
10. Interviews with Kwamsisi village officials and former MTUU officials. See also Rajabu and Shayo 1978: 174–176.
11. See, for example Mitande 1978: 54.
12. See, for example Rajabu and Shayo 1978: 180–187; Meena 1983: 125–126.
13. Interviews with former MTUU officials, Kwamsisi village officials and parents; Ministry of Education, *Progress Reports 1973–1975*; Meena 1978: 128–31; Mwajombe 1978: 80–91.
14. Interviews with former MTUU officials, Kwamsisi village officials, parents, former students and former teachers. See also Kilimhana 1975: 113–14; Rajabu and Shayo 1978: 178–80.

15. Interviews with Kwamsisi village officials, parents and former and present students.
16. Interviews with Kwamsisi village officials, parents, former MTUU officials and former teachers.
17. Interviews with Kwamsisi village officials, parents and former and present students. See also Meena 1983: 127.
18. Interviews with Kwamsisi village officials, former MTUU officials and former teachers. See also Meena 1983: 135.
19. Interviews with Kwamsisi village officials and former MTUU officials.
20. Interviews with former MTUU officials.
21. Interviews with Kwamsisi village officials, parents and former MTUU officials.
22. Katunzi 1988: 166–67.
23. Katunzi 1988: 169–73; Interview with Kwalukonge headteacher.
24. Kwalukonge village statistics; Chama cha Mapinduzi-Ofisi ya Tavi Magamba Kwalukonge 1990.
25. Kwalukonge village statistics; interviews with Kwalukonge village officials.
26. Kwalukonge village statistics.
27. Interviews with Kwalukonge village officials; Chama cha Mapinduzi-Ofisi ya Tavi Magamba Kwalukonge 1990.
28. In 1977, TANU merged with the Zanzibari Afro-Shirazi party and became the Chama cha Mapinduzi (CCM).
29. Interviews with Kwalukonge village officials; Chama cha Mapinduzi-Ofisi ya Tavi Magamba Kwalukonge 1990.
30. Interviews with former MTUU officials, Kwalukonge village officials and teachers.
31. Interviews with Kwalukonge village officials, teachers and parents.
32. Interviews with Kwalukonge teachers and former and present students.
33. Interviews with Kwalukonge village officials, teachers and parents.
34. Interviews with Kwalukonge village officials, teachers and parents.
35. Interviews with Kwalukonge village officials, teachers and parents.

Eight

▼▼▼
◆❖◆◆❖◆◆❖◆◆❖◆◆❖◆◆❖◆◆❖◆◆❖◆◆❖◆
▲▲▲

Education in the
Context of Structural Adjustment
1982–90

During the 1980s, the strategy of Socialism and Self-Reliance, though still officially defended by government leaders, was abandoned under the impact of the structural adjustment programmes, which were implemented in virtually all sub-Saharan countries in the context of the world-wide recession. These programmes introduced new goals for the development process in Tanzania and redirected the functions of education. In contrast to the former emphasis on equality and participation, economic recovery through the establishment of a market economy and political pluralism were the new central notions. In education, the previous key reform areas of access and equity were replaced by a concern with the academic quality of education, its cost and its training role. While there were some positive indications with respect to economic recovery during the 1980s, the impact of the recession and the structural adjustment programmes on the social sectors and social equality, including equity in education, was negative. This situation led to renewed discussions at the end of the 1980s and in the early 1990s on the relative balance between the different sectors of the economy, and the balance between and content of the sub-sectors of education in the context of the new declared international strategy of Education for All.

Altered Development Priorities

In the early 1980s, Tanzania was caught in an international economic depression, which affected the whole of Africa as well as other continents and added to the severe macro-economic difficulties in the country. With respect to the most indebted and least developed countries, the World Bank and the International Monetary Fund (IMF) assumed the major role as lending institutions. They set definite

144

economic and political conditions related to structural adjustment as terms for their lending policy. These conditions also, by extension, determined assistance from other Western donors as aid to individual countries was coordinated by the above-mentioned international bodies.[1]

The Tanzanian government introduced a number of short term emergency packages and economic recovery programmes during the 1980s in replacement of its former long-term economic plans. They included the Structural Adjustment Programme (SAP) in 1982, the Economic Recovery Programme (ERP) in 1986 and the Economic and Social Action Programme (ESAP) for the years 1989/90–1991/92. The ERP was influenced by the stipulations of the IMF agreement in 1986 and, thus, represented a severe tightening of the policies of SAP. While the Tanzanian government in its negotiations with the IMF laid emphasis primarily on external factors as being important in its economic decline, the IMF identified primarily domestic policy errors as the main cause of Tanzania's problems. The signing of the agreement with the IMF, therefore, demanded the adoption by the Tanzanian government of further domestic policy measures identified by the IMF as necessary to secure economic recovery and political stability.[2]

Under the impact of the IMF, economic recovery was related to the development of a market economy through a blending of private and public enterprise. The goal was to increase the gross national product (GNP) per capita and, in the long term, to secure a higher quality of life and social equity. There was renewed emphasis on investment in the directly productive sectors of the economy and specific efforts to stimulate agricultural production through increased producer prices and credit schemes. Leasing of land was permitted for commercial farming, individual land-holding was relegitimised, private investment was welcomed and parallel marketing was allowed to function side by side with the state trading structures. In addition, wage and salary levels were adjusted to ease the situation for the non-agricultural population. Privatisation and cost-sharing were introduced as counteracting measures to public responsibility and control in order to alleviate the pressure on national financial resources.[3]

There were some positive indications of improvement of the agricultural sector related to both export and food crop production and declining food imports during 1983–84.[4] There was also an increased output of export crops and of some of the major food crops in 1990/91 compared with the previous year.[5] (In terms of GDP at factor cost, the performance of the economy was positive with a real change from 2.6 per cent in 1985 to 3.6 per cent in 1990. In terms of real change of the GDP per capita, the performance was initially positive, increasing from −0.2 to 2.2 during 1985–87, followed by a decline to 0.7 per cent in 1990.[6]

Many of the underlying structural barriers to development also remained. While the value of exports increased during 1986/87–1987/88, the tendency towards import dependency was so high that it undermined the restoration of agricultural exports, and severe infrastructural deficiencies further hampered agricultural development. The government budget deficit did not fall and total outstanding debt increased from US\$ 3,431 million to US\$ 4,918 million during 1984–89.[7] Inflation also continued to be so high that the purchasing powers of the people were eroded and the general social conditions were badly affected. The growth of the labour force outpaced that of the formal labour market, creating a huge informal sector, which is estimated to have absorbed 40–60 per cent of the urban labour force by the end of the 1980s.[8]

Politically, reforms in the early 1980s addressed the balance of power between the ruling CCM party and the government. In 1982, their responsibilities were separated at the local level, when elected district councils were reintroduced. The district councils were in the 1984/85 budget given charge of a number of public services (for instance education, health and small roads) on the basis of a reduced subvention from the central government and the introduction of a new development tax, as another attempt at increased cost-sharing through local participation and self-help in development efforts.[9] This step was followed in 1985 at the national level by the separation of the party chairmanship from the presidency, when Mwinyi took over as president and Nyerere continued as party chairman. They were recombined, however, in 1990, when Mwinyi also became party chairman after Nyerere stepped down. This took place at a time when external pressure for a multi-party political system was reinforced by the adoption of the IMF-designed structural adjustment programmes which, in addition to the need for the correction of certain domestic economic policy measures, saw the lack of 'good governance' as a major reason for the economic decline in countries like Tanzania.[10] In 1990, a presidential commission began to investigate the popular response to a possible return to a multi-party system. On 17 June 1992 opposition parties were legalised and constitutional amendments were made. The first multi-party elections are likely to be held sooner than the elections currently scheduled for October 1995.[11]

Both the economic liberalisation measures and the move towards political pluralism were the subject of intense debate and controversy among different social groups within Tanzanian society. Due to the fact that the economic and political measures were pushed by external agencies, overarching issues and principles related to the question of national sovereignty, the right to self-determination, national self-reliance and the direction of the economic development process were dominant in the debate.[12] As during the 1970s, there was in the 1980s and early

1990s, continuous discrepancy between official defence of the originally stipulated socialist goals and the implementation of liberalisation policies, which themselves promoted development towards a pluralistic market-oriented society. The emerging contradictions, ambivalences and variety of interests created new patterns of social differentiation and social inter-action and a more varied social structure, which could not easily be encompassed within the existing political system.[13] These social changes also led to the need for formation of new values and attitudes and for new skills. Rethinking the purposes of the educational system in societal development in the light of these changes, therefore, continued to be important.

The Redirection of Education

The priority given to the directly productive sectors, the emphasis on cost-sharing and the reduced public responsibility for education in the context of structural adjustment all affected the previous central importance of education as a sector and the relative priority placed on its sub-sectors. This affected the former high importance of mass educa-tion, in particular adult education, and the goal of equality in education, including aspects relating to gender. The changed priorities corres-ponded to changed emphases within the international aid community, which eventually resulted in the formulation of the strategy of Education for All in 1990.

In 1980, an advisory commission to the President of Tanzania was set up to plan the future of education in Tanzania towards the year 2000. Its recommendations were accepted in 1982 as the guidelines towards the future. While reaffirming Education for Self-Reliance as the 'cornerstone of educational plans and practices [towards] the twenty first century',[14] the specification of the concept noticeably excluded the radical strain of educational thinking which dominated during the early to mid-1970s. Science, technology and vocational training were stipu-lated as the keys at all educational levels with which to understand, analyse and make the best use of the environment and the country's natural resources. The basic concern of the commission was the academic quality of education, its costs and its training role, particularly at the post-primary level, rather than the previous issues of access, equity and 'relevance' related to mass education reforms. This was reflected in the acknowledgement of English as the medium of instruction at the post-primary level, whereas Kiswahili was maintained at the primary level.

The Ministry of Education simultaneously transferred additional authority to the regional education officers in order for them to consolidate the policy of decentralisation and improve the status of primary education in cooperation with the reintroduced district and town authorities.[15]

These changed goals were further reinforced because of the increased concern during the 1980s among the international donor agencies, headed by the World Bank, with the cost and efficiency of education. In 1990, the strategy of Education for All was adopted at a world conference in Jomtien, Thailand, organised by the key United Nations organisations and with widespread participation from bilateral and non-governmental organisations, national governments and academic research institutions. The overall goals of the strategy combined the need for broad access to and equity in education with overriding concerns for the quality, efficiency and effectiveness of education. In the constrained economic situation internationally and nationally, it was seen as important to develop new cost-sharing partnerships in education with private and non-governmental organisations, parents, religious groups and others. In order to achieve maximum benefit from educational policies, it was suggested that supporting policies in other sectors of the economy had to be designed, and international solidarity be developed to reduce existing global inequalities.[16]

The changed commitment to education in Tanzania in the 1980s is reflected both in the overall expenditures to the educational sector and in the financing of its sub-sectors.[17] As a percentage of the gross domestic product, total educational expenditures dropped from approximately 5 per cent in 1982 to approximately 2 per cent in 1988.[18] While education constituted approximately 12 per cent of the total recurrent budget in 1981/82, only approximately 6 per cent was allocated to education in the recurrent budget during the period 1985/86–1989/90.[19] At the same time external influence on educational financing was increasing. In the total education budget (recurrent and development), the component of external aid increased from 9 per cent in 1981/82 to 15 per cent in 1986/87. As a proportion of the development expenditure of the Ministry of Education alone, the increase was from 62 per cent in 1983/84 to 81 per cent in 1986/87.[20] Within the educational sector, support for primary and adult education from the recurrent budget increased from approximately 54 per cent of the total in 1981 to 63 per cent in 1985/86 but dropped to 37 per cent in 1989/90. During the same period (1980/81–1989/90), expenditure on secondary and technical education increased from 11 to 26 per cent, teacher training from 3 to 11 per cent and higher education from 12 to 19 per cent.[21]

During 1982–89, the gross enrolment figure in Tanzania was declining at the primary level. It increased somewhat at the secondary level and in technical education, teacher training and higher education (see Table 8.1). At the primary level, net enrolment dropped from approximately 70 to 60 per cent.[22] Female enrolment, however, continued to constitute 50 per cent in standard I and increased from 44 to almost 50 per cent in standard VII during 1982–89. This positive effect, however, was not sustained at the top of the post-primary level. In secondary education, the number of institutions and students enrolled in the private sector outnumbered the public ones. Female participation increased from approximately 37 to 44 per cent of the total form I enrolment in public and private secondary schools during 1982–89. It was, however, unchanged in form VI (23 per cent) in 1989 and highest in the private secondary schools. Of the four vocational secondary school biases, females continued to be concentrated in the traditional female subject areas, in particular domestic science, while very few attended the technical bias. As in the formal system in general, there was no attempt at gender sensitivity in the curriculum.[23] At the post-primary level, the female university undergraduate body declined from 21 to 17 per cent of the total during 1982–89 and female technical students from 11 to 7 per cent, while female participation in teacher training increased from approximately 37 to 41 per cent of the total.

Official statistics also indicate a decline in the national adult illiteracy rate from approximately 20 to 10 per cent during 1982–86. While the male illiteracy rate dropped from approximately 15 to 7 per cent, that of females declined from approximately 27 to 12 per cent.[24] No official rate has been released since 1986, but there are indications that the national illiteracy rate has been increasing since the mid-1980s.[25] This is confirmed by the decreased number of functional literacy learners and of students in folk development colleges in 1989 compared with earlier (see Table 8.1). It is also confirmed by the following study of adult literacy in Dodoma rural district. The increased number of illiterates is partly related to the higher drop-out rate from primary schools and, as reflected in the gross enrolment figures of Table 8.1, to the shifting of support to the post-literacy level by the Tanzanian government and international donors as a consequence of the priority of quality over equality in education. It was probably also affected by the cost-sharing arrangements involved in the delegation of responsibility for basic education to the regional and district levels.

While the expansion of the private secondary school sector in Tanzania can be interpreted as a positive popular response to unfulfilled demands for education in a tight economic situation, such a response may be very different when related, not to the reproduction of the future politico-economic elite in geographical areas which are both relatively well-off and experiencing land pressure, but to the less prestigious adult literacy programmes serving the broad population. Regions and districts in Tanzania which are unable to increase the level of taxation cannot uphold or improve the existing educational situation

Table 8.1 Formal and Adult Education in Tanzania 1982–89 by Category: Schools and Enrolment

Category	1982 Schools	1982 Enrolment	1985 Schools	1985 Enrolment	1989 Schools	1989 Enrolment
Formal (govt)						
Primary (stds I–VII)	10,002	3,503,729	10,147	3,160,145	10,404	3,252,934
Secondary (forms I–IV)	}85	35,074	}86	37,733	}124	57,482
Secondary (forms V–VI)		3,909		4,589		5,340
Technical	2[a]	1,409[b]	3[c]	1,449[b]	3[c]	1,927[b]
Teacher training	7	12,926[d]	39	12,311[d]	40	13,263[d]
Higher	1[e]	2,980	2[f]	3,414	2[f]	3,327
Higher (overseas)	–	1,244	–	1,066	–	1,287
Sub–total	10,097	3,561,271	10,277	3,220,707	10,573	3,335,560
Formal (private)						
Primary (stds I–VII)	33	9,070	26	9,614	27	5,667
Secondary (forms I–IV)	}82	29,761	}104	39,647	}195	75,003
Secondary (forms V–VI)		401		1,108		1,761
Sub-total	115	39,232	130	50,369	222	82,431
Grand total	10,212	3,600,503	10,407	3,271,076	10,795	3,417,991
Adult						
Functional literacy	n/a	2,958,910	n/a	2,493,234		1,639,350
Post-literacy	n/a	1,198,156	n/a	1,586,297		2,001,442
Folk dev. college	n/a	13,901	52	16,419	52	11,625
Illiteracy rate (%)	–	20[g]	–	10[h]		n/a
Total		4,170,987	52	4,095,960	52	3,652,417

n/a   Not available.
Notes: a Dar es Salaam and Arusha technical colleges.
   b Excluding students in vocational training centres and post-primary vocational centres under the Ministry of Labour and Manpower Development.
   c Dar es Salaam, Arusha and Mbeya technical colleges.
   d Including diploma, grade A, grade C, inservice.
   e University of Dar es Salaam.
   f University of Dar es Salaam and the Sokoine University of Agriculture.
   g 1981 figure.
   h 1986 figure.

Sources: Ministry of Education, *Basic Education Statistics in Tanzania (BEST) 1981–1985, 1985–1989.*

and are likely to be most affected by the changed public and international commitment to education. This relates both to the functioning of educational programmes and to participation by specific groups, including women, as will be discussed in the context of Dodoma rural district.

The Establishment of Adult
Functional Literacy Schemes in Tanzania

The idea of combined literacy and community development activities, which were implemented during a restricted period of the British administration, were readopted by the Tanzanian government after the announcement of Education for Self-Reliance in 1967. They merged into the concept of functional literacy and were, as before independence, implemented under the strong influence and participation of international organisations. The concept was first applied in the work-oriented adult literacy pilot project of UNESCO and the United Nations Development Programme (UNDP) in the Lake regions during 1968–72. Furthermore, extensive adult education campaigns were implemented in Tanzania from the late 1960s to the mid-1970s, which focused on selected topics of national importance, for instance health, food production and politics. They were implemented through innovative teaching methods and were perhaps the most successful of all measures adopted to fulfil the goals of Education for Self-Reliance.[26]

Underlying these functional literacy and adult education programmes was the belief that they would yield certain benefits in terms of economic development, political integration, reinforcement of cultural identity and overall social well-being for the individual participants and for the nation. The functional literacy concept combined the teaching of literacy (in Kiswahili) with the teaching of different vocational skills which were particularly useful for the varied local economies. Furthermore, it aimed at heightening the understanding of and participation by the mass of the population in the local and national political and economic development efforts through the teaching of political education. The teaching was based on 12 different primers focusing individually, for instance, on the production of maize, wheat, rice, cotton, cattle or fishing, and on political education. The implementation of the campaign was supported heavily by government and donor resources. Adult education coordinators were appointed at each layer of the decentralised administrative structure, which was established in 1964.[27]

Functional literacy classes were to be taught in the classroom during the dry season (May–November) and as practical lessons during the rainy season (December–April). The teaching in practice merely involved demonstrations of what had been taught in the classroom, for instance, the application of certain 'modern' production methods on a demonstration plot by an agricultural extension officer. Classroom teaching was to involve the meeting of classes three times per week for two hours, but no strict schedule was established for the practical lessons. The teachers came from a range of different backgrounds, for instance, professional teachers, students trained on the job, volunteers and TANU and religious officials.

A set of definitions was adopted to identify a literate person. All incorporated the achieved reading and writing skills with the ability to engage in activities for which literacy was required to function effectively at the personal level, and in the context of the wider community. The learners were tested nationally in six different years during 1975–89, according to different levels of achievement. A person was considered to be a literacy graduate if he or she passed levels III or IV in reading, writing and arithmetic combined. He or she was functionally literate after achieving level IV. Functional literates could proceed to the post-literacy levels V and VI.[28]

The following investigation of the functioning of the adult literacy programmes in Dodoma region during 1975–90 is based on field visits in spring 1991 to three different village sites – Bahi, Dabalo and Mvumi Makulu (see Map 3) – located in three different divisions of Dodoma rural district. During the visits, statistical materials related to the characteristics of the sites and the literacy programmes, and qualitative oral evidence, related to the functioning of the schemes, in particular with respect to the original Education for Self-Reliance goals of agricultural innovation and politicisation, were collected. Other interviews concerning the functioning of the schemes were conducted with district and regional educational officials in Dodoma, where supplementary educational statistics were also gathered.[29]

The Local Context in Dodoma Rural District

Dodoma region is exposed to poor socio-economic and harsh climatic conditions similar to those in neighbouring Singida. Of the five districts in the region, Dodoma rural district is the most densely populated, the (1988) total number being 353,478 people, of whom 164,181 were males and 189,297 (56 per cent) females. The economy combines agricultural and pastoral activities and the soils are relatively deficient. The district is partially incorporated in the maize belt and also has sizeable vineyards and other economic activities, such as fishing. The dominant ethnic group is the Gogo. Around 13.5 per cent of the population was estimated to be illiterate in 1991. While this indication is close to the estimated 10 per cent national illiteracy rate in 1986, the likely illiteracy rates in the three sites were much higher.[30]

The three selected villages represented the variety of socio-economic conditions in Dodoma rural district. Mvumi Makulu is relatively 'urban' and located in the proximity of Dodoma city. Its economic activities are limited to farming and concentrated on the production of maize, millet, groundnuts, castor seeds and sunflower. The village is mechanised, with privately and communally owned lorries, tractors and milling machines. There are electricity, water facilities, a dispensary, two schools, a co-operative shop, a rural library and an impressive assembly hall. The total (1988) population, which was mostly Gogo, numbered 6,680 (2,909 males and 3,771 females).[31]

Bahi is peri-urban and is located on the border of the Manyoni district of Singida region near the main road to Singida town. The village has a public and a private (missionary) dispensary, a primary school, water facilities and a rural library, but no village or privately owned mechanisation and transport facilities (except for a public bus service). Its mixed farming activities are concentrated on millet, rice and groundnuts. They are supplemented by a sizeable fishing industry which brings widespread trading activities. The total (1991) population of 11,595 people (5,451 males and 6,144 females) is of a mixed ethnic origin. The number of females in the age group beyond 14 was, like the proportion of the total, higher than the male (3,605 females compared with 3,071 males).[32]

Dabalo is rural, located several hours' drive from Dodoma city in a remote part of the district with no private or public transport facilities. It has a dispensary, a school, water facilities and a rural library, but no equipment for mechanised agriculture. The agricultural activities are concentrated on maize, millet and groundnuts, which, in some of the households, are supplemented by fishing, bee-keeping and pottery. Market activities are only conducted within the village. The total (1990) population amounted to 2,637, of whom 1,198 were males and 1,439 females. In the age group above 14, females numbered 583 and males 507. The Nguu and the Gogo were the largest ethnic groups.[33]

The Participation in Adult Literacy Programmes in Mvumi Makulu, Bahi and Dabalo 1977–89

During 1975–86, the enrolment of learners in functional literacy classes in Dodoma rural district as a whole was fairly constant, seen as a proportion of the total number of learners in Dodoma region (between

31 and 36 per cent of the total). The female proportion was higher than the male at all levels and the learners were concentrated in the age group 15–50. From 1986, new learners have appeared in the age group 10–14, of whom females constitute the major part (73 per cent in 1986).[34]

There seems to have been no common pattern of development of adult literacy in the three selected villages during 1977–89 (Table 8.2). Females constituted half or more than half of the number of learners in Mvumi Makulu and Bahi, but half or less than half in Dabalo. In Bahi and Dabalo, the female pass rate was generally higher than the overall

Table 8.2   Measures of Basic Literacy in Mvumi Makulu, Bahi and Dabalo 1977–89

Measures by village	1977	1981	1983	1986	1989
Mvumi Makulu					
Total no. of learners	n/a	n/a	n/a	1,408	770
Females	n/a	n/a	n/a	706	536
Evaluated	956	1,505	1,178	866	608
% of eval. who passed	16	19	14	70	85
% of eval. females who passed	11	14	11	69	84
Bahi					
Total no. of learners	2,727	3,072	2,351	2,284	2,201
Females	1,660	2,000	1,140	1,456	1,295
Evaluated	1,559	2,369	2,015	1,853	1,872
% of eval. who passed	55	82	71	71	80
% of eval. females who passed	30	90	74	74	84
Dabalo					
Total no. of learners	1,563	852	722	1,143	1,367[a]
Females	870	317	363	594	724[a]
Evaluated	1,006	800	665	1,143	988
% of eval. who passed	64	76	72	65	80
% of eval. females who passed	100	75	62	71	85

n/a   Not available.

Note: a   When compared with the population figures, enrolment numbers seem to be flawed. The 1990 female population figure beyond the age of 14 was 583. The number of 724 is likely to include learners in the 0–14 age group.

Sources: Bahi, Dabalo and Mvumi Makulu adult education statistics.

pass rate, whereas the opposite was the case in Mvumi Makulu. While deficiencies of the population statistics and enrolment figures hamper the calculation of the illiteracy rate in the three sites, it seems that it is vastly above the declared national and regional averages. In Dabalo, the total number of learners in 1989 indicates an illiteracy rate of 80 per cent (based on the 1990 population figures). This high rate was indirectly confirmed by the fact that interviews there had to be conducted in the local language, Kigogo, instead of Kiswahili. In Bahi, the 1989 figures point to an illiteracy rate of 33 per cent, the female rate alone being 42 per cent based on the number of 1991 females above 14 (3,071). Both rates compare well with the official literacy rate for the village of 56 per cent.[35] In Mvumi Makulu, the relatively small number of learners seen in relation to population size and the relative persistence of learners at the lowest level (see Table 8.3) seems to indicate that it is a comparatively small group of the oldest people in the village that remains illiterate.

During 1981–86, more than half of the basic literacy learners were concentrated at the lowest levels (below level I and level I) in Dodoma region and Dodoma rural district, whereas more than half were enrolled at the highest levels (levels III and IV) in 1986 (Table 8.3). Females, who constituted more than half (60–65 per cent) of all learners in the region and the district, were generally disproportionately represented at the lowest levels. This same pattern also existed in Dabalo, where half or more of the learners were enrolled at the lowest levels (below level I and level I) during 1977–83, and more than half of the learners at the highest levels (levels III and IV) during 1986–89. Female enrolment was always highest, but only during 1986–89 proportionately higher than the male at the highest level. In contrast, half or more of the learners in Bahi were enrolled at the highest levels (levels III and IV) during 1977–89, female representation being above that of male at the highest level during the whole period. In Mvumi Makulu, half or more of the learners were enrolled at the lowest level (level I) during 1977–89 and male enrolment was higher than female at the highest level.

Compared with basic literacy, participation in post-literacy level V and VI was limited both in the individual sites and in the district and region as a whole. In 1986, the numbers tested at level V in Dodoma region and Dodoma rural district constituted approximately 19 per cent of the total number of learners at the basic level, male participation being slightly higher than female participation (by approximately 5 per cent). This same pattern was expressed in the three sites, where the number of evaluated learners constituted between 13 and 18 per cent of the number of basic learners, with the male proportion being above the female (between 59 and 69 per cent of all of those being evaluated).[36]

The participation rates, if not the achievement of the students enrolled in the adult literacy programmes in the three sites, therefore,

Table 8.3 Relative Levels of Basic Literacy Learners in Mvumi Makulu, Bahi, Dabalo, Dodoma Rural District and Dodoma Region 1977–89

Levels by entity	1977				1981				1983				1986				1989			
	M	F	Total	Total %	M	F	Total	Total %	M	F	Total	Total %	M	F	Total	Total %	M	F	Total	Total %
Mvumi Makulu																				
Below level I	–	–	0	–	–	–	0	–	–	–	0	–	–	–	0	–	–	–	0	–
Level I	164	537	701	80	185	617	802	53	206	640	846	72	147	462	609	70	67	387	454	75
Level II	34	68	102	12	73	140	213	14	59	110	169	14	18	98	116	13	10	46	56	9
Level III	20	22	42	5	89	119	208	14	45	61	106	9	22	54	76	9	22	40	62	10
Level IV	15	17	32	4	146	142	288	19	27	30	57	5	12	53	65	8	13	23	36	6
Total	233	644	877	101	493	1,018	1,511	100	337	841	1,178	100	199	667	866	100	112	496	608	100
Bahi																				
Below level I	85	72	157	10	–	–	0	–	83	66	149	7	79	98	177	10	–	–	0	–
Level I	176	182	358	22	85	58	143	6	108	84	192	10	55	59	114	6	80	90	170	9
Level II	364	–	364	23	203	72	275	12	105	140	245	12	90	153	243	13	100	90	190	10
Level III	102	138	240	15	364	447	811	34	292	349	641	32	192	404	596	32	319	655	974	52
Level IV	191	289	480	30	326	814	1,140	48	291	497	788	39	220	503	723	39	217	323	540	29
Total	918	681	1,599	100	978	1,391	2,369	100	879	1,136	2,015	100	636	1,217	1,853	100	716	1,158	1,872	100
Dabalo																				
Below level I	90	38	128	13	69	120	189	23	41	102	143	21	72	44	116	10	–	–	0	–
Level I	214	400	614	61	76	130	206	26	94	156	250	37	88	48	136	12	58	36	94	9
Level II	40	55	95	9	62	111	173	22	134	6	140	21	70	79	149	13	54	44	98	10
Level III	45	41	86	9	65	90	155	19	41	46	87	13	121	91	212	18	215	329	544	55
Level IV	62	21	83	8	47	30	77	9	21	24	45	7	198	332	530	46	122	132	254	26
Total	451	555	1,006	100	319	481	800	99	331	334	665	99	549	594	1,143	99	449	541	990	100

Number of Learners

Table 8.3 cont.

Levels by entity	1977 M	1977 F	1977 Total	1977 Total %	1981 M	1981 F	1981 Total	1981 Total %	1983 M	1983 F	1983 Total	1983 Total %	1986 M	1986 F	1986 Total	1986 Total %	1989 M	1989 F	1989 Total	1989 Total %
Dodoma rural district																				
Below level I	n/a	n/a	n/a	–	8,975	19,724	28,699	39	6,522	15,849	22,371	38	1,607	2,325	3,932	8	n/a	n/a	n/a	–
Level I	n/a	n/a	n/a	–	7,378	14,022	21,400	29	6,260	12,595	18,855	32	2,373	3,070	5,443	11	n/a	n/a	n/a	–
Level II	n/a	n/a	n/a	–	4,353	5,668	10,021	14	3,707	5,541	9,248	15	4,367	3,710	8,077	16	n/a	n/a	n/a	–
Level III	n/a	n/a	n/a	–	3,811	3,839	7,650	10	2,820	2,984	5,804	10	3,164	8,989	12,153	24	n/a	n/a	n/a	–
Level IV	n/a	n/a	n/a	–	3,227	2,287	5,514	7	1,615	1,555	3,170	5	6,936	13,784	20,720	41	n/a	n/a	n/a	–
Total					27,744	45,540	73,284	99	20,924	38,524	59,448	100	18,447	31,878	50,325	100				
Dodoma region																				
Below level I	n/a	n/a	n/a	–	18,355	40,351	58,706	29	14,150	34,065	48,215	29	5,488	10,666	16,154	11	n/a	n/a	n/a	–
Level I	n/a	n/a	n/a	–	19,643	39,079	58,722	29	15,487	32,715	48,402	30	6,686	11,405	18,091	13	n/a	n/a	n/a	–
Level II	n/a	n/a	n/a	–	14,258	21,116	35,374	17	10,787	16,566	27,353	17	11,268	14,846	26,114	18	n/a	n/a	n/a	–
Level III	n/a	n/a	n/a	–	3,283	14,051	17,334	13	9,466	11,649	21,115	13	13,203	23,893	37,096	26	n/a	n/a	n/a	–
Level IV	n/a	n/a	n/a	–	12,605	10,083	22,688	11	7,513	7,360	14,873	9	16,284	26,685	42,969	30	n/a	n/a	n/a	–
Total					68,144	124,680	202,824	99	57,403	102,355	159,958	99	52,929	87,495	140,424	98				

n/a   Not available.

Note: The extremely high number of enrolled learners could possibly be explained by the fact that either the same person follows more than one learning level simultaneously, i.e. is registered more than once, or that primary school-age children are included in the numbers.

Sources: Bahi, Dabalo and Mvumi Makulu, adult education statistics; Wizara ya Elimu ya Taifa 1981, 1983; Wizara ya Elimu 1986.

157

point to localised strong needs for further educational efforts. While there was some improvement in the level of literacy over time, there was no widespread participation in post-literacy classes. This indicates that the major part of the population in the selected sites, in the district and in the region as a whole has still not reached the levels of declared literacy and functional literacy, despite the fact that some learners have participated in classes since the start of the nationwide literacy campaign at the beginning of the 1970s. The situation is worse for women than for men. The variety across the three sites in the same district of one particular region underlines the impact of local contextual factors, even at the village level, on the performance of the schemes.

The Functioning of the Classes[37]

The visits to the selected villages in 1991 confirmed that there were serious problems with the functioning of the adult literacy schemes. According to the interviewed regional and district education officers, the adult education situation in the region as a whole had worsened in recent years, partly because the responsibility for the classes had been transferred to the district level. In general, after 1986, they argued, there was little interest in adult education at the national and regional levels and also among donors who formerly sponsored the adult literacy programmes, perhaps in particular the Swedish International Development Authority (SIDA). As the lack of donor, national and regional resources could not be compensated for through increased taxation at the district level, the performance of the adult literacy classes in the villages was highly dependent on specific initiatives and support at the village level by the village chairman and the broader leadership.

There were indications of different degrees of conflict about and co-ordination of the adult literacy classes in the three sites. This, combined with the comparative remoteness of the villages and the different importance of pastoral production, influenced the functioning and achievements of the adult literacy classes, along with the impact of national and regional decision-making and support. Mvumi Makulu seemed to be the best organised and most settled village. There were regular coordinating meetings between the adult education officer and the headteacher, who was responsible for the conduct of adult literacy classes. These meetings did not, however, include the adult literacy learners. As in the other sites – and in other educational efforts in Tanzania, such as the community school movement – little or no attempt was made to base the adult literacy classes on the identified needs and wishes of the learners, and to incorporate the learners in the planning and running of the activities. Participation in the classes was not necessarily voluntary. In all sites village officials had encouraged, if not demanded, that villagers attended the classes, and in two of the sites learners were fined for non-attendance.

Bahi and Dabalo were both drought-stricken and on the brink of famine at the time of the field visits. This, in combination with the higher emphasis on pastoral production, made regular attendance in adult literacy classes difficult. The fact that basic literacy learners complained about irregular classes and that basic statistics on enrolment were unavailable tends to indicate a more disrupted local situation than expressed in the official statistics of Table 8.3. There was also a lack of mutual understanding among the village chairman, the adult education coordinator and the teachers concerning the conduct of adult literacy activities, in particular with respect to the use of resource persons in class. While teachers were reluctant to use outside expertise because they believed this had to be arranged 'at higher levels' (by the village chairman), the village chairman claimed that teaching in adult literacy classes was part of the duty of experts, such as the agricultural extension officer. Dabalo seemed to be the most disorganised of the three sites, with no functioning adult literacy classes since 1988, despite official statistics to the contrary (cf. Table 8.3). This was explained by both teachers and learners by the total lack of interest by the village chairman and leadership in the functioning of the classes, perhaps because they themselves were illiterate.

The purpose of the literacy classes was clearly understood by most teachers and learners in all sites as a narrow one, 'to teach and learn how to read and write and count'. The broader concept of functional literacy was not referred to and the connection between literacy and self-reliance or individual and community development, through the teaching, for instance, of improved agricultural methods and political education, was not immediately evident either to teachers or learners. Teachers and learners who had participated in the nationwide literacy campaign of the 1970s pointed to a clear difference in enthusiasm, efficiency and performance between then and now. The present low performance was explained by both teachers' and learners' lack of interest and participation in the educational process. The lack of resource inputs into the teaching–learning process, including follow-up materials such as zonal newspapers and other readings, were, however, also setting strong limitations to the achievement in class.

With respect to the motivation of teachers, basic literacy learners in two of the sites complained that their teachers 'were no longer interested in teaching because they had become money-minded'. This view was partly confirmed by the teachers, but explained by the fact that, since 1989, it was no longer volunteer teachers who chose to teach adult literacy, but primary school teachers who had to teach adult literacy classes in addition to teaching in primary school. While some primary school teachers were clearly not interested in teaching adults or felt overburdened by the workload, many felt that they should be paid a reasonable amount and, at least, be provided with basic support materials (such as notebooks) in order for the work to be worthwhile compared with other activities, such as private shamba work.[38]

The teaching results were, therefore, low. With respect to the teaching of improved agricultural practices, this was merely didactic and took place in the classroom for lack of school or village demonstration plots where teaching in practice could be undertaken. Both female and male teachers and learners were of the opinion that the teaching of improved agricultural methods could lead to individual and village development if the teaching in class was supplemented by teaching in practice. In cases such as Dabalo, where the learners had to use modern practices related to maize production on the communal farm,[39] only in exceptional cases did this lead to similar practices on the private plots. For lack of the additional inputs, such as fertilisers in the case of maize production, modern farming methods (row-planting and spacing of maize) were not economically beneficial measured against the time-consuming labour inputs. In general, the learners could not afford to buy fertilisers and they had no expectation that either the respective village leadership or outside donors would provide fertilisers for their private plots.

The teachers had received little or no specific training in the teaching of adults and, generally, did not know how to modify their normal teaching practice for an adult audience. They, generally, did not supplement the basic primers with further specialised readings on agriculture, even when available, or use radio programmes or appearances by village officials, such as the agricultural extension officer, as additional resources in class. They also did not encourage the learners to use the rural libraries and the radio as sources of information, for instance on agriculture and politics, outside of the class. This was probably partly because teachers and learners who did have access to radios generally were not interested in the programmes that were intended to stimulate learning concerning agricultural production and party politics, but preferred entertainment programmes, such as sports and news programmes.

The particular skills focused on in the primers were apparently not the most relevant for the particular local environments in the three sites and did not go beyond the rural modernisation efforts that existed before the announcement of Socialism and Self-Reliance. None of the primers used at the time of the field visit had been updated since they were produced in the 1970s. Some which might have been particularly relevant were never supplied (for example fishing in Bahi and Dabalo) and, according to the learners, 'books cannot solve our basic problem which is the lack of rain'. It was noteworthy that, despite the fact that Bahi and Dabalo are located near huge lakes, the question of irrigation was reportedly never discussed in class, not even on a small scale related to the vegetable gardens. The learners favoured the millet primer, which was produced at the regional level in Dodoma in 1986, but suggested that primers written at the ward level might better relate to their specific circumstances. Teachers and learners were also of the opinion that primers on some of their cash crops, like groundnuts and castor seeds, would be valuable. This idea was unrelated to the likely restricted benefits for women of such teaching, unless production of and incomes from cash crops come under female control.

The likely but small effect in the three communities of the teaching of modern farming methods through the literacy classes was also reflected in a similarly small impact of the teaching of political education. In contrast to the originally stipulated wider purposes of participation in decision-making and control of individual living circumstances, political education for most of the current teachers and learners implied knowledge about the party and the political system of their country. At none of the sites were learners involved in decision-making concerning the teaching–learning activities. Moreover, the question of decision-making was not related to wider cultural issues in the context, for instance, of the family, the village organisation, and the village and higher administrative levels. Generally speaking, learners indicated that village matters were decided by the village leadership or at higher administrative levels, and learning activities by educational officials. Learners who held official positions in the village or who participated in organised village activities pointed out that they did so out of their own interest, and not as a result of the literacy classes or because they had been encouraged by their teachers. Some of the teachers maintained that they tried to promote the participation of their learners in certain village organisations and to discuss national and village matters in class. Female teachers seemed to be particularly active and successful in incorporating learners in the local branches of the women's organisation, Umoja wa Wanawake wa Tanzania (UWT). A national event like the change of the party chairmanship from Nyerere to Mwinyi in 1990, which was recent to the field visit, had, however, not been part of the teaching in any of the sites and was generally unknown to the inter-viewed basic literacy learners.

There were, thus, obvious parallels between the implementation of the community school movement and the functional literacy schemes in terms of impeding factors. These related to national and regional decision-making processes and to the lack of attention to crucial qualitative factors in the teaching–learning process, such as appropriate teacher training, adequate resources and integration of the learners as participants in the process. There were also parallels concerning the nature of village life and the impact of the village leadership on the functioning of the schemes. Similar to the situation in Singida before independence, the local socio-economic circumstances were strongly influential on the performance of the schemes at specific times of the year and when outside changes in the politico-economic environment occurred. Thus, while the teaching of adult functional literacy could possibly have contributed to societal development, it could only have met with the planned goal of long-term change in attitudes and skills if it had been closely related to wider socio-economic and political opportunities and had been implemented in due consideration of the local context.

The Prospect for Educational Transformation in the 1990s:
Concluding Remarks

The use and functioning of the adult literacy programmes in the selected sites of Dodoma region seem to indicate a wide discrepancy between the goals set in the 1970s and their realisation today. This seems to be partly related to the lower priority now given to adult education by the national government and donor agencies compared with other subsectors of education, and partly to the generally reduced public responsibility for basic education related to the introduction of the structural adjustment programmes in the 1980s.

While the originally formulated goals for adult literacy programmes were transformative, their implementation was far more modest. The two key aspects of the programme, improved agriculture and political education, were implemented without touching deeper questions of power and position in general, and particularly related to gender. The information, knowledge and technology passed on through the programmes had little or no effect on agricultural practices. With the possible exception of the engagement of women in the UWT, the teaching of political education seemed not to have created the desired participating citizens with a higher awareness of political and economic circumstances that should have contributed to wider societal change at the local and national levels, as outlined in the Education for Self-Reliance policy.

This reality does not, however, mean that the original ambitious and sophisticated goals could never be achieved under different circumstances. Such would require renewed priorities in national and international policy-making, differentially applied cost-sharing arrangements determined by the existing resources at the regional and sub-regional levels, and long-term, consistent and persistent implementation of the programmes. To be fully effective, such programmes would have to employ the original idea of voluntary participation of teachers and learners who can see the personal and societal benefits of the schemes. Furthermore, more effort would be required to control strongly interfering contextual factors at the village and ward levels and to ensure that the basic inputs into the educational process in terms of relevant training, relevant materials and supplementary inputs were supplied.

The variety of the local circumstances would also have to be taken into consideration in the design of the functionally related aspects of the programmes, and women's disfavoured positions in the production and reproduction processes must be considered. New skills areas for women, for instance the production of cash crops, would have to be reinforced by securing their control of the income from such production. Similarly, the teaching of political education or other 'consciousness-raising' topics would have to go beyond the mere passing of information in class to securing the engagement of participants, including women, in different kinds of decision-making bodies. In order to contribute to the longer term changes in the traditional roles in society, national initiatives would have to be created and policies formulated which could then secure an interaction with and possible parallel development at sub-national and national levels.

The likelihood that such transformative aims and purposes will be revived and the needed procedures and resources provided in the 1990s is, however, slight. The international dominance of other concerns in the Education for All strategy is reflected in Tanzania and reinforced by increased donor coordination in educational activities and specific demands on the national government for adherence to particular aspects of the strategy.[40] This is taking place at a time when the national government has itself redirected the originally set goals of Education for Self-Reliance through emphases on post-primary education and on quality of rather than equality in and through education.

Investment in people has been designated in the present international thinking as one of the four key elements needed to secure economic development.[41] While this has been formulated in part in reaction to the increased awareness of the negative impact on the social sectors of the structural adjustment programmes, the immediate concern of such programmes is economic growth combined with a long-term concern with securing quality of life and social equity. With respect to education, however, the investment in people in order to achieve economic development will only also secure long-term social equity, if equity concerns are reflected in positive short-term access for disfavoured social groups. This is particularly so because the recent emphasis on the quality of the educational process has limited the expansion of education in a climate of restricted funding, cost-sharing and decentralised responsibility for basic education to the local levels.

In the same way, long-term improved quality of life for the mass of the population can only be established if the provision and content of education reflect a society with widespread opportunities for the many rather than the few. In the present constrained economic context, the best potential for growth and individual opportunity may exist in the rapidly growing informal sector and the rural sector of the economy, rather than in the modern sector, which has failed to absorb the majority of students from the formal educational system. The current strong focus on the quality of education and the downgrading of skills development through the formal educational system may, therefore, delay rather than advance prospects for disfavoured groups in Tanzania and contribute little or nothing to the solution of their critical unemployment problems. If the 'vocational school fallacy' is to be disproved, this will occur because of attitudes and beliefs, such as those of parents and students in the investigated community schools and of teachers and learners in the functional literacy schemes, that education can help in societal development. Such a role will only be successful, however, if it is effectively integrated with wider economic and political reform and related to the creation of realistic and improved opportunities.

Notes

1. See, for example, Svendsen 1986.
2. See, for example, Singh 1986.
3. See, for example, World Bank 1988; Campbell and Stein 1991.
4. Raikes 1986; Svendsen 1986.
5. Economist Intelligence Unit 1991: 13.
6. Economist Intelligence Unit 1991: 9.
7. Economist Intelligence Unit 1991: 29.
8. Wagao 1990.
9. See, for example, Svendsen 1986.
10. World Bank 1989: 60–61.
11. Economist Intelligence Unit 1992: 4, 8–12.
12. See, for example, Campbell and Stein 1991; Moshi 1992.
13. Hartmann 1991.
14. Ministry of Education 1984a: 1.
15. Ministry of Education 1984a.
16. Inter-Agency Commission 1990.
17. Samoff (1991) convincingly argued that official Tanzanian educational

statistics on expenditure and enrolment are highly unreliable. This is reflected in the sources applied here, which indicate different figures for the same years and do not list them systematically. Margins of error of ± 10–20 per cent even eliminate the soundness of relative trends based on the same source. Indicated figures and trends are here exclusive of expenditures at the local level, of which the availability and accuracy are as problematic as, if not more problematic than, those of the Ministry of Education. The development budget was from 1985 under local government control and is generally considered to be less reliable than the recurrent budget. For lack of any alternative to the use of official statistics, the assumption here is that an established correlation between changes in formulated policies and changes in relative trends of government expenditures and enrolment may heighten the probability of the identified trends without proving the accuracy of the figures.

18. Lugalla 1992: 15.
19. Ministry of Education 1990a, 1990b.
20. Wagao 1990: 32.
21. Ministry of Education 1990b.
22. Ministry of Education 1990a.
23. Mbilinyi 1991.
24. Ministry of Education 1986, 1990a, 1990b.
25. Lugalla 1992.
26. See, for example, Mpogolo 1980: 45–46.
27. See, for example, Mpogolo 1980: 46–54, 1983: 170–187.
28. Ministry of Education 1985: 7-10.
29. The oral evidence from the three sites was collected through semi-structured interviews with groups of basic literacy learners, post-literacy learners, basic literacy teachers and post-literacy teachers. Most groups had both men and women. The number of women was highest for basic literacy learners, whereas the groups of post-literacy learners and one group of teachers had no or only few women. The oral evidence primarily aimed at highlighting the use and effect of the literacy programmes with respect to improved agriculture and political participation. It also served as a partial check on the statistical materials and of the exploration across sites of the relative impact of village conditions on the functioning of the adult literacy classes.
30. Dodoma regional statistics.
31. Mvumi Makulu village statistics.
32. Bahi village statistics.
33. Dabalo village statistics.
34. Dodoma regional statistics; Wizara ya Elimu ya Taifa 1981, 1983; Wizara ya Elimu 1986.
35. Bahi village statistics.
36. Dodoma regional adult education statistics; Bahi, Dabalo and Mvumi Makulu adult education statistics.
37. Further information on the schemes can be found in Buchert 1993.
38. Primary school teachers are entitled to an honorarium of sh. 300 per month for their teaching of adult literacy classes. There have, however, been severe problems in securing the payment of the honorarium.

39. Like the adult literacy classes, the communal farm was no longer functioning at the time of the field visit.
40. Buchert 1994.
41. See, for example, World Bank 1991.

Nine

Education
in the Development of Tanzania
Conclusions & Perspectives

Summary

Looked at in Braudel's multi-layered time perspective, there has probably been more continuity than change in the long term development of Tanzania and in the function of education in this regard. Both the British administration and the independent Tanzanian government designed specific educational policies to fulfil goals for the economic and political development of the country. In both cases, there were wide discrepancies between stated goals and implemented reality.

As appears from Figure 9.1, there were contrasting medium-term development policies during the period of the British administration. The important dividing line was the Second World War when the adaptation philosophy was replaced by a more vigorous modernisation strategy. Both before and after the Second World War, short-term sub-periods can be identified when there were alterations to the implemented economic policies. This same pattern was repeated after independence, when the year 1967 represented a clear break with the past in terms of the underlying ideology of the formulated strategy of Socialism and Self-Reliance. From the beginning of the 1980s, the goals of the strategy were redirected under the impact of the structural adjustment policies. As before independence, there were different emphases on specific economic policies in sub-intervals of the medium-term period.

The relative importance of the educational sector changed with the alterations in the overall development strategies. This was, furthermore, reflected in changing priorities on different sub-sectors of education and in the intended relative importance of the use of education to implement economic, political and socio-cultural purposes. As appears in Figure 9.2, at the level of formulation, the move from adaptation to modernisation during the British administration period led to changed emphases on developing the modern sector of the economy rather than

167

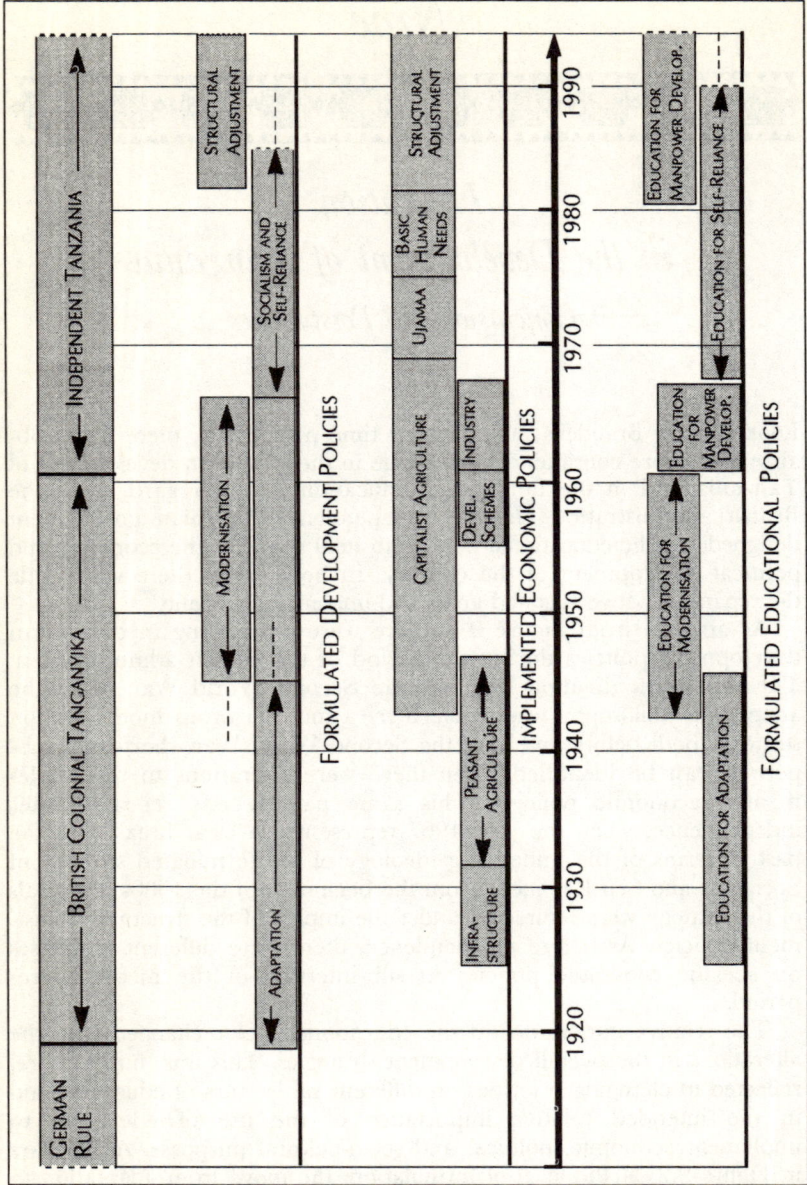

Figure 9.1 Historical Time-Line of Policy Development and Implementation in Tanzania 1919–90

the traditional rural sector, on establishing central political institutions rather than strengthening the indirect rule system, and on forming Western values rather than blending local with Western values. With respect to education, the adaptation philosophy relied heavily on mass educational efforts for Africans, emphasising the transfer of Western values and attitudes in terms of 'civilisation' and Christianity and, perhaps, less on knowledge through the transfer of literacy, the three Rs and vocational agricultural skills to develop the traditional rural sector. Modernisation, on the other hand, relied on mixed mass and elite educational efforts which were implemented on a differential and segregated racial basis, Africans being provided with mass education and non-African communities with elite education. The implemented educational efforts emphasised more strongly the development of the modern sector through the teaching of literacy and academic knowledge, particularly of English, and some vocational agricultural and technical skills. The transmission of values in terms of 'citizenship' was of less importance.

The strategy of Socialism and Self-Reliance, in some respects, led to a return to some of the emphases of the early British period. The key economic focus was, again, the rural sector. Attitudes were to reflect the interpreted African heritage rather than the Western one, and politically, the centralised system in the form of the one-party state was to combine with a decentralised administrative system. Education, again, became a mass education concept which was implemented in an integrated system and had about equal emphases on the general areas of underlying economic, political and socio-cultural goals. Literacy, the three Rs and vocational skills were to support the development of the rural sector, and the reinterpreted African values of cooperation and social commitment were underlined in order to further national and local, economic and political development. With the introduction of structural adjustment programmes, there was renewed emphasis on a Westernisation process, which had some resemblance to the modernisation policies. Western political ideals of pluralism were to be followed, a market economy was advocated which blended public and private enterprise, and attitudes and values related to enterprise and initiative were to further the altered goals for economic and political development. In education, there was now renewed attention to the post-primary level, stressing academic knowledge and vocational, technical and science skills. At the basic level, the quality of education was underlined at the expense of equality of education. The formation of attitudes, related to the need for enterprising and respectful citizens, was of less importance compared with the transfer of needed knowledge and skills and, similarly, compared with the earlier use of education to stimulate the socio-cultural goals of cooperation and social commitment.

Figure 9.2 Major Attributes of Formulated Development and Educational Policies in Tanzania 1919-90

Policies	Dev.: / Educ.::	Economic / Knowledge	Political / Skills	Social/cultural / Attitudes
Dev. Adaptation (laissez-faire)	Dev.	Traditional agricultural sector	Indirect rule	Local/Western
Educ. Education for Adaptation (mass education)	Educ.	Literacy, 3Rs — (traditional rural sector)	Vocational agriculture —	'Civilisation', 'Christianity'
Dev. Modernisation (GNP/capita)	Dev.	Modern sector	Central Western political institutions (political self-government)	Western
Educ. Education for Modernisation (mass/elite education)	Educ.	Literacy/academic (English) — (traditional rural sector/modern sector)	Vocational/agric./techn. —	'Citizenship'
Dev. Socialism and Self-Reliance (equality and participation)	Dev.	Self-reliant economy based on local resources (rural sector)	One-party state (decentralized admin. structure)	Reinterpretation of African heritage
Educ. Education for Self-Reliance (mass education)	Educ.	Literacy, 3Rs — (traditional rural sector)	Vocational agriculture —	Cooperation and social commitment
Dev. Structural Adjustment (growth, quality of life, social equity)	Dev.	Market economy (private/public)	Pluralism (democracy)	Western market behaviour
Educ. Education for Manpower Development (elite education)	Educ.	Academic — (modern sector)	Vocational/techn./science —	Enterprise, initiative

The Possibility of the Use of Education in Development

There were clear discrepancies between the stated goals for education and their implemented reality in the entire period of Tanzania's history investigated here. There were also in different sub-periods fundamentally different beliefs as to whether education should follow or lead societal development and whether developments were best achieved through investment at the base or the top of the educational pyramid.

The strongest belief in education as a guiding tool in development was expressed in the policy of Education for Self-Reliance. It led to investment in mass education and reforms of the inherited educational system related to issues of access, equity and relevance. Its achievements in terms of virtually full enrolment of the primary school age group and limited adult illiteracy have been subsequently negatively affected by the reforms of the 1980s, which stressed quality over quantity of education and growth over equality. Underlying this change was apparently the notion that the goals of the policy of Education for Self-Reliance had not been achieved and, perhaps, never could be achieved. Besides, the historical lesson from the experiences of the Western world was that education for the masses followed after adequate education for the elite had been provided and at a time when mass education was required by expanded economic development. The contemporary advice by the Western world, as reflected in current and dominant World Bank thinking, was that combined theoretical academic learning and practical work could not fulfil the intended goals, was too expensive, and was not worth while compared with less expensive conventional academic education of a satisfactory quality. This argument was reinforced in the situation of the severe economic difficulties which were facing Tanzania and which partly resulted from overspending on the social services.

Innovative educational experiments were undertaken at the height of the implementation of Education for Self-Reliance and were analysed here in terms of the community school movement. While this movement can hardly be called successful in terms of implementation of its announced goals, the question is whether it could have been successful if it had been given a high enough priority. Such a level of priority would have been reflected in serious attention to the generic and specific local factors impeding the experiment and which were also experienced as impediments to the innovative efforts before independence and in the functional literacy scheme.

The most important outcome of these educational innovations is not that the 'vocational school fallacy' has yet again been overwhelmingly proved right. The lesson rather is that with due incorporation of the local communities, with due attention to their wishes and needs, and with due understanding of the interaction between educational and non-educational variables at different national and sub-national levels, then perhaps, the educational thinking reflected in the philosophy of Education for Self-Reliance, rather than how it was implemented, is the most appropriate for societies which suffer from lack of growth of the modern sector of the economy, from rapid growth of the informal sector and from a continuously dominant rural sector operating at low technological levels. Such schemes ought also, however, to be well and appropriately balanced with more traditional educational efforts that can stimulate the removal of structural barriers to development related to, for instance, industrialisation and export diversification.

The general counter argument derived from the 'vocational school fallacy', that parents always hope that their particular son and daughter is the lucky one to proceed to higher levels of education and, therefore, would take any short cut to academic education which secures access to further education, is not immediately reflected in the attitudes and beliefs reported from the community schools analysed here. Parents expressed support for skills development through the formal educational system, and adult literacy learners were certain that economic development could take place through the teaching of better vocational practices. Impeding factors were rather that innovative educational efforts were not satisfactorily integrated with adequate continuing opportunities for graduates in the local context and with adequate resource inputs and follow-up support.

The reality of Tanzania in the early 1990s is that a growing number of school leavers have to rely on their capacity for enterprise, because of lack of formal sector opportunities and capital inputs needed in order to survive well in the rural sector. If education is to lead development, this situation should be reflected in the content of education in terms of curricula which promote knowledge and skills for enterprise, could lead to fulfilling informal sector jobs, and could promote a possible growth potential in the dominant informal and rural sectors.

Such a more skills-oriented emphasis should not outweigh the kind of skills and knowledge which are needed to stimulate the removal of the structural barriers to economic development. Overcoming these barriers demands a richer supply of middle- and high-level manpower and is the justification for the stronger emphasis on post-primary education now than at the height of Education for Self-Reliance. However, an appropriate balance should also be upheld between the former strong emphasis on equality in education and the current strong emphasis on quality in education. Neither the limits to expanded educational efforts set by restricted funding nor the real need for an enhancement of the quality of education at all levels of the system precludes that efforts should continue to exist which promote participation in education for disfavoured geographical areas and social groups, including increased female participation at the higher educational levels.

The collapse of the state, the decentralised responsibility for basic education, and the increased donor coordination in fulfilment of the goals of the strategy of Education for All, however, all set limits to an effective, consistent and integrated national educational effort in Tanzania which could be socially and economically innovative and politically feasible. Education for All, with its emphasis on quality, efficiency and effectiveness, is not Education for Self-Reliance in disguise. While ostensibly emphasising access to education for all people, the new strategy, compared with Education for Self-Reliance, downgrades the question of social equity, lacks attention to basic adult literacy and, furthermore, displays no coherent view on the interplay between basic and higher education seen in relation to the specific needs and circumstances in individual countries like Tanzania. Like the structural adjustment programmes, Education for All, tends to be implemented across the sub-Saharan countries irrespective of local differences and, perhaps, even irrespective of national wishes. Even if determined national efforts were made in these countries to protect nationally designed, more integrated, innovative educational goals and efforts, national governments would probably have difficulty withstanding the new international sweep of quality and efficiency in a situation of increased dependency.

Practical and Research Implications

This historical investigation may point to the significance of forming a more complex view than often expressed of the function of education in development. Such a view would, in effect, integrate the objectives of education in Braudel's three-dimensional time scale according to the level of change which can be achieved through, respectively, the educational process, the educational institution and the wider society.

In the short-term and within the process of education itself, additional inputs of scarce resources – such as exercise books, chalk, primers and appropriate teacher training – the lack of which hinders basic educational achievements, could improve the situation. These would have to be supplemented by more broad-scale educational changes to have any reasonable impact on either institutional or societal life. In the medium-term, the performance of educational institutions could be improved by a careful investigation of their strengths and weaknesses and a consequent improvement in leadership, and the application of identified needed facilities and resources. The wider impact of the institution would, similarly, depend on synchronism with larger societal reforms, such as the creation of further educational and employment opportunities. Only in the long term can education be expected to contribute to a change of

173

Braudel's conditions of material life, states of mind and the natural environment. Such changes are unlikely to occur unless fundamental attention to the functions of both the educational and non-educational societal dimensions are made. The lack of achievement of some of the stipulated educational goals in Tanzania, undoubtedly, related to an ineffective partnership between educational and non-educational variables in the development process. This explains why, in the 1990s, one must reflect on how far we have moved away from the attempts at educational innovations made decades ago by other authorities in Tanzania.

There are also more specific factors which have to be considered by policy-makers and implementors in order to maximise the effect of innovative schemes. Based on the schemes analysed here across time and space in Tanzania, the following, in particular, should be given attention: the design of effective criteria for the selection of prototypes for particular experiments; the need to gain acceptance of the innovative idea by the local community concerned before the initiation of such experiments; the full integration of the local community in the implementation of any scheme; the design and use of assessment criteria properly selected according to the overall purposes of the scheme; an ongoing evaluation of any innovative process, including a thorough evaluation of medium- and long-term sustainability; and an examination of the timing and nature of adoption of successful dimensions of innovative experiments into the larger system.

Related to these larger and more specific recommendations are some fundamental gaps in existing theory, knowledge and methods which can be used to isolate and examine education as a variable in societal development. Expanded understanding of its function could possibly be made through long-term tracer studies undertaken to examine working hypotheses on the possible effect of education in national development. Combined macro- and micro-level studies aiming at identifying stimulators of and barriers to development at the national and sub-national levels should be expanded in various countries and settings in order to highlight the complexity, variation and interaction of the different variables within a specific country. Such studies could be supported by comparative regional and wider international studies, which could lead to higher levels of theoretical understanding and to the refinement of approaches, concepts and methodologies. All of this could further inform policy-making processes. The strategy of Education for All is an expression of the present high interaction of research and policy-making at the international and national levels. However, the historical experiences of Tanzania point to the need for more subtle, integrated and balanced approaches which are responsive to factors and forces at the sub-national level, in order to solve the dominant development issues which continue to exist in low-income countries.

Bibliography

Official Primary Sources

Government of Tanganyika/ The United Republic of Tanzania

Annual Plan for 1977–78. Dar es Salaam 1978.

Annual Report of the Ministry of Education 1962 and *1966.* Dar es Salaam.

Annual Report of the Social Development Department 1949–1960. Dar es Salaam.

Appropriation Accounts, Revenue Statements, Accounts of the Funds and Other Public Accounts of Tanzania for the Year 1975/76. Dar es Salaam 1977.

Background to the Budget. An Economic Survey 1966/67 and *1968/69.* Dar es Salaam.

Budget Survey 1964–65. Dar es Salaam 1964.

Department of Agriculture. *Annual Reports 1913–1946.* Dar es Salaam.

Department of Education. *Annual Reports 1923–1959.* Dar es Salaam.

Development of African Education. Sessional Paper No. 5. Dar es Salaam 1956.

Development of Non-African Education. Sessional Paper No. 6. Dar es Salaam 1956.

Development Plan for Tanganyika 1961/62–1963/64. Dar es Salaam 1962.

Economic Survey 1977–78. Dar es Salaam 1979.

Education Act. Bill Supplement to the Gazette of the United Republic of Tanzania, No. 43, Vol. L, dated 3 October; No. 11, 8 October. Dar es Salaam 1969.

Estimates of the Revenue and Expenditure of Tanganyika 1st July 1962–30th June 1963, 1st July 1963–30th June 1964, Dar es Salaam. *Estimates of the Revenue and Expenditure of Tanzania 1st July 1966–30th June 1967* Dar es Salaam.

Five Year Plan for African Education 1957–1961. Dar es Salaam 1958.

Five Year Plan for Economic and Social Development 1st July, 1964–30th June, 1969, Vol. I: General Analysis. Vol. II: The Programmes. Dar es Salaam 1967.

Memorandum on African Education in Tanganyika. Tanganyika Territory No. 68. Dar es Salaam 1933.

Memorandum on Education in Tanganyika. Sessional Paper No. 4. Dar es Salaam. 1934.

Ministry of Agriculture. 1983. *The Agricultural Policy of Tanzania.* Dar es Salaam.

Bibliography

Ministry of Education. 1961. *Annual Summary of the Ministry of Education. Statistics.* Dar es Salaam.

Ministry of Education. *The Tanzania/UNICEF/UNESCO Primary Education Reform Project (MTUU). Progress Reports 1973–1989.* Dar es Salaam.

Ministry of Education. 1984a. *Educational System in Tanzania Towards the Year 2000. Recommendations of the 1982 Presidential Commission on Education as Approved by the Party and Government.* Dar es Salaam.

Ministry of Education. 1984b. *Recent Educational Developments in the United Republic of Tanzania (1981–1983).* Country Report submitted to the 39th session of the International Conference on Education, Geneva, 16–25 October 1984. Dar es Salaam.

Ministry of Education. 1985. *Translated Report on the Impact of Adult Education in Tanzania.* Dar es Salaam.

Ministry of Education. 1986. *Basic Education Statistics in Tanzania (BEST) 1981–1985.* Dar es Salaam.

Ministry of Education. 1990a. *Basic Education Statistics in Tanzania (BEST) 1985–1989.* Dar es Salaam.

Ministry of Education. 1990b. *The Development of Education 1988–1990.* National Report of the United Republic of Tanzania. International Conference on Education, 42nd session, Geneva. Dar es Salaam.

Ministry of Labour and Social Welfare. 1983. *Proposal on Technical and Vocational Teacher Education and Management Training 1984/85–1990/91.* Dar es Salaam.

Ministry of Local Government and Housing. 1964. *Annual Report of the Community Development Division, 1961.* Dar es Salaam.

Ministry of National Education. 1978. *MTUU. Its Role in the Reform of Primary Education in Tanzania 1969–1976, Vol. I.* Dar es Salaam: Printpak.

Ministry of National Education. 1981. *Enrolment Statistics 1980, Primary Education: Analysis and Comments.* Dar es Salaam: Statistics Section.

National Accounts of Tanzania 1960–62, 1964–72, 1970–82. Dar es Salaam.

National Education Act. Acts Supplement to the Gazette of the United Republic of Tanzania, No. 49, Vol. LIX, dated 8 December, No. 5. Dar es Salaam 1978.

Non-African Education. Report by Donald Riddy and Leslie Tait. Dar es Salaam 1955.

Ordinance to make Provision for a Single System of Education in the Territory. Tanganyika No. 37 of 1961. Dar es Salaam.

Proceedings of the Tanganyika Advisory Committee on African Education, 1926–1952. Dar es Salaam.

Report of the Education Conference. Dar es Salaam 1925.

Report of the Special Committee on European Education. Dar es Salaam 1948 and 1951.

Report of the Special Committee on Indian Education. Dar es Salaam 1948 and 1951.

Report on the Census of the Non-Native Population of Tanganyika taken on the night of the 25th February, 1948. Dar es Salaam 1953.

Report on the Census of the Non-African Population taken on the night of 13th February, 1952. Dar es Salaam 1954.

Report on the Census of the Non-African Population taken on the night of the 20th/21st February, 1957. Dar es Salaam 1958.

Report on Social Welfare, 1946, 1947, 1948. Dar es Salaam.

Revised Development and Welfare Plan for Tanganyika 1950–56. Dar es Salaam 1951.

Bibliography

Second Five Year Plan for Economic and Social Development 1st July, 1969-30th June, 1974, Vol. I: General Analysis. Dar es Salaam 1969.

Speech by the Minister of State for Planning and Economic Affairs in the Vice-President's Office, Prof. K.A. Malima, MP, Presenting the Economic Survey for 1980/81 and the Annual Plan for 1981/82 on June 17, 1981. Dar es Salaam 1981.

Statistical Abstract 1957, 1962, 1964. Dar es Salaam.

Ten Year Development and Welfare Plan for Tanganyika. Sessional Paper No. 2. Dar es Salaam 1950.

Ten Year Development and Welfare Plan for Tanganyika Territory. Dar es Salaam 1946.

Ten Year Plan for the Development of African Education. Dar es Salaam 1947.

Third Five Year Plan for Economic and Social Development 1st July 1976–30th June 1981, Vol. I. Dar es Salaam 1976.

Wizara ya Elimu. 1984. *Tathmini Ya Shule Za Kijamii* (evaluation of community schools). Dar es Salaam: Idara ya Mafunzo ya Ualimu.

Wizara ya Elimu. 1986. *Matokeo ya Upimaji wa Tano wa Maendeleo ya Kisomo Chenye Manufaa Kitaifa* (5th national evaluation report on adult literacy). Dar es Salaam.

Wizara ya Elimu ya Taifa. 1981. *Matokeo ya Upimaji wa Tatu wa Maendeleo ya Kisomo Kitaifa* (3rd national evaluation report on adult literacy). Dar es Salaam.

Wizara ya Elimu ya Taifa. 1983. *Matokeo ya Upimaji wa Maendeleo ya Kisomo Chenye Manufaa* (4th national evaluation report on adult literacy). Dar es Salaam.

Others

League of Nations. 1922. *British Mandate for East Africa.* London.

United Kingdom. *Report by Her Majesty's Government in the United Kingdom of Great Britain and Northern Ireland to the General Assembly of the United Nations on the Administration of Tanganyika under United Kingdom Trusteeship for the year(s) 1919–1938, 1947–1960.* London: HMSO.

United Kingdom. 1923. *Indians in Kenya.* Cmd. 1922. London: HMSO.

United Kingdom. 1925. *Education Policy in British Tropical Africa.* Cmd. 2374. London: HMSO.

United Kingdom. 1929 and 1940. *Colonial Development Act 1929* and *Colonial Development and Welfare Act 1940.* London: HMSO.

United Kingdom. 1932. *Report by Sir Sydney Armitage-Smith on a Financial Mission to Tanganyika.* Cmd. 4182. London: HMSO.

United Kingdom. 1935. *Memorandum on the Education of African Communities.* Col. no. 103. London: HMSO.

United Kingdom. 1937. *Higher Education in East Africa.* Col. no. 142. London: HMSO.

United Kingdom. 1943. *Mass Education in African Society.* Col. no. 186. London: HMSO.

United Kingdom. 1945. *Report of the Commission on Higher Education in the Colonies.* Cmd. 6647. London: HMSO.

United Kingdom. 1948. *Education for Citizenship in Africa.* Col. no. 216. London: HMSO.

United Nations. 1946. *Text of Trusteeship Agreement as approved by the General Assembly of the United Nations.* Cmd. 7081. New York.

Bibliography

United Nations, Trusteeship Council. 1949 and 1955. *Visiting Mission to Trust Territories in East Africa, 1948 (and 1954): Report on Tanganyika together with Related Documents.* New York: United Nations.

Unofficial and Semi-Official Primary Sources

Tanzania National Archives, Dar es Salaam

TNA SMP 10514/Vol. I – Schools Lake Province (1927–1935).

TNA SMP 19141 – Provincial Advisory Education Committee Bukoba.

TNA SMP 19972 – Central School for Tabora and Mwanza Provinces.

TNA SMP 22337/Vol. II – Agricultural Development Lake Province (1938–1942).

TNA SMP 23271/Vol. I – Nyakato Agricultural Training Centre, Bukoba District, 1933–1938.

TNA SMP 23271/Vol. II – Nyakato Government Secondary School, 1939–1942.

TNA SMP 23437/Vol. I – Memorandum on Education of African Communities (1935–1939).

TNA SMP 23765 – Financial Assistance to Pupils Leaving Nyakato (1936–1937).

TNA SMP 24523 – Future of Bwiru School (1936–1937).

TNA SMP 25083/Vol. I – Agricultural Schools for Africans (1937–1938).

TNA SMP 36164 – Development of Adult Education (Prof. Philips).

TNA Acc. 215/E.1/44 – Advisory Committee on Native Education.

TNA Acc. 215/26/Part I – Education and Schools (1924–1928).

TNA Acc. 215/26/Part II – Education and Schools (1929–1932).

TNA Acc. 215/617/Vol. I – Education. Nyakato School (1932–1934).

TNA Acc. 215/617/Vol. II – Education. Nyakato School (1934–1936).

TNA Acc. 215/617/Vol. III – Education. Nyakato School (1936–1939).

TNA Acc. 215/827A/Vol. I – Native Schools. General (1933–1935).

TNA Acc. 215/827A/Vol. II – Native Schools. General (1936–1937).

TNA Acc. 215/827A/Vol. III – Native Schools. General (1938–1942).

TNA Acc. 302/LGS 1/1 – Social Development and Welfare (1954–1961).

TNA Acc. 302/LGS 1/7 – Community Development Reports (1961–1962).

TNA Acc. 68/R.3/1 – Returns and Reports (1954–1957).

TNA Acc. 68/S.1/1 – Social Development and Welfare (1956–1963).

TNA Acc.68/S.1/5 – Social Development and Welfare (Adult Literacy Campaigns) (1955–1961).

TNA Acc. 68/S.1/5/II – Community Development and Welfare (Adult Literacy Campaign) (1961–1962).

Others

Bahi adult education statistics [provided by the district education officer, Dodoma at the request of the author].

Bibliography

Bahi village statistics [provided by the ward adult education officer at the request of the author].

Chama cha Mapinduzi-Ofisi ya Tavi Magamba Kwalukonge. 1990. *Historia Fupi Ya Kikiji Cha Magamba Kwalukonge* (CCM office Kwalukonge, A history of the Kwalukonge ujamaa village). Kwalukonge.

Dabalo adult education statistics [provided by the ward adult education officer at the request of the author].

Dabalo village statistics [provided by the ward adult education officer at the request of the author].

Dodoma regional and adult education statistics [provided by the regional education officer in Dodoma at the request of the author].

Kwalukonge village statistics [provided by the village secretary at the request of the author].

Kwamsisi village statistics [provided by the village secretary at the request of the author].

Mvumi Makulu adult education statistics [provided by the ward adult education officer at the request of the author].

Mvumi Makulu village statistics [provided by the ward adult education officer at the request of the author].

Secondary Sources

Anderson, C.A. and M.J. Bowman (Eds). 1966. *Education and Economic Development.* Chicago: Aldine.

Austen, R.A. 1968. *Northwest Tanzania Under German and British Rule. Colonial Policy and Tribal Politics, 1889–1939.* New Haven: Yale University Press.

Barkan, J.D. (Ed.). 1984a. *Politics and Public Policy in Kenya and Tanzania.* Revised Edition. New York: Praeger.

Barkan, J.D. 1984b. Comparing politics and public policy in Kenya and Tanzania. In J.D. Barkan (Ed.) *Politics and Public Policy in Kenya and Tanzania.* Revised Edition. New York: Praeger, pp. 3–42.

Beck, R.S. 1963. *An Economic Survey of Coffee-Banana Farms in the Central Machame Area, 1961.* Mimeo. Dar es Salaam.

Boesen, J. and A.T. Mohele. 1979. *The 'Success Story' of Peasant Tobacco Production in Tanzania.* Uppsala: Scandinavian Institute of African Studies.

Boesen, J., K.J. Havnevik, J. Koponen and R. Odgaard (Eds). 1986. *Tanzania – Crisis and Struggle for Survival.* Uppsala: Scandinavian Institute of African Studies.

Boesen, J., B. Storgaard Madsen and T. Moody. 1977. *Ujamaa – Socialism from Above.* Uppsala: Scandinavian Institute of African Studies.

Bowles, B.D. 1980. The political economy of colonial Tanganyika 1939–1961. In M.H.Y. Kaniki (Ed.) *Tanzania Under Colonial Rule.* London: Longman, pp. 164–191.

Braudel, F. 1967. *Civilisation matérielle et capitalisme. XVe–XVIIIe Siècle, Tome I.* Paris: Librairie Armand Colin.

Braudel, F. 1969. *Ecrits sur l'histoire.* Paris: Flammarion.

179

Bibliography

Brett, E.A. 1973. *Colonialism and Underdevelopment in East Africa.* London: Heinemann.

Bryceson, Deborah Fahy. 1986. *Household, Hoe and Nation: Development Policies of the Nyerere Era.* Paper presented at *Tanzania After Nyerere.* An International Conference on the Economic, Political and Social Issues facing Tanzania. London, Centre for African Studies, School of Oriental and African Studies, June.

Bryceson, Deborah Fahy. 1990. *Food Insecurity and the Social Division of Labour in Tanzania, 1919–85.* London: St Anthony's/Macmillan.

Buchert, Lene. 1991. *Politics, Development and Education in Tanzania 1919–1986. An Historical Interpretation of Social Change.* PhD dissertation, University of London.

Buchert, Lene (Ed.). 1992a. *Education and Training in the Third World. The Local Dimension.* CESO Paperback no. 18. The Hague: CESO/CDR.

Buchert, Lene. 1992b. The community school as an instrument of social innovation in Tanzania: an analysis based on two cases. In L. Buchert (Ed.) *Education and Training in the Third World. The Local Dimensions.* The Hague: CESO/CDR, pp. 23–139.

Buchert, Lene. 1993. A Gender Perspective on Adult Literacy Programmes in Tanzania: Some lessons from Dodoma region. *Journal of the African Association for Literacy and Adult Education,* Vol. 7, No. 1, pp. 7–25.

Buchert, Lene. 1994. Education and development: a study of donor agency policies on education in Sweden, Holland and Denmark. *International Journal of Educational Development,* Vol. 14, No. 2.

Campbell, Horace and Howard Stein (Eds). 1991. *The IMF and Tanzania. The Dynamics of Liberalisation.* Harare: SAPES.

Carr–Hill, R. 1984. *Primary Education in Tanzania. A Review of the Research.* Education Division Documents No. 16. Stockholm: SIDA.

Carron, G. and Ta Ngoc Châu (Eds). 1980. *Regional Disparities in Educational Development. Diagnosis and Policies for Reduction.* Paris: UNESCO/IIEP.

Cliffe, L. 1972. Nationalism and the reaction to enforced agricultural change in Tanganyika during the colonial period. In L. Cliffe and J.S. Saul (Eds) *Socialism in Tanzania.* Nairobi: East African Publishing House, pp. 17–24.

Cliffe, L. and J.S. Saul (Eds). 1972. *Socialism in Tanzania, Vol. 1 Politics, Vol. 2 Policies.* Nairobi: East African Publishing House.

Cooksey, B. 1985. *A Critical Review of Policy and Practice in Tanzanian Secondary Education Since 1967.* Paper presented at the IDR and Research Information Sharing Meeting, Nairobi, 3–6 October.

Coulson, Andrew (Ed.). 1979. *African Socialism in Practice: The Tanzanian Experience.* Nottingham: Spokesman Books.

Coulson, Andrew. 1982. *Tanzania. A Political Economy.* New York: Oxford University Press.

Court, D. 1973. The social function of formal schooling in Tanzania. *African Review,* Vol. 3, No. 4, pp. 577–593.

Court, D. 1984. The education system as a response to inequality. In J.D. Barkan (Ed.) *Politics and Public Policy in Kenya and Tanzania.* Revised Edition. New York: Praeger, pp. 265–295.

Court, D. and K. Kinyanjui. 1980. Development policy and educational opportunity: the experience of Kenya and Tanzania. In G. Carron and Ta Ngoc Châu (Eds) *Regional Disparities in Educational Development. Diagnosis and Policies for Reduction.* Paris: UNESCO/IIEP, pp. 325–409.

Bibliography

Crouch, S.C. 1987. *Western Responses to Tanzanian Socialism 1967–83*. Aldershot: Avebury.

Economist Intelligence Unit. 1991. *Tanzania. Country Profile 1991–92. Annual Survey of Political and Economic Background*. London: Business International Limited.

Economist Intelligence Unit. 1992. *Tanzania, Mozambique. Country Report No. 3 1992. Analysis of Economic and Political Trends Every Quarter*. London: Business International Limited.

Egerö, B. and R.A. Henin (Eds). 1973. *The Population of Tanzania. An Analysis of the 1967 Population Census. Census Vol. 6*. Dar es Salaam: BRALUP and Bureau of Statistics.

Ehrlich, C. 1964. Some aspects of economic policy in Tanganyika, 1945–60. *Journal of Modern African Studies*, July, pp. 265–277.

Fanon, F. 1963. *The Wretched of the Earth*. New York: Grove Press.

Foster, P.J. 1966. The vocational school fallacy in development planning. In C.A. Anderson and M.J. Bowman (Eds) *Education and Economic Development*. Chicago: Aldine, pp. 142–166.

Foster, P. 1969. Education for Self-Reliance: a critical evaluation. In R. Jolly (Ed.) *Education in Africa*. Nairobi: East African Publishing House, pp. 81–101.

Freire, P. 1977 (1970). *Cultural Action for Freedom*. Harmondsworth: Penguin.

Freire, P. 1982 (1972). *Pedagogy of the Oppressed*. Harmondsworth: Penguin.

Goranson, U. 1981. *Development Assistance to the Education Sector in Tanzania Since Independence*. Dar es Salaam: Ministry of National Education/Department of Planning.

Gordon, D.F. 1984. Foreign relations dilemmas of independence and development. In J.D. Barkan (Ed.) *Politics and Public Policy in Kenya and Tanzania*. Revised Edition. New York: Praeger, pp. 297–335.

Gottlieb, M. 1973. The extent and character of differentiation in Tanzanian agricultural and rural society 1967–1969. *African Review*, Vol. 3, No. 2, pp. 241–261.

Green, R.G. 1978. Basic Human Needs: concept or slogan, synthesis or smokescreen? *IDS Bulletin*, Vol. 9, No. 4, pp. 7–11.

Hailey, Lord. 1938. *An African Survey*. London: Oxford University Press.

Hailey, Lord. 1942. *Native Administration and Political Development in British Tropical Africa*. London: HMSO.

Hartmann, Jeanette. 1983. *Development Policy-Making in Tanzania 1962–1982: A Critique of Sociological Interpretations*. PhD dissertation, University of Hull.

Hartmann, Jeannette. 1988. President Nyerere and the state. In Michael Hodd *Tanzania After Nyerere*. London: Pinter Publishers, pp. 165–174.

Hartmann, Jeannette. 1991. The state in Tanzania: yesterday, today and tomorrow. *Occasional Papers*, 12. University of Helsinki: Institute of Development Studies.

Haule, R.M. (Ed.). 1979. *MTUU. Basic Education – A Community Enterprise, Vol. 3*. Dar es Salaam: Printpak.

Hodd, Michael (Ed.). 1988. *Tanzania After Nyerere*. London: Pinter Publishers.

Hunter, G. 1963. *Education for a Developing Region. A Study of East Africa*. London: Allen and Unwin.

Hunter, Jannie and Christo Lombard (Eds). 1992. *Multi-Party Democracy, Civil*

Bibliography

Society and Economic Transformation in Southern Africa. Papers from the 14th Southern African Universities Social Science Conference. Windhoek: SAUSSC.

Hyden, G. 1980. *Beyond Ujamaa in Tanzania.* London: Heinemann.

Iliffe, J. 1971. *Agricultural Change in Modern Tanganyika,* Nairobi: East African Publishing House.

Iliffe, J. 1972. Tanzania under German and British rule. In L. Cliffe and J.S. Saul (Eds) *Socialism in Tanzania.* Nairobi: East African Publishing House, pp. 8–17.

Iliffe, J. 1979. *A Modern History of Tanganyika.* Cambridge: Cambridge University Press.

Inter-Agency Commission. 1990. *World Declaration on Education for All and Framework for Action to meet Basic Learning Needs.* New York: UNICEF.

International Bank for Reconstruction and Development (IBRD). 1961. *The Economic Development of Tanganyika.* Baltimore: Johns Hopkins University Press.

International Bank for Reconstruction and Development (IBRD). 1983. *World Development Report.* Washington: Oxford University Press.

International Institute for Educational Planning (IIEP). 1983. *Planning and Administration of National Literacy Programmes.* Paris: IIEP.

International Labour Organisation (ILO). 1978. *Towards Self-Reliance, Development, Employment and Equity Issues in Tanzania.* ILO, Jobs and Skills Programme for Africa. Addis Ababa: Artistic Printers.

International Labour Organisation (ILO). 1982. *Basic Needs in Danger. A Basic Needs Oriented Development Strategy for Tanzania.* ILO, Jobs and Skills Programme for Africa. Addis Ababa: United Printers.

Ishumi, Abel G.M. 1984. *The Urban Jobless in Eastern Africa.* Uppsala: Scandinavian Institute of African Studies.

Ishumi, Abel G.M. 1988. *Institutional Framework for Education for Self-Reliance: Adequacies and Inadequacies.* Paper for presentation at the National Symposium on Twenty Years of Education for Self-Reliance, Marangu, 12–17 September.

Jellicoe, M. 1961. An experiment in mass education among women: Singida district, Tanganyika, July to December 1960. *Occasional Papers on Community Development,* 1. Dar es Salaam: East African Literature Bureau.

Jellicoe, M. 1962. *An Appraisal of the Success of the Literacy Campaign in Singida Area.*

Jellicoe, M. 1978. *The Long Path. A Case Study of Social Change in Wahi, Singida District, Tanzania.* Nairobi: East African Publishing House.

Jolly, R. (Ed.). 1969. *Education in Africa.* Nairobi: East African Publishing House.

Kahama, C.G., T.L. Maliyamkono and S. Wells. 1986. *The Challenge for Tanzania's Economy.* London: James Currey.

Kaniki, M.H.Y. (Ed.). 1980. *Tanzania Under Colonial Rule.* London: Longman.

Katunzi, N.B. 1988. *Implementing Education for Self-Reliance through the Community School in Tanzania.* PhD dissertation, University of Calgary.

Kayuza, M.M.G. 1979. Tanzania/UNESCO/UNICEF cooperation. In R.M. Haule (Ed.) *MTUU. Basic Education – A Community Enterprise, Vol. 3.* Dar es Salaam: Printpak, pp. 97–107.

Kilimhana, S.N.M. 1975. *An Evaluation of the Kwamsisi Experimental Project in Tanzania.* MEd dissertation, University of Alberta.

Kimambo, I.N. and A.J. Temu (Eds). 1969. *A History of Tanzania.* Nairobi: East African Publishing House.

Bibliography

King, K. 1971. *Pan-Africanism and Education. A Study of Race Philanthropy and Education in the Southern States of America and East Africa.* Oxford: Clarendon Press.

King, Kenneth. 1984. The end of education for self-reliance in Tanzania? *Occasional Papers No. 1.* University of Edinburgh: Centre of African Studies.

King, Kenneth. 1988. Evaluating the context of diversified secondary education in Tanzania. In Jon Lauglo and Kevin Lillis (Eds) *Vocationalizing Education. An International Perspective.* Oxford: Pergamon Press, pp. 279–292.

Kjekshus, H. 1977. *Ecology Control and Economic Development in East African History.* London: Heinemann.

Komba, D. and E.B. Temu. 1987. *State of the Art Review of Evaluation of 'Education for Self-Reliance' Implementation.* A Study co-sponsored by Ministry of Education, Dar es Salaam, Tanzania and Foundation for Education with Production, Gaborone, Botswana. Dar es Salaam.

Koponen, J. 1988. *People and Production in Late Precolonial Tanzania. History and Structures.* Jyväskylä: Gummerus Kirjapaino Oy.

Koponen, J. n.d. *African Education: State and Missionaries.* Unpublished ms.

Lauglo, J. and K. Lillis (Eds). 1988. *Vocationalizing Education. An International Perspective.* Oxford: Pergamon Press.

Lawuo, Z.E. 1984. *Education and Social Change in a Rural Community.* Dar es Salaam: Dar es Salaam University Press.

Leonard, D.K. 1984. Class formation and agricultural development. In J.D. Barkan (Ed.) *Politics and Public Policy in Kenya and Tanzania.* Revised Edition. New York: Praeger, pp. 141–170.

Lewis, L.J. (Ed.). 1962. *Phelps–Stokes Reports on Education in Africa.* London: Oxford University Press.

Little, A.D. 1966. Tanganyika industrial development. In H.E. Smith (Ed.) *Readings on Economic Development and Administration in Tanzania.* London: Oxford University Press. pp. 269–285.

Lugalla, Joe L.P. 1992. *Structural Adjustment Policies and the Education Sector in Tanzania. A State of the Art Paper.* Paper prepared for the workshop on social impact of SAP policies in sub-Saharan Africa. Harare, March.

Lugard, F.D., Sir. 1965 (1922). *The Dual Mandate in British Tropical Africa.* London: William Blackwood and Sons.

Mählck, L. and E.B. Temu. 1989. Distance versus college trained primary school teachers: a case study from Tanzania. *IIEP Research Report No. 75.* Paris: IIEP.

Malekela, G.A. 1983. *Access to Secondary Education in Sub-Saharan Africa: The Tanzanian Experiment.* PhD dissertation, University of Chicago.

Mathews, K. and S.S. Mushi (Eds). 1981. *Foreign Policy of Tanzania 1961–1981: A Reader.* Dar es Salaam: Tanzania Publishing House.

Mbilinyi, Marjorie 1977. Basic education: tool of liberation or exploitation? *Prospects,* Vol. 7, No. 4, pp. 489–503.

Mbilinyi, Marjorie 1979. Contradictions in Tanzanian education reform. In A. Coulson (Ed.) *African Socialism in Practice: The Tanzanian Experience.* Nottingham: Spokesman Books, pp. 217–227.

Mbilinyi, Marjorie (Ed.). 1991. *Education in Tanzania with a Gender Perspective.* Dar es Salaam.

Meena, E.A.K. 1978. The itinerant tutor educators as agents of change. In

Bibliography

Ministry of National Education *MTUU. Its Role in the Reform of Primary Education in Tanzania 1969–1976, Vol. I.* Dar es Salaam: Printpak, pp. 125–133.

Meena, E.A.K. 1983. *Some Aspects of Education in Tanzania.* Dar es Salaam: Longman.

Memmi, A. 1974. *The Colonizer and the Colonized.* London: Souvenir Press.

Mitande, P.K. 1978. Why community school? In Ministry of National Education *MTUU. Its Role in the Reform of Primary Education in Tanzania 1969–1976, Vol. I.* Dar es Saalaam: Printpak, pp. 49–57.

Mmari, G.R.V. 1976. Implementation of the Musoma resolutions: the University of Dar es Salaam admissions experience. *Papers in Education and Development,* No. 3, pp. 15–51.

Morris-Hale, W. 1969. *British Administration in Tanganyika from 1920 to 1945.* PhD dissertation, University of Geneva.

Morrison, D.R. 1976. *Education and Politics in Africa. The Tanzanian Case.* London: Heinemann.

Moshi, H.P.B. 1992. Structural adjustment programmes and Africa's future political face. In J. Hunter and C. Lombard (Eds) *Multi-Party Democracy, Civil Society and Economic Transformation in Southern Africa.* Papers from the 14th Southern African Universities Social Science Conference, Windhoek: SAUSSC, pp. 103–110.

Mpogolo, Z.J. 1980. *Functional Literacy in Tanzania.* Dar es Salaam: Swala Publications.

Mpogolo, Z.J. 1983. Planning and administration of national literacy programmes in the United Republic of Tanzania. In IIEP, *Planning and Administration of National Literacy Programmes.* Paris: IIEP, pp. 166–195.

Mwajombe, R.Z. 1978. MTUU administration, finance and relationship with UNICEF and UNESCO. In Ministry of Education *MTUU. Its Role in the Reform of Primary Education in Tanzania 1969–1976, Vol. I.* Dar es Salaam: Printpak, pp. 80–91.

Nyerere, J.K. 1961. Independence address to United Nations. In J.K. Nyerere 1967a. *Freedom and Unity: A Selection from Writings and Speeches 1952–65.* London: Oxford University Press, pp. 144–156.

Nyerere, J.K. 1962. Ujamaa – The basis of African socialism. In J.K. Nyerere 1967a. *Freedom and Unity: A Selection from Writings and Speeches 1952–65.* London: Oxford University Press, pp. 162–171.

Nyerere, J.K. 1965. Agriculture is the basis of development. In J.K. Nyerere 1968a. *Freedom and Socialism. A Selection of Writings and Speeches 1965–1967.* Dar es Salaam: Oxford University Press, pp. 385–409.

Nyerere, J.K. 1966a. The role of universities. In J.K. Nyerere 1968a. *Freedom and Socialism. A Selection of Writings and Speeches 1965–1967.* Dar es Salaam: Oxford University Press, pp. 179–186.

Nyerere, J.K. 1966b. The power of teachers. In J.K. Nyerere 1968a. *Freedom and Socialism. A Selection of Writings and Speeches 1965–1967.* Dar es Salaam: Oxford University Press, pp. 223–228.

Nyerere, J.K. 1967a. *Freedom and Unity: A Selection from Writings and Speeches 1952–65.* London: Oxford University Press.

Nyerere, J.K. 1967b. The Arusha Declaration: Socialism and Self–Reliance. In J.K. Nyerere 1968. *Freedom and Socialism. A Selection of Writings and Speeches*

1965–1967. Dar es Salaam: Oxford University Press, pp. 231–250.

Nyerere, J.K. 1967c. Education for Self-Reliance. In J.K. Nyerere 1968a. *Freedom and Socialism. A Selection of Writings and Speeches 1965–1967.* Dar es Salaam: Oxford University Press, pp. 267–290.

Nyerere, J.K. 1967d. Socialism and rural development. In J.K. Nyerere 1968a. *Freedom and Socialism. A Selection of Writings and Speeches 1965–1967.* Dar es Salaam: Oxford University Press, pp. 337–366.

Nyerere, J.K. 1967e. The purpose is man. In J.K. Nyerere 1968a. *Freedom and Socialism. A Selection of Writings and Speeches 1965–1967.* Dar es Salaam: Oxford University Press, pp. 315–326.

Nyerere, J.K. 1967f. After the Arusha Declaration. In J.K. Nyerere 1968a. *Freedom and Socialism. A Selection of Writings and Speeches 1965–1967.* Dar es Salaam: Oxford University Press, pp. 385–409.

Nyerere, J.K. 1967g. Progress in schools. In J.K. Nyerere 1968a. *Freedom and Socialism. A Selection of Writings and Speeches 1965–1967.* Dar es Salaam: Oxford University Press, pp. 410–414.

Nyerere, J.K. 1968a. *Freedom and Socialism. A Selection from Writings and Speeches 1965–1967.* Dar es Salaam: Oxford University Press.

Nyerere, J.K. 1968b. The intellectual needs society. In J.K. Nyerere 1973. *Freedom and Development.* New York: Oxford University Press, pp. 23–29.

Nyerere, J.K. 1968c. Freedom and development. In J.K. Nyerere 1973. *Freedom and Development.* New York: Oxford University Press, pp. 58–71.

Nyerere, J.K. 1969. Adult Education Year. In J.K. Nyerere 1973. *Freedom and Development.* New York: Oxford University Press, pp. 137–141.

Nyerere, J.K. 1970a. *Non-Alignment in the Seventies.* Dar es Salaam: Government Printer.

Nyerere, J.K. 1970b. The church and society. In J.K. Nyerere 1973. *Freedom and Development.* New York: Oxford University Press, pp. 213–228.

Nyerere, J.K. 1972. *Decentralization.* Dar es Salaam: Government Printer.

Nyerere, J.K. 1973. *Freedom and Development.* New York: Oxford University Press.

Nyerere, J.K. 1974a. Economic development through self-reliance: the Tanzanian experience. In K. Mathews and S.S. Mushi (Eds) 1981. *Foreign Policy of Tanzania 1961–1981: A Reader.* Dar es Salaam: Tanzania Publishing House, pp. 295–300.

Nyerere, J.K. 1974b. Education and liberation. *Development Dialogue,* No. 2, pp. 46–52.

Okumu, J.J. with F. Holmquist. 1984. Party and party–state relations. In J.D. Barkan (Ed.) *Politics and Public Policy in Kenya and Tanzania.* Revised Edition. New York: Praeger, pp. 45–69.

Oliver, R. 1965 (1952). *The Missionary Factor in East Africa.* London: Longman.

Omari, I.M. 1991. Innovation and change in higher education in developing countries: experiences from Tanzania. *Comparative Education,* Vol. 27, No. 2, pp. 181–205.

Ploeg, A.J. van der. 1977. Education in colonial Africa: the German experience. *Comparative Education Review,* February, pp. 91–109.

Pratt, R.C. 1972. *The cabinet and presidential leadership in Tanzania in 1960–66.* In L. Cliffe and J.S. Saul (Eds) *Socialism in Tanzania.* Nairobi: East African Publishing House, pp. 226–240.

Bibliography

Pratt, C. 1976. *The Critical Phase in Tanzania, 1945–1968*. Cambridge: Cambridge University Press.

Prewitt, K. 1971. *Education and Political Values*. Nairobi: East African Publishing House.

Psacharopoulos, G. and W. Loxley. 1984. *Diversified Secondary Education and Development: A Report on the Diversified Secondary Curriculum Study*. Washington: World Bank.

Raikes, P. 1972. *Differentiation and Progressive Farmer Policies*. Paper presented to the East African Agricultural Economics Society, Kampala, June.

Raikes, P. 1976. Coffee production in West Lake region, Tanzania. *IDR Project Papers, West Lake Tanzania* D.76.9. Copenhagen: Institute for Development Research.

Raikes, P. 1986. Eating the carrot and wielding the stick: the agricultural sector in Tanzania. In J. Boesen, K.J. Havnevik, J. Koponen and R. Odgaard (Eds) *Tanzania – Crisis and Struggle for Survival*. Uppsala: Scandinavian Institute of African Studies, pp. 105–141.

Rajabu, A.R.M.S. and G.E. Shayo. 1978. The community school. In Ministry of National Education *MTUU. Its Role in the Reform of Primary Education in Tazania 1969–1976, Vol. I*. Dar es Salaam: Printpak, pp. 172–190.

Resnick, I.N. (Ed.). 1968. *Tanzania: Revolution by Education*. Arusha: Longman.

Resnick, I.N. 1981. *The Long Transition. Building Socialism in Tanzania*. New York: Monthly Review Press.

Rodney, W. 1980. The political economy of colonial Tanganyika 1890–1930. In M.H.Y. Kaniki (Ed.) *Tanzania Under Colonial Rule*. London: Longman, pp. 128–163.

Ruthenberg, H. 1964. *Agricultural Development in Tanganyika*. Berlin: Springer-Verlag.

Rweyemamu, J. 1973. *Underdevelopment and Industrialization in Tanzania*. Oxford: Oxford University Press.

Samoff, J. 1974. *Tanzania. Local Politics and the Structure of Power*. Madison: University of Wisconsin Press.

Samoff, J. 1979. Education in Tanzania: class formation and reproduction. *Journal of Modern African Studies*, Vol. 17, pp. 47–69.

Samoff, J. 1987. School expansion in Tanzania: private initiatives and public policy. *Comparative Education Review*, Vol. 31, No. 3, pp. 333–360.

Samoff, Joel. 1991. The façade of precision in education data and statistics: a troubling example from Tanzania. *Journal of Modern African Studies*, Vol. 29, No. 4, pp. 669–689.

Schultz, Theodore W. 1961. Investment in human capital. *American Economic Review*, Vol. 51, pp. 1–17.

Shivji, I. 1982. *Class Struggles in Tanzania*. London: Heinemann.

Singh, A. 1986. Tanzania and the IMF: the analytics of alternative adjustment programmes. *Development and Change*, Vol. 17, No. 3, pp. 425–453.

Skorov, G. 1966. Integration of educational and economic planning in Tanzania. *African Research Monographs* 6. Paris: UNESCO/IIEP.

Svendsen, K.E. 1986. The creation of macroeconomic imbalances and a structural crisis. In J. Boesen, K.J. Havnevik, J. Koponen and R. Odgaard (Eds) *Tanzania – Crisis and Struggle for Survival*. Uppsala: Scandinavian Institute of African Studies, pp. 59–78.

Bibliography

Temu, A.J. 1969. The rise and triumph of nationalism. In I.N. Kimambo and A.J. Temu (Eds) *A History of Tanzania*. Nairobi: East African Publishing House, pp. 189–213.

Temu, A.J. 1980. Tanzanian societies and colonial invasion 1875–1907. In M.H.Y. Kaniki (Ed.) *Tanzania Under Colonial Rule*. London: Longman, pp. 86–127.

Temu, E.B. and D. Komba (Coord.). 1987. *Education with Production in Tanzania: Implementation of Education for Self-Reliance in 1985*. Report of a FEP/Ministry of Education Research Project. Dar es Salaam.

Thomas, R.L. 1968. Problems of manpower development. In I.N. Resnick (Ed.) *Tanzania: Revolution by Education*. Arusha: Longman, pp. 106–122.

Thompson, A.R. 1965. *Partnership in Education in Tanganyika 1919–1961*. MA dissertation, University of London.

United Nations Educational, Scientific and Cultural Organisation (UNESCO). n.d. *Conference of African States on the Development of Education in Africa, Addis Ababa, 15–25 May 1961. Final Report*. Paris: UNESCO.

United Nations Educational, Scientific and Cultural Organisation (UNESCO). 1963. *Report of UNESCO Educational Planning Mission for Tanganyika. June to October 1962*. Paris: UNESCO.

United Nations Educational, Scientific and Cultural Organisation (UNESCO). 1977. *Statistical Yearbook 1976*. Paris: UNESCO.

United Nations Educational, Scientific and Cultural Organisation (UNESCO). 1978. The school and community interact: community-centred education in the United Republic of Tanzania. In UNESCO, *Basic Services for Children: A Continuing Search for Learning Priorities. Part I. Experiments and Innovations in Education*, 36, pp. 72–90. Paris: UNESCO.

United Nations Educational, Scientific and Cultural Organisation (UNESCO). 1991. *Statistical Yearbook 1991*. Paris: UNESCO.

von Freyhold, M. 1979. *Ujamaa Villages in Tanzania. Analysis of a Social Experiment*. London: Heinemann.

Wagao, Jumanne H. 1990. Adjustment policies in Tanzania 1981–1989: the impact on growth, structure and human welfare. *Innocenti Occasional Papers*, No. 9.

World Bank. 1988. *Education in Sub-Saharan Africa: Policies for Adjustment, Revitalization and Selective Expansion*. Washington: World Bank.

World Bank. 1989. *Sub-Saharan Africa. From Crisis to Sustainable Growth. A Long-Term Perspective Study*. Washington: World Bank.

World Bank. 1991. *World Development Report 1991. The Challenge of Development*. Oxford: Oxford University Press.

Wright, M. 1971. *German Missions in Tanganyika 1891–1941. Lutherans and Moravians in the Southern Highlands*. Oxford: Clarendon Press.

Wright, M. 1976. Missions and educational policies between the wars in Tanganyika. *Papers in Education and Development*, No. 2.

Index

Index

Index

curriculum of, 39-41
Nyerere, 91-97, 101, 123, 146, 161

one-party state, 97; authority structure, 97, 101, 146

paramountcy, principle of, 8, 12, 53
peasant, income, 102; mode of production, 92; production, 7, 12-15, 30, 35, 55-56, 123; sector 31, 92; societies, 12-15, 35, 45; *see also* education, vocational agricultural, Nyakato
periods, historical, 1-2, 4-6, 124, 167-171
Phelps-Stokes Commission, 18
Philips, C.H., 73-74
plantation industry, 12-14, 16, 30, 53-56, 76
political pluralism, 144, 146
political, setting, 7-9, 31, 52-53, 146-147
Pratt, C., 53, 97, 99-100
provision, of education, 5-6, 14, 16, 20-21, 23-30, 37, 59-65, 69, 106-112, 148-150

Raikes, P., 35, 40, 55, 145
reciprocity, principle of, 9, 91-92
Rodney, W., 13-14
Ruthenberg, H., 13, 54-57

Samoff, J., 114, 164 fn 17
schools, number of, *see* provision, education
secondary education, *see* education
self-government, 18, 49-52, 57, 59, 72
self-reliance, *see* Education for Self-Reliance, Socialism and Self-Reliance
Singida, 5, 69, 75, 78, 83-86, 100, 152-53, 162; district, 72, 78-80; mass literacy and education programme, 5, 69, 72, 75-85; women's mass education programme, 83-86; conversion of primary schools, 124, 133
sisal, 14, 54, 59, 101, 126, 134; *see also* plantation industry
Social Welfare (Development) Department, 58, 73-74, 79-80
Socialism and Self-Reliance, strategy of, 5-6, 90, 93, 96-97, 100, 103, 116, 144, 160, 167-170; development, 123; state, 142
socialist development, 4-5; goals, 147; socialism, 91
socio-economic setting, of Tanganyika, 2-15, 53-57; of Tanzania, 98-103, 144-

147; of Singida 76-78; of Kwalukonge, 134-136; of Kwamsisi 126-127; of Dodoma rural district, 152-153
southern highlands, 13-14
stratification, 9, 14; *see also* differentiation
structural adjustment, policies of, 6, 120, 124-125, 142, 147, 167-168, 170; programmes of, 144-146, 169, 173
Svendsen, K.E., 98, 101, 145-146

Tabora, 13; central school of, 27, 33 fn 54, 39-40, 43
Tanga, 76, 124, 135, 138; government school, 15-16
TANU, 57, 72, 79, 97, 99, 152; Youth League, 115
trade, 14, 43-44, 53, 99, 101-102
Turu, 76, 79, 81, 84; social organisation of, 76-77

ujamaa, philosophy of, 91-93, 137; implementation of, 100-101, 119-120, 125, 127-128, 133, 168
UNESCO, 57, 72, 93, 124, 113 fn 47; primary education reform project, 126; *see also* MTUU; functional literacy, 151
UNICEF, 69, 72, 82-83, 85, 124, 125 fn 6, 133-134; primary education reform project, 126; *see also* MTUU
United Nations, 7, 56-57, 97, 148; trusteeship agreement of, 52, 70 fn 32
UWT, 161-162

Vischer, Hanns, 18
vocational education, *see* education
vocational school fallacy, 6, 69, 133, 141, 164, 171-172

West Lake Province (region), 12, 35, 44, 101, 113-114, 151
White Fathers Mission, *see* missionary organisations
white settler, interests of, 8, 12, 52; production, 12-14, 30, 54; agriculture, 91
World Bank, 56, 98, 116-117, 144-146, 148, 163, 171
women (females), 18, 38, 51-52, 72-77, 83-85, 112, 152-153; *see* education, differentiation, UWT

Zigua, 127, 131, 134